The Play
—— of ——
Mahamudra

The Play
of
Mahamudra

SPONTANEOUS TEACHINGS
ON VIRUPA'S MYSTICAL
SONGS

Lama Migmar Tseten

Wisdom Publications
199 Elm Street
Somerville, MA 02144 USA
wisdomexperience.org

Library of Congress Cataloging-in-Publication Data
Names: Tseten, Migmar, author.
Title: The play of Mahamudra: spontaneous teachings on Virupa's mystical songs /
Migmar Tseten.
Description: Somerville, MA: Wisdom, 2021. | Includes index.
Identifiers: LCCN 2020043886 (print) | LCCN 2020043887 (ebook) |
ISBN 9781614297031 (hardcover) | ISBN 9781614297765 (ebook)
Subjects: LCSH: Virūpa. | Mahāmudrā (Tantric rite) | Tantric Buddhism—Rituals. |
Spiritual life—Tantric Buddhism. | Buddhist poetry, Tibetan—History and criticism. |
Songs, Tibetan—History and criticism. | Songs, Sanskrit—History and criticism.
Classification: LCC BQ8921.M35 T73 2021 (print) | LCC BQ8921.M35 (ebook) |
DDC 294.3/925—dc23
LC record available at https://lccn.loc.gov/2020043886
LC ebook record available at https://lccn.loc.gov/2020043887

ISBN 978-1-61429-703-1   ebook ISBN 978-1-61429-776-5

25 24 23 22 21
5 4 3 2 1

Cover image by David Talamas. Cover design by Marc Whitaker.
Interior design by James Skatges.

Printed on acid-free paper that meets the guidelines for permanence
and durability of the Production Guidelines for Book Longevity
of the Council on Library Resources.

Printed in the United States of America.

Please visit fscus.org.

Contents

Preface

The teachings in this book on the Mahasiddha Virupa's mystical songs were conducted over the course of several months by Khenpo Lama Migmar at the Sakya Institute in Cambridge, Massachusetts. The classes were then transcribed and adapted to book form.

In the interest of making this work widely available to fellow yogis, and to preserve the spontaneous nature of these teachings, we have chosen to leave the transcriptions much as they were. For this reason, the book remains conversational and informal in nature.

It is our hope that the following pages offer a window into the awakened state of one of India's greatest masters, and that the profound words of his song inspire you in your own practice. May all sentient beings everywhere experience peace.

1

Completely Pure by Nature, Like Space

THE TEACHINGS IN THIS book concern Virupa's *Treasury of Dohas*. Virupa is one of the eighty-four *mahasiddhas*, the Indian masters who practiced meditation according to the Vajrayana or tantric Buddhist path and achieved high levels of realization.

Why are these masters called mahasiddhas? *Siddha* means "accomplishment." If we examine the different practices in Buddhism, we'll see that there are four common siddhis, or accomplishments, that one can achieve. These siddhis are also called the *four karmas*. This means that meditation practice can be used to (1) pacify negativities, (2) increase all of our positive qualities, (3) achieve power and empower ourselves, or (4) destroy that which cannot be subdued. All meditation practice has a component of achieving one or more of these four siddhis or achievements.

We can address the many different needs in our lives while on the path to achieving buddhahood and awakening ourselves completely. By *needs* I mean that sometimes we experience sickness, for example.

So to pacify our sickness, we cultivate practices such as Medicine Buddha or White Tara. If we experience too much poverty, we will not be able to practice, so that's why we have developed magnetizing practices, which attract positive circumstances. We have different practices to address the different challenges that may arise.

The main purpose of any meditation practice should be to achieve buddhahood or enlightenment. This experience of attaining enlightenment is known as the *uncommon siddhi*. In all of the meditation practices that we do, our ultimate purpose is to achieve the uncommon siddhi of buddhahood. All of the common siddhis are there to support the practitioner to achieve the uncommon siddhi. Mahasiddhas are called mahasiddhas—literally, "great siddhas"—because they have achieved the uncommon siddhi, which is awakening within themselves.

Mahasiddha Virupa was one of the eighty-four mahasiddhas. In Indian Buddhist history, we see that these eighty-four mahasiddhas were the greatest practitioners of tantra, the highest system of practice transmitted by the Buddha. They were the masters who achieved the very highest level of accomplishment, which is equal to awakening and becoming a buddha. From this realization many transmissions and many blessings were passed on to other disciples.

We have received many teachings from Mahasiddha Virupa. Many meditation practices like Hevajra came from Mahasiddha Virupa. Naropa is another mahasiddha; from him we received Vajrayogini practices.

In Sanskrit, Virupa's mystical song is traditionally called a *doha*. A doha is very different from commentarial writings, or *shastras*. A doha is also different from the Buddhist discourses, or sutras. A doha is something spontaneously sung or spoken by the master based on his meditative experience.

We don't find many scholarly technicalities in dohas. Scholarly books are very dense and dry, and it takes a long time to understand them. If you study texts like the Abhidharma, there is a lot of counting, and the language is not very lively.

These scholarly texts are mostly based on technical information. They are very useful for students who are pursuing knowledge, because students will learn a great deal. However, there is not much wisdom there. Wisdom comes from within us. Wisdom is not something we can gain from the outside world or external study.

It is very important to make a distinction here between knowledge and wisdom. Knowledge is information you have collected. The more information you have stored, the more knowledge you have. Knowledge tends to be focused on learning about others.

Scholars are always investigating something outside of themselves, such as studying plants, oceans, astronomy, or history. As scholars we can accumulate a tremendous amount of information about others, but this information rarely helps us to truly know ourselves.

As a result, scholars are not necessarily transformed, despite a lifetime of study, because their focus is primarily external. The physical universe is so big, and each new discovery acts merely to incite more hunger for knowledge and exploration. Meanwhile, our short lives will pass, and at the time of our death, there is not much in essence that we have achieved from all of that knowledge.

On the other hand, those students who have some meditation experience will have the opportunity for internal realization. If they have even a glimpse of wisdom, then that glimpse of wisdom is extremely precious and has the potential to be very transformative.

These mystical songs of Mahasiddha Virupa are coming from that wisdom that has been awakened within. I can share Virupa's words with you, but how far that wisdom can be realized through you depends on the level of your mental cultivation. If our mental cultivation is not up to a certain level, then the words that we receive will not be very transformative.

But we can study these dohas and aspire to make a deeper connection. This is a fresh English translation that we have done from the original text. It is very challenging to attempt to translate from Sanskrit and Tibetan because those languages are very highly developed as far as spirituality is concerned. Perhaps they cannot contend with other languages when it comes to computer terminology or scientific language, but spiritually, Sanskrit and the Tibetan language are very advanced.

As a result, sometimes when we try to translate these ancient texts into English, it can become very challenging to find equivalent words. We must also constantly ask the question, which approach is more important? Should we choose a translation that will ultimately make the meaning clearer to the listener, or should we adhere more literally to the words of the original text? If we try to translate verbatim from the original text, then due to the limitations of the English language, it may be more difficult for the English reader to understand.

When we attempt to translate a doha word for word, then some of the original meaning may be lost. But if we try to translate focused only on transmitting the deeper meaning, then inevitably some words are missing. As a translator it is difficult to navigate these challenges.

In the original Sanskrit and Tibetan, even one word is imbued with many profound meanings. The power of these multiple meanings simply cannot be translated into English. Sometimes we have opted to leave the original word in Sanskrit, like all of the Tibetan masters have done, since most of the Mahayana and Vajrayana Buddhist teachings were originally in Sanskrit. When these original texts were translated into Tibetan, there were many words that the masters could not translate, so they left them in Sanskrit as we have done here.

These dohas are coming from the realization and experience of Mahasiddha Virupa. We can see by reading through them that when there are attempts to sing the words that express very profound and deep meditation experiences, even in Sanskrit, there will always be the limitations of language.

• • • • •

In the beginning, Virupa made two homages:

Homage to Shri Vajrasattva.
Homage to blessed Nairatmya.

This tradition of paying homage has been adopted in almost all Tibetan Buddhist works. First we pay homage to a buddha or bodhisattva. The purpose of this is to accumulate more merit. Whatever work we are going to do, in order to achieve complete success and accomplishment, we always pay homage.

In this case, Virupa paid homage to Vajrasattva because Virupa was a Vajrayana practitioner. He also paid homage to Nairatmya. Vajra Nairatmya is the consort of Hevajra.

According to Tibetan works on the history of Buddhism in India, while Virupa was teaching Buddhism during the day as the abbot of Nalanda University, he was using his nights to practice many different forms of meditation. It is said that he practiced for years without seeing any progress.

Eventually he grew discouraged, and in his frustration, he threw his *mala*, or rosary, into the latrine.

The following day, at dawn, Nairatmya appeared to him. She encouraged him to continue his meditation practice, saying that now he was very close to achieving some higher realization.

After the vision of Nairatmya, Virupa's realizations became stronger and stronger. We have many records that tell of these experiences. This is why Virupa pays homage to Nairatmya. The first song begins:

The mahamudra of samsara and nirvana
is completely pure by nature, like space.

"Mahamudra" is a very important term used in Tibetan Buddhism. *Maha* means "great" and *mudra* means "seal." This mahamudra also refers to a profound meditation experience.

The experience of mahamudra, for the yogi and for the meditator, is like space. We understand this inner space better when we look at external space. Outer space is unconditioned. It is not born, it will never cease, it is infinite, and it has been there from beginningless time.

How many planetary systems have come and gone? How many nations have come and gone? We are able to go back ten thousand or twenty thousand years through history, but beyond that, although civilizations have come and gone, space has remained unconditioned. Space is unchanged, unborn, and unceasing. It is there all the time.

This outer space, in some sense, is a reflection of our inner space. For those who have had great meditation experience, that glimpse of inner space they achieve is actually similar to the outer space.

It is similar to outer space in the sense that inner space is also unconditioned. It is there infinitely and is also not born and will never cease. It is beyond time and beyond space. It is always there. In this way we see that outer space can be a reflection of that inner space.

In the doha, Virupa is expressing his experience of this space. How many of us have had this kind of experience? The experience of inner space is very rare. We have so much internal expression, so much inner chattering. When we try to meditate, we are seldom in that inner space between our thoughts.

Instead we are full of ideas and constantly engaged in an inner dialogue with ourselves. As a result of this, all of our physical actions and our speech are merely the expression of those thoughts which are firing rapidly, one after another, in our mental continuum. We rarely have any experience of that inner space.

For someone like Virupa, who lives in that inner space all the time, there is no such thing as samsara or nirvana. Samsara is the cycle of birth, death, and rebirth. Nirvana refers to when that cycle has ceased. Unlike Virupa, because we have thoughts, our thoughts create karma. Thought and karma create our birth and fuel our entire cycle of life and death. As a result, we are constantly trapped in samsara.

Until we can achieve nirvana, samsara and nirvana will seem to be two separate things to us. We will live in samsara and be bound by our karma and our emotions. We will think of nirvana as something separate that we think we can achieve.

For Virupa, though, because he is in that state of inner space, samsara and nirvana are the same thing. Both samsara and nirvana are like space, and the nature of space is empty. In that empty space, then, both samsara and nirvana are the same.

When we have a very profound meditation experience and all of our inner chattering and thoughts are calmed and dissolved, then gradually we will know that space between our thoughts.

As that inner space between our thoughts grows bigger and bigger, we are no longer even conscious of who we are. We lose ourselves. Not only do we lose ourselves, we also lose our idea of the "other." When one's self dissolves, then the concept of "other" will also cease to exist.

While we are self-conscious, we create the idea of other. Self and other are a dualism. Because we have self-consciousness, then everything else, the whole universe, becomes the other, separate from us. The tension of attraction and aversion is born in that dualism. In that separation of self and other, there is tremendous emotional and mental conflict.

When we don't have that self-consciousness, then there is no such thing as the other. We go beyond both. Not only do we go beyond both, we also don't have any awareness of time. We don't have any consciousness of the past or future. We are always in the present.

Those of us who bring all of our past to the present will not have that experience because we can't remain in that state of inner space. We drag all of our past into the present moment, and then we lose the present. Even if we are remembering only the wonderful times we've had, our attachment to those pleasurable memories will still make it impossible for us to live in the present. The same is true if we dwell on the pain and suffering that we have experienced in the past.

If we are immersed in thoughts of attachment to all the good things of the past, or in aversion to all the pain and suffering we've endured, these thoughts will create a reaction in us. This will perpetuate the cycle of action and reaction, which will then continue into the future, and our present will be lost.

Meditators who are in that space do not react. They are not attached to all the experiences of their past. Therefore they are not creating future reactions. They have abandoned the idea of a self, so they no longer have the aversion and the attachment related to that self. They are beyond object and subject. They are also beyond time, because they are always in the present. They have even gone beyond space.

When meditators are in that inner space, they almost become omnipresent. They also become omniscient because they have dissolved the dualism, so they are not separate from the universe. They are one. One space.

Through this you can prove that when you are more awakened, you are more omnipresent, because you go beyond time. You are also more omniscient, because you have gone beyond space. This is why mahamudra is like space. The outer space is the reflection of the inner space. The realization of that inner space within the mind is mahamudra.

> Since the reality of the demonstrated object does not exist,
> it cannot be expressed through the medium of conventional
>   words.

We might be curious about the experience of that inner space. In that inner space there is no dualism. No dualism of the subject (the ego) and the object (the universe). They are all one.

This is something you will discover only through meditation experience. When you are in that deep meditation where all your thoughts and emotions and actions have calmed down, you will be at peace. You will not be conscious of a self or of others. You will become whole. You and the universe will be one and the same.

Normally we have so many attachments because we have this self-consciousness, this self-identity, and this ego. Because we have this ego, "I" is so important. Because "I" is so important, then "my" is important. So all of my possessions are the territory of the ego.

Whenever we say something is "mine" because it is attached to "I" and "me," suddenly its value goes way up. Its importance is increased dramatically because of the attachment and emotional involvement we have with it.

We can see this everywhere in our lives. We may go to a shop where many beautiful things are displayed. We may appreciate them to some extent, but the moment at which we purchase one of these objects on display, and suddenly we own it, our level of attachment immediately changes.

When we purchase something, we then identify that object as a part of ourselves, because if we exist, then that object must also exist. When we own something, the emotional involvement is increased, and so many new feelings are generated.

The realist thinks that because "I" exist, then my object should also exist. However, the teaching says, "the reality of the demonstrated object does not exist." We live in a world where "I" exist and "my object" exists. Now concerning those who are enlightened in that inner space, their egos are dissolved. When the ego is dissolved, then its object is also dissolved. In that inner space the masters could not find anything that exists independently.

Right now, for us, the outer object exists because of our emotional attachment, based on our ego in reference to that object. "I" and "my" are very strong concepts for us. But when you are in that inner space, whatever is experienced by you, the yogi, cannot be expressed in any conventional words. The experience is beyond the confines of language.

The words that we experience are mostly an expression of our emotions. Language is an expression of our thoughts and therefore of our karma. So when you are forced to express something through language, it cannot convey the experience of the ultimate. The doha says, "It cannot be expressed through the medium of conventional words," meaning that inner space cannot be expressed by language. Words are conventional and were created to express our emotions and thoughts. Since the inner space is beyond thought, beyond emotion, and beyond words, it is impossible to describe.

The essence without proliferation
by nature is free from all dependent phenomena.

The essence here refers to that inner space, and that inner space is free from dependent origination, relativity, and interdependency. It is free from all of the extremes. "Without proliferation by nature" refers to freedom from all of the extremes of our conceptual thinking. Inner space is free from existence, free from nonexistence, free from both existence and nonexistence, and free from neither existence nor nonexistence.

In our realm, almost everything is included in one of these extremes. That is why that inner space cannot be relative. It cannot be a dependent or interdependent phenomenon.

Normally, when we discuss the truth, we distinguish between "relative truth" and "ultimate truth." Relative truth is that which is created by causes and conditions and has a result. The whole principle of karma is part of relative truth.

For example, when we see a flower, it has a cause, which is the seed, as well as all of the conditions of the soil, of the minerals, of the temperature, of the sunlight, and so on, which allow for growth. Gradually this will yield a variety of results. All of the results, however, are part of karma, and therefore they are all part of the relative world.

On the other hand, if you examine that same plant very closely, piece by piece, you will not find a cause. You cannot find the conditions, and you also will not find the result. If you don't investigate, you will just assume the reality of all of this interdependence and relativity.

When you examine something very closely, however, you will find no independent existence. Without investigation and deep study, though, when you look at any of these things, you will see only relative truth.

There are many ways to understand relative truth. We can study this in more detail at the subjective level or at the objective level. When relativity is there, there is no independent existence.

Independent existence is also called ultimate truth. In this case, ultimate truth refers to the inner space. Although we can refer to that inner space as ultimate truth, as long as we have to refer to it, then that ultimate truth can only be suggested by the words we use; it cannot be realized.

The term mahamudra does not just refer to experience. It is an actual meditative state. This meditative state that yogis can experience simply cannot be expressed through language. The text says:

> It cannot be investigated or examined,
> it is free from demonstrative examples

That inner space that is called mahamudra cannot be investigated. You can investigate something only if it has parts and is relative, but this does not apply to mahamudra. We use different examples to attempt to express inner space, but no example can actually express it. The inner space of mahamudra is beyond examples. We may use examples as a reference point, but they cannot entirely convey that experience.

> it is also not abiding in freedom from examples,
> beyond the domain of the mind

All of these relativities and all of these investigations are done by the mind. When something is beyond mind, it cannot be comprehended by the mind, so that is our challenge.

When there is inner space, there is no mind. Mind is only drops of continuing thoughts, like a river. A river is made up entirely of drops of water. Between the drops, when there is a significant gap, where is the river? The river is only there when the drops of water are connected.

In the same way, the mind is merely drops of thoughts. Between our thoughts, if there is a gap, then where is the mind? You cannot examine that gap; you cannot find anything. You cannot find any conditions.

The doha is saying that the inner space is free from all of the conditions that the discursive mind creates. When something is beyond thought and beyond mind, however, then there are no conditions. This is why the outer space is a reflection of the inner space.

Where are the conditions for outer space? If there are conditions, then we can prove that outer space was born during a certain century and will cease to exist at a particular age. Outer space is the environment that allows all of the interdependency to arise. This is how we have all of these limitless planetary systems.

Within a planet like our earth, how many nations are there? How many things have come and gone? There is constant evolution. But outer space will remain the same, undisturbed by all of these changes. In a similar way, our inner space will never be affected by our emotions, our karma, and our thoughts. It is there from beginningless time until you become a buddha.

One meaning of tantra is "continuum." Continuum refers to the duration from beginningless time until you become a buddha. Inner space is unconditionally present all the time, and that is called tantra or continuum.

That continuum is there within all of us. Our sadhana practice and meditation practice allow us to see that inner space present in the mind. We rarely see that because our mind is always busy with thoughts and emotions—with action, reaction, and karma. We are consumed by our inner chattering. When we try to meditate, we see how our mind is busy with so many different things. Our mind is rarely calm because we are not seeing that inner space.

Outer and inner space are the same in the sense that both are by nature empty. The only difference is that our inner space is not only empty by nature; there is also the wisdom to see that emptiness. That is the only difference.

When our mind sees its own true empty nature, which is space, then that is wisdom. In order to realize that wisdom, we need to do all of this practice. Then we need to go beyond all these conditions to that unconditioned state.

Our meditation practice and all our accumulations of merit and wisdom allow us to go beyond these clouds of ignorance to see that inner space. Clouds come and go, but that inner space remains clear all the time.

not eternal, not annihilated, not samsara or nirvana,
not apparent, not empty, not real, not unreal, not nonarising,
not the original dharmata, and also not beyond mind

Once you are in that inner space, it's inexpressible. You are rendered speechless; it is impossible to express. You cannot say that the inner state is there or not there. You cannot say it is samsara or nirvana; you cannot possibly express it in words.

You can realize that inner space, however. You can have the experience, but you cannot express it. So this is why in the *Heart Sutra* it says "no eye, no ear, no nose" and so forth. When someone is in that inner space, then they cannot project any identification to any object. Identification is there only at the relative level, not at the ultimate level.

2

Not Eternal,
Not Annihilated

THOSE WHO HAVE STUDIED Buddhism and particularly Vajrayana may have heard the word mahamudra quite often. It is a very technical Sanskrit word, and it has many different interpretations according to different traditions.

If we look at the two components of the Sanskrit term, *maha* means "great," and *mudra* means "seal" or "stamp." When something is stamped or sealed then there is a certification that it is authentic or empowered.

This is why in ancient times whenever kings would make an important declaration, they would always place their stamp to seal that document. And instead of using a signature to authenticate or certify something, they would use this stamp or seal.

In mahamudra, the "great seal" has a meaning that is based on meditation experience. Until you have that profound meditation experience directly, then mahamudra is just a word. It is just another expression.

Mahasiddha Virupa is a very highly realized person. He is enlightened. He is another buddha. So he is trying to share his wisdom with us through these mystical songs.

Although he may be sharing a great deal and communicating so much wisdom to us, what we gain from this depends entirely on how we receive it. In one class a teacher may be teaching the same subject to many different students, but students will understand only at their own respective levels.

So that's why this is a meditation experience. If we have some meditation practice and realization, then I think we can relate to these expressions more profoundly.

There are numerous kinds of practice, and we are all doing many different meditations. Some students may be doing just *shamatha* meditation. Others may be doing some mindfulness meditation. Some may be doing contemplative meditations, and others may be doing visualization meditations. But whatever we may be doing, based on that meditation, everyone has some personal experience. People come to see me, and in the interviews, they say, "In my meditation I have this vision." People have many different experiences to report.

What we really need to know is what this experience of meditation is. Can the real experience be shared? Is it even possible for it to be expressed?

Often what we are sharing about our personal experience seems more like an extension of our inner chattering during the course of meditation. Although we may be sitting and meditating, we very rarely have that real experience of the meditative state.

We are mostly experiencing our inner chattering when we are trying to meditate. When we sit, we no longer have all the external busyness to engage us and stimulate our senses with outer objects. Instead we become more introspective, and we tend to remember more experiences related with past incidents.

It is quite common that when these thoughts and memories surface in meditation, we mistakenly think we are having some meditative experience. Perhaps these thoughts have been repressed because circumstantially we have been so busy with other things for so long. We haven't given these repressed memories a chance to arise until we sit still.

Since our senses are not stimulated by outer objects during meditation, then we have more inner room to express. When all our outer senses are closed, that basic mind is now expressing all these buried thoughts. Quite often we think that these are meditation experiences that we are having, but they rarely are.

Virupa says that mahamudra is completely pure by nature and similar to space. We all know something about outer space, right? But if we want to describe that space, how will we? At this point we will describe outer space based on whatever that space is in reference to our inner conditions.

As long as we have some object, even something as vast as outer space, that is still not a real meditation experience. For that reason, I emphasize that the outer space is just another reflection of the true meditative state, which is the inner space.

So imagine that the drops of thoughts in our mental continuum are rushing rapidly through our minds. These drops of thoughts are coming and going so rapidly that they have become a rushing river. In the midst of that rushing river, how many of us have experienced that space between our thoughts?

If we have never experienced the space between our thoughts, then even though we may be trying to perfect our meditation, whatever experience we discuss stems from those drops of thoughts and not from the space between them.

But if you do become familiar with that state, that space between our thoughts, then what will there be to express? Who is the expresser, what is the expression, and what is it that we can possibly express?

This all may sound very impersonal. But as long as we have thoughts rushing one after another, these thoughts are there because of the person, because of the ego involved. So if something is experienced in that space between our thoughts, then that will be impersonal. And if something is impersonal, then how can you convey it by saying, "I have had this experience?"

Sometimes that state of meditation, that space between our thoughts, is beyond time and beyond space. You don't even feel your physical body anymore. That's why sometimes it is called bliss or joy. It is beyond any feeling based on the ego because the ego is dissolved. The ego is gone. The ego has disappeared, and that's why the experience is beyond any time or space or any feeling.

Now it is possible that when you emerge from that state, you may think that you have had such a great feeling or experience. But if you want to express that experience in words, it will be very challenging.

Even though mystics are always trying to express their experiences, their expressions are mere words—they are just a reference point for us. They do not really express what the masters have experienced.

We can take an example from ordinary life. What if we try to share the experience of eating sugar? We say sugar is sweet, but how will you possibly describe what sweetness is to someone who has not experienced it? You may try to describe it with words and analogies to other things. But no matter what words you use, you will still be unable to express the real experience to someone who has never tasted anything sweet.

Furthermore, we face so much miscommunication. We face miscommunication caused by different languages. For example, the word for sugar may mean something different in Hindi than it does in Sanskrit. We presume our native language should be the only language in the universe, but that, of course, is not the case.

Language is something man has created for reference and communication. It is man-made; it is not a universal or divine method of communication! It is not based on natural law. It is something humans have created. For this reason, all languages have tremendous limitations.

In order to communicate the sweetness of sugar to the seven billion people of the world, we would need to create a language that would have the same meaning for everyone—a universal language.

But as we know, this is not the case. Within a given culture and a given time period, people have agreed to common interpretations of particular words. But the ways in which we understand and use those words has constantly changed throughout history. So language is always relative.

The scientific approach is to try to explain and prove the sweetness of sugar based on its chemical components. But understanding the chemical makeup of sugar will still not tell us anything about what it is to taste that sweetness. Science cannot explain that experience to us. Someone with certain neurological impairments or with no sense of taste will never know the experience of sweetness. Only when someone has tasted sugar will it be possible to say, "Sweetness is like this." But still it is very subjective.

Whatever you have tasted or experienced on your tongue, with your senses, is very personal. So even our own personal sensory experiences are impossible to communicate to others completely.

This is how it is in the relative world. In order to discuss mahamudra, the ultimate nature, the individual ego has to dissolve. When we have transcended the ego and ceased to see ourselves as individuals, then our experience will be very different.

In that space between your thoughts, where is your subjective "I"? Where is the person? Where are your feelings? The moment that emotion and individuality arise, then you lose that space. But if you are in that space between your thoughts, all your ideas, feelings, and activities dissolve. That state of dissolution is the meditative state. All of the various types of meditation are trying to reach that same experience.

Those who believe they have experienced that meditative state may try to describe their experience to others. In their attempt to share, much is lost in translation. If we personalize that experience, speak of it as something we have accomplished, then in the moment we express it, something immediately is lost. Here it says:

not eternal, not annihilated, not samsara or nirvana

Those who are in that space cannot find any existence. We can begin to understand this by examining outer space. There are so many things that appear in space. The clouds come and go in the open space of the sky. All these planetary systems and galaxies come and go. The whole universe is subject to change.

In the nature of space can you find any permanent, unconditioned existence? You cannot. But if you have strong attachment, you will not experience that space. Our attachment is the beginning of all of our creations. If you are very attached to the idea of having a house, then you will work very hard to buy or build that house in order to satisfy your desire.

So that intense need comes from the seeds of attachment inside our mind. In a similar sense our physical body is also a home. Although we don't remember this, even our physical body was formed and created based on attachment. We can easily see how much attachment we have to others, but our primary attachment is to our idea of ourselves. It is because of our self-attachment that we grow attached to others.

Although we cannot remember the moment of conception, our current life is proof of that conception. Our present life is also in some sense the witness who knows how we have lived our life from conception.

Our lives are full of attachment. As long as we have attachment, we will always project some kind of existence—they go together. Attachment cannot live without the idea of existence. This applies not only to our attachment to objects but also to our attachment at the level of ideas, at the level of feelings, and at the level of actions.

As we become better meditators, we may grow more detached from outer objects. But until we have experienced mahamudra, that space between our thoughts, then we may still remain attached to some ideas.

Why are we so fixated on wanting something to be permanent? In very basic ways in our own life we know that some things are not real or lasting, but still the power of our attachment wants to make them so.

We all know that one day we will die. This is very difficult news because most of us want to live forever. Our attachment to permanence creates tremendous conflict in us. Who wants to die? Because we desire to live forever, when death is forced on us, it is often extremely painful on all levels. This is proof of how attachment is so related to existence.

If we look closely at our minds, we see that as long as we have attachment, we endlessly project different objects that we think we need in order to live comfortably. These objects could be material, they could be at the feeling or idea level, or they could even be at the level of the divine. Perhaps we are even clinging to our idea of a God in order to feel safe and comfortable.

Based on our attachment we project something we desire. It is our clinging to that thing we want that creates eternalism. Even from a purely psychological standpoint we can prove this. So this is why Virupa says "not eternal." When you want something to be eternal, then based on your strong attachment you will have insecurity and fear.

Attachment, fear, and eternalism all go together and perpetuate each other. When you experience fear, then you need something to cling to, and you are always looking for something to make you more comfortable. In this way our whole psychology and mental involvement becomes very dependent.

In this weakened state we are much like babies who need a mother or father to depend on. When fathers and mothers are around, we feel good, self-confident, and secure. We see this all the time. Children are very happy and relaxed when their parents are around. But when their parents leave, they often become very sad and insecure. Our life is often controlled by these polarities.

Where there is attachment we project the eternal. But where there is aversion and anger we project nihilism. Attachment starts our life, and anger causes our death—death in the sense of nihilism. We hear many tragic stories about people who have ended their own lives due to so much self-hatred, despair, or mental illness. They may feel hatred toward the universe and anger at themselves. These emotions drive them to commit suicide because they believe the mind will cease. So this nihilism formed by anger and hatred is another extreme, another polarity.

Eternalism and nihilism are both extremes. They arise in us because we have a lot of attachment and aversion. Due to attachment and aversion we create and express these conditions. If you are a very centered and wholesome person, then you will not feel that same need to have some object to cling to. By "wholesome" I mean someone who is in that state between our thoughts where there is no attachment and no aversion. When you are in that inner space, you won't feel the need to hate anyone. You will be free from both of these extremes.

You will only experience this centered state when your meditation experience becomes better and better. When you begin to have that glimpse of inner space between our thoughts, then that is proof that there is a middle, that there is a center that is free from these two extremes.

The experience of mahamudra is an experience that is free from all extremes. Our daily life is full of extremes. We are always living in polarities. We have excitement due to attachments, and we have depression due to anger. All of our feelings and projections are based on these extremes.

The state that is "not eternal, not nihilistic" is the state of mahamudra, the great seal. This is the space between our thoughts in meditation that is free from all the extremes. For those who are in that state, they no longer have any inner chattering. For those who are not in that state, then regardless of what type of meditation they are doing, it is really just another occasion for more inner chattering.

Early in your meditation practice you will have more and more inner chattering. One effective way to monitor your meditation experience is to keep a meditation journal. This is a journal where you can write about all your meditation experiences. When you go back and read them, you will have a good sense for how your practice is progressing.

If the thoughts that surface in your meditation are thoughts of attachment, or if you are angry and imagining killing something, this is a good indicator that you are still caught in extremes. Your mind is still working in polarities. You are not in the center. You are not in the present yet.

These impulses toward attachment and aversion are very related with our thoughts of the past. If you are truly in the present, you will not fall into these extremes. The mahamudra experience is free from all the extremes including samsara and nirvana. This is very important.

Over and over again we are born, we live, and we die in this perpetual cycle of existence. As long as we do not know that inner space of mahamudra, we will be trapped in this cycle of birth, life and death. Our attachment will lead us to desire an object, and this will force our conception.

If you read the *Tibetan Book of the Dead*, it describes the whole journey of living, the dying process, the bardo, and conception. Although we have experienced endless cycles of birth and death, we cannot remember them. For some of us this may be too much to consider at present. It may be easier to think of death as being similar to sleep. When we have a very deep sleep, we completely forget everything about the world. We don't remember any thoughts.

The cycle of sleeping and waking is a good way to contemplate death and birth. The buddhas or enlightened ones who have gone through all the stages of death, bardo, and rebirth are even able to remember conception and being just a fetus. These enlightened ones describe sleeping and waking up as an experience that is similar to death and rebirth. This may be challenging for us at this point because we cannot remember these experiences, and we may not be sure that there is rebirth.

We fall asleep and wake up over and over again because there is a continuum. What is continuing is our consciousness. In the consciousness there is the ego with its attachment and aversion. So even deep in our dreams we have nightmares based on these emotions.

It's been said that everyone dreams regardless of whether you remember your dreams or not. In a sense your journey after death through the bardo experience is similar to dreaming. You will have scary dreams when you have lots of anger and hatred repressed inside your mind. And if there is something you've wanted very badly and you have not gotten it, then that unexpressed desire will also affect your dreams.

The process is very similar to death. When we have these unsettling dreams, it means that there are still lots of emotions repressed in our mind and mental consciousness. These emotions propel us to wake up, to live, and to go back to sleep in this continuous cyclic journey.

Samsara is a continuation of the emotions in the mind from moment to moment. And based on those emotions we create all of our actions repeatedly. Due to these actions we create more karma and emotion, and this forces our mind to continue from one moment to another. This is how we remain in samsara.

Every moment we are continuing. Every moment we are born, every moment we are dying, every moment we are awake. That is samsara. So as long as we have ego and emotions, we are living.

Meditators who have seen that space are no longer attached to self and other. There is no attachment, and because there is no attachment, there is also no longer any aversion. In that inner space there is no ego, and the self is gone. Without the self, the concept of other also dissolves.

For those who have gone beyond self and other, there is no samsara. They are not forced to be born because they don't have the ego to create attachment. And they don't have attachment to create any aversion.

It is important to make the distinction that mahamudra is not nirvana. Nirvana is the cessation of your karma, your feelings, your actions and everything. Nirvana is when you cease to be forced by karma to be reborn again and again.

Samsara and nirvana are opposite extremes. Samsara is life continuing one moment after another, and nirvana is the cessation of that life. For those who have achieved nirvana, life based on the ego has disappeared, leaving only enlightenment and wisdom. But the important distinction is that mahamudra is beyond both samsara and nirvana.

Those who have studied Indian and Tibetan Buddhism know that mahamudra is the highest experience. Nirvana, on the other hand, is simply the experience of understanding selflessness and freeing yourself completely from suffering and rebirth.

Mahamudra is the nature of the mind, which is the union of wisdom and compassion. Mahamudra is also described as the realization of the union of clarity and emptiness. Clarity is that wisdom, and emptiness is free from all destructive emotions.

Because mahamudra is the union of wisdom and compassion, the power of that compassion is what inspires the conscious reincarnation of enlightened beings. It is the compassion that activates the wisdom so that, even after becoming enlightened, a buddha will take rebirth in order to benefit others. In this way, mahamudra is not a cessation. It is beyond cessation and beyond both samsara and nirvana.

In contrast to this, the whole purpose of Theravada practices such as mindfulness meditation is to achieve nirvana. That is the ultimate goal of all Theravada training.

But the purpose of Vajrayana and Mahayana practices is to experience mahamudra, which is the union of wisdom and compassion. Mahamudra is beyond both samsara and nirvana, so for enlightened beings who have experienced it, reincarnation is not forced, but rather a conscious choice, made with deep compassion for the sake of all sentient beings.

Now for those of us who do not have this enlightened understanding, our actions and emotions have forced us to be reborn again and again. For us, forced rebirth is painful. Living is also painful both physically and emotionally, and death is very painful.

Enlightened beings who have chosen to be reincarnated are not subjected to this same pain and suffering. They have chosen to take rebirth out of their own free will. They are reincarnating to benefit others. In this way, mahamudra is beyond both samsara and nirvana.

Mahamudra is neither eternal nor nihilistic. Mahamudra is also not samsara or nirvana. So with this one line from Virupa, what we understand is that the meditative state of mahamudra is free from all extremes. It is beyond the cycle of birth, life, and death.

3

Not Apparent, Not Empty

VIRUPA'S MYSTICAL SONG IS based on meditative realization. As we meditate more, these words will make more and more sense to us. However, if we have never done any meditation, then it is very likely that reading and discussing these songs will not make much sense.

In fact, if we have no meditation experience, studying these songs and teachings could actually create more conflict in us. Our life is conceived with conflicting emotions. Our strong emotions of attachment inspire our feelings of aversion as well. We carry these conflicting emotions into our present lives, and as a result, we are very restless, very eager for distraction.

So we can prove this through personal experience. When we are not doing meditation, all of our senses are externally pursuing sensual objects. The song says:

not apparent, not empty, not real, not unreal, not nonarising

The mystical song is challenging how we perceive things in our life. If we reflect on how we live, we see a paradoxical life of conflicting emotions. This is why we have all these objects of desire and attachment. We see that when this desire is not fulfilled, we have anger.

In some sense our life is based on this interaction between desirable objects and the objects of aversion. When our desire is fulfilled, we feel pleasure, we feel happy. When our desire is not fulfilled, we feel angry. Out of that anger we have pain.

When Virupa says "not apparent," he is challenging how we interact with the universe and how our feelings, ideas, and so forth are based on these emotions. What are the causes of these emotions? If we can just examine how we act in the universe in the first place, we will develop a deeper understanding.

We have eyes, and because we have eyes, we see something. We have visual objects. Ordinarily the deciding factor in proving whether something exists depends on whether you have seen it or not. For example, in jury duty, in the conventional legal process, what you have seen is taken as the truth, the proof that something happened or exists.

This may be the case in our ordinary life. But here in the songs, when it says that mahamudra or mystical realization is "not apparent," it is challenging how we perceive our life. This reference to "not apparent" is also reflected in the profound words of the *Heart Sutra*, which say:

No eye, no ear, no nose, no tongue, no body, no mind, no
form, no sound, no smell, no taste, no touch, no dharmas.

For those of us who do not have mystical realization, when the sutra says "no eye," and that ultimate realization or truth is not apparent, it doesn't make sense to us. We know we have an eye! And because our vision is the basis on which to prove that something exists or not for all of the visual objects, we are convinced that everything we see exists.

We don't have the required realization to go beyond both seeing and not seeing because we never have lived that life, and we don't have that understanding. We operate as if everything in our lives is based on whether we have seen or not seen something.

Seen and not seen are there because, in the first place, we have the eye organ. This does not apply to blind people who never have seen anything. For them, seen or not seen will not apply. Only for those who have healthy eyes will apparent visual objects apply. Whether you have seen or not seen is based on whether you have a working eye organ.

So we've established that to prove whether something exists or not we rely on the eye organ. We make the eye organ so important in our lives that it is almost like the judge of everything we do and experience. But when the *Heart Sutra* says "no eye," it is challenging us to ask how truthfully we are seeing things. When our eye is perceiving, how truthfully are we actually seeing that object? This is the wonderful challenge we face, the paradigm shift our spiritual practice demands of us.

For those who are not doing any meditation, this challenge may not even surface in their consciousness. For most people, if the eye sees it, it exists. That is what is valid in shaping all of their decisions and reactions.

But for those who have meditation experience, the more practice you have done, the more you can begin to go beyond what you have seen. Now you are not just relying on this flesh and blood and whatever organ is experiencing the world. You are going beyond those basic sense perceptions to see things with the wisdom eye. That seeing that is born from wisdom is a kind of seeing without eyes.

Of course, most of the time we see *with* our eyes, and that's why we presume that what we see is actually universal. We assume that what we see must be the same for everyone. With a little examination we learn that this is not the case. What we've seen is shaded by our emotions. My eye organ is reliable only according to my inner conditions.

For example, when we meet people, if we don't have any information about them, and we are seeing them for the first time, we have no preconceived idea of who they are. But the more we spend time with them, the more information we gather about them; although we are still seeing the same person, we are beginning to see them in very different ways.

As we gather more information about them, we begin to form concepts. We determine their value to us. We come to recognize either an attachment, an aversion, or an indifference to them. So although our eye organ is still looking at the very same people, we may see them very differently after we've spent more time with them.

So that's why we say, "Beauty is in the eye of the beholder." Beauty is just an idea that we have formed based on our inner conditions that are based on our emotions. The same person may appear beautiful to one beholder and very ugly to another.

We certainly see that definitions of beauty on a broader cultural scale are radically different. I come from Asia, so the standards for what is desirable may be very different from the ideals of beauty here in the West. If someone has access to a lot of food, they may become bigger, and in some Asian cultures this is a sign of wealth, a sign of abundance! Only the beggars on the street are skinny. In a country that has famine, thinness is not something people value or aspire to!

Then we look at the Western world, and we see that all the models are skinny, and that thinness is seen to be beautiful. All the rich people try to be so thin as a sign of their success!

So in some countries being bigger is very beautiful. Even the buddhas are very fat! And in other countries being overweight is a sign of ugliness. But if we don't have any cultural preconditioning, then neither is ugly nor beautiful. They are the same.

We have to look more closely at who created the idea to project that value onto that object. And also, even within a given culture, our ideas of what's desirable are constantly changing. Our ideas change as often as the design of our clothes. When I was growing up in India, young people liked to wear bell-bottom pants that flared at the bottom. They wanted their pants to be very big! Then later that grew out of fashion, and now jeans are supposed to be very skinny.

So everything changes according to the times. And then according to these changes, our emotions are also affected. When everybody is wearing bell bottoms, if we don't have them, then we may experience so much pain worrying that we are not like everyone else!

Our values are based on the concepts we have formed through the influence of family and cultural conditioning. Then according to that conditioning, we project all the values and judgments onto the world around us.

When a meditator like Virupa says that the meditative state of mahamudra is "not apparent," what he is really saying is that whatever is apparent is not reliable. What he's saying is that this relationship between the ideas in your mind, your six sense organs, and the six sense objects taken together form what seems apparent.

When we see, when we hear, when we smell, when we touch, when we taste—how reliable are these experiences? This is the question Virupa is challenging us to ask.

We are under the mistaken impression that we don't have a life if we are not constantly pursuing these sensual objects based on our emotions. Our eyes are always grasping at visual objects according to our attachments and desires. The whole entertainment industry is based on this pursuit of sensory distraction.

The same applies to our other senses, which are always craving sound, smell, taste, and touch. This is the driving force in our daily existence. We are desperately pursuing these sensual objects in the hopes of experiencing more sustained pleasure and happiness.

Our focus in meditation is the opposite of this pursuit of sensory pleasure. We are focused inward, and we are practicing renunciation from worldly activities. If you become a great yogi, however, and if you have gained deep meditative experience, it may be possible to carry that meditative state into all of your activities regardless of what you are doing.

At the moment we constantly carry conflicting emotions around with us. But if you are a great yogi, then outwardly you may appear to be doing ordinary activities, but really you are remaining in an extraordinary and constant state of meditative wisdom. That state is a place of total freedom, complete independence. Existence is a very different experience for those who have achieved this level of realization.

For most of us, however, in order to practice meditation, we first need to become very introverted. We need to try to bring all our focus and attention onto one object. This is because in the beginning our attention is dispersed across so many activities. We are constantly multitasking, and our focus is very scattered. Due to this frenetic pace, our minds are extremely restless and unpeaceful.

Our mind is not capable of accomplishing all of these things we expect of it because we have underlying conflicting emotions. These conflicting emotions, when they escalate, become the cause of all of our stress and anxiety.

Early in our meditation practice we attempt to develop some attention by focusing on one object. As we progress in our practice, we see that in meditation we become capable of abandoning our dependence on outer objects, and we also are no longer relying on our sense organs. We begin to rely more on the mind and mental activities, and then we must attempt to go beyond even those. Meditators who have gone beyond mental activities have profound mystical experiences.

For us, we may be moving away from reliance on outer objects through our meditation. But still we are dependent on something like our breathing. Still we are relying on the mind, and we have not gone completely beyond.

Occasionally in our meditation we may gain some glimpse of that mystical experience in which we experience that freedom. In that glimpse we are not depending on the object, the sense organ, or the mind. In that glimpse we will understand what Virupa is referring to when he said, "not apparent."

"Not apparent" is when you have the experience of going beyond both the sense organ and the sense object. In this way you will have no eye, and you will have no object of the eye, and so no form. This is what is meant when the *Heart Sutra* says "no eye, no ear, no nose . . ." and lists all the sense organs as well as the sense objects, that is, "no form, no sound, no smell. . . ." This experience of going beyond both sense organ and sense object will become your experience only through the meditative state.

When you experience that mystical meditative state, then for the first time you are free of conflicting emotions. This is an incredible new freedom. You suddenly have inner independence.

Until this point, although we may think we have some freedom, really we are controlled by our emotions. Our whole universe is divided into three groups in our mind. And, based on those mental categories, every object we encounter will invoke an emotional response of some sort.

Based on these reactions to the objects in our lives, we are trapped in this cycle of pain and pleasure, of happiness and unhappiness, and we are even trapped in our neutral feelings of indifference to objects. But this experience of "not apparent" that Virupa speaks of is challenging the truth of not only the object but also your sense organ and your mind and mental activities.

This is the meditative way in which the yogis have examined these questions. But it is also possible to explore this in a more scientific manner. Buddhist philosophers have examined this through a very logical process of inquiry. Ultimately they have realized that what you see, those apparent objects you perceive, have no inherent independent existence.

If you examine any object, reducing it down to the smallest atom, you cannot find any validity or independent existence. Buddhist scholars came to this conclusion through logical examination 2500 years ago. And now scientists are experimenting and coming to the very same conclusions.

There is very active engagement now between Buddhism and science. When you listen to these discussions between leading scientists and Buddhist practitioners, although they may use different terms to describe these same principles, increasingly we find that science is now proving what philosophers have believed for hundreds and hundreds of years.

So whether it is examined through philosophy or through science, the truth should be the same. You can also apply this to the actual sense organs themselves. Sense organs are also made up of atoms, and in a similar way, you can reduce them down to the last atom and realize there is no inherent existence. And this same process can also be applied to the mind. Even the mind does not exist independently.

If you cannot find any independent existence in even one of these three, the sense organ, sense object, or mind and mental consciousness, then it is very challenging to prove that there is ultimate existence in any of them.

Without examination, in the course of our conventional life in relativity, we say, "Yes, we have eyes, and yes, we absolutely see things, and they appear very real to us!"

But ultimately what we learn from the great masters is that in a higher meditative state, the sense organ, sense object, and mind do not exist. So when the song is saying "not apparent" and when the *Heart Sutra* says "no eye, no ear, no nose, no tongue, no body, no mind, no form, no sound" and so forth, they are speaking of the same experience. When you investigate, ultimately you cannot find eyes, you cannot find form, you cannot find ears, you cannot find sound, and this is true of all sense organs and perceptions.

not apparent, not empty, not real, not unreal, not nonarising

So the great yogis not only examine this conclusion of nonappearance, but they also integrate conventional experience into their spiritual cultivation.

For example, when Mahasiddha Virupa was teaching the three visions, he was also teaching about this same topic. As sentient beings with afflictive emotions, we experience constant suffering of one sort or another, and that is the nature of our existence.

Out of the triad of sense organ, object, and mind, the inner condition in the mind has the most power over our sense organ and object. This is why our conflicting emotions in the mind then manifest in the sense organ and affect how it perceives the sense object. So, based on our desire, we have pleasure and happiness. Based on our aversion, we have anger and pain. These inner conditions define all of our sensory experiences.

As long as we have afflictive emotions causing all of this inner mental turmoil, we will also perceive the world around us through all of our sense organs with this same level of conflicting feelings.

Now Mahasiddha Virupa said that for those who are on the spiritual path, we can use these same conflicting emotions to cultivate something positive, to encourage our spiritual growth. So through our own experience of pain and suffering we deepen our compassion for all living beings. And from our desire for happiness we cultivate loving kindness for others.

For yogis, these afflictive emotions become the basis of all of positive emotional development. Without desire and anger, without pain and pleasure, you cannot develop loving-kindness and you cannot develop compassion. And at some point when your love and compassion are integrated with wisdom and become mystical experience, then your perception of the universe will completely change.

In this mystical state you will no longer categorize anything in the universe into groups of enemies, friends, desirable, or undesirable objects. Everyone and everything will be the same. You will be free from all of the emotions that separate you from the universe.

This is why Mahasiddha Virupa said that those who have been transformed through spiritual practice and have a mystical experience will have the experience of total purity. Because you have achieved this purity inside of you, which is free from all of the discursive emotions, you are able to see the outer world with this same purity.

You have abandoned all judgments. You no longer call something good or bad. You no longer call someone a friend or enemy. You no longer assign different values to different objects because now you have seen the purity within you. And because you have seen that purity, everything around you becomes pure. This is the realization that is the goal of tantric practice.

If I am here in the universe of impurity and encountering Virupa who is singing this mystical song from that place of purity, then naturally we have a paradox. Virupa's songs will be very challenging for us to understand here in the relative world.

This is why it takes meditation to integrate our ordinary way of life with that extraordinary way of the mystical experience. Without meditation, the meaning of these songs will be hard to perceive because we are not at that level of wisdom.

So things can only become "not apparent" for people who are now in that state of purity. Now they have gone beyond seeing something as ugly or beautiful, as good or bad. They have gone beyond both. They are seeing the universe through the wisdom eye. They go beyond conventional seeing to see reality. That's why it is not just apparent, it is beyond apparent. Someone like Virupa has gone beyond seeing the apparent and nonapparent, because now he has seen true wisdom. His seeing is not based on the eye organ.

So if we examine the meaning of "not real, not unreal," first we have this apparent object that we experience with our sense organs. Whether something is valued as real or not is based entirely on what we carry inside of our minds. Whether something exists to us is dependent on what our sense organs have connected to different objects. And how much those objects have been impressed on our minds will then determine whether we perceive something as being real or not.

Based on our emotions, based on the attachment inside our minds, we can project things as being real. Sometimes if we are possessed by very strong emotions, then even those objects that we don't ordinarily see may appear real to us because our feelings are so intense.

Whether something appears real or not is very much based on our emotions. But those yogis who have mystical experiences—because they have gone beyond all of those emotions—at the mental level do not have that experience of reality anymore. Their experience of reality is now based on wisdom. And that wisdom is free from all emotion.

Those highly realized yogis are even free from the question of whether something is real or not. Real or unreal is based on your own ideas—ideas that you have formed in your mind based on experiences with apparent objects.

For example, if you have met someone, and then due to some emotional connection you carry that person in your mind, then even if that person is gone for many years, they still remain very clear and very real in your mind.

So although the person as a physical being is gone, really for you that person still exists because he or she is still so present in your head. And what exists in your head can still make you do things. It can still be a cause of action and reaction.

Yogis do not have that problem. They remain in the present. They don't have that inner chattering to incite feelings and fantasies and memories inside their minds.

This means that "not real, not unreal" is referring to the things that you carry inside you. Most of the time the things you carry inside you depend on how much emotional involvement you have in reference to those objects. The more attached you are to someone or something, the more you carry it in your mind. You become bound to this object of your attachment. If the attachment is strong enough, then sometimes you will even carry this bond into the next life.

Yogis don't have this problem because they have the realization of wisdom. Wisdom is there within us all the time; we just have to discover it through meditation. That wisdom that we have within us is not born because of meditation. It has always been there. We simply have to see it again.

As we already addressed at the beginning of the doha, the wisdom of mahamudra is similar to space. Space is not born from somebody else. Space is not created by something else, by some other object. Space is not born because of the clouds. Space is not born because of the wind or the ocean. Space is there unconditionally. In the same way, the inner space without emotions and without karma—the inner space that yogis experience—is there all the time.

This is why this tradition of practice is called tantra or continuum. It is there for all time. It has been there from beginningless time, and it is still there inside us. We only have to discover it again. And once we have discovered it, we cannot say that our discovery has created or caused that wisdom. That wisdom has been in us the whole time. It is simply that the clouds that have obscured our wisdom are removed, and now we can recognize that inner space again.

Similarly, when the clouds of your emotions are gone, you see that inner space within you. That inner space is unconditioned. It is nonarising because it has always been there.

If something arises for the first time, then maybe there is some cause for its existence, and it may also come to an end when that cause expires. But this space is there all the time within you. That is why it is not born, and it does not cease. It is nonarisen because it doesn't have a first cause, and it is not nonarisen because it doesn't have an end.

Only when something has a first cause should it be understood as arising. Anything that is born has some beginning. But this inner space of wisdom doesn't have a beginning or an end. It has gone beyond both.

These are the different expressions through which Mahasiddha Virupa is trying to share his experience with us. Only when you have some glimpse of this experience will these teachings make sense. If you have never done any meditation, and if you don't have a glimpse of that inner space, then these lines may not resonate with you.

These dohas are just a reference to inspire us to do more practice. To encourage us that through meditation there is another way to experience our lives, another way to experience reality. That's why the yogis and mystics wanted to share their mystical experiences with us. They inspire us not to become too dependent on conventional life. Being trapped in the values of conventional life is not how we will achieve our highest potential. Our minds are capable of far more.

With dedication, our meditative practice will uncover this unconditioned inner space of wisdom that has always been inside us.

4

Not Real, Not Unreal, Not Nonarising

not apparent, not empty, not real, not unreal, not nonarising

IN THIS LINE, VIRUPA is referring to the mystical experience of the wisdom you have gained through meditation practice. But for those like us who have not achieved that experience, then the meaning of arising is different.

At our level, "arising" refers to birth. Due to our birth we are then able to experience the universe. Because we have a physical body, then we have all the sense organs to see, to smell, to taste, to register sound, and to feel the tangible through touching. Through our sense organs we make contact with the apparent objects, which we then hungrily consume.

After we make contact with apparent objects, if we don't have that mystical experience of wisdom, then our consumption of these objects will create many emotional responses in us. And these feelings will then give rise to so much inner chattering in our minds as we respond to and categorize our experience.

As we have mentioned earlier, when you see something for the first time, without any prior information, you won't have much emotional involvement with it. But after that initial meeting, when you learn more about that person or that object, then you begin to form an image in your mind.

Based on our inner conditions of emotions and karma, we begin to project more concepts onto that object or person. We begin to create our individual reality with our inner chattering, and it dramatically alters how we perceive things. We project these values onto objects, and then we carry these ideas in our minds as truth, as reality.

But this exploration of arising and nonarising can have a much deeper level. If we don't have the mystical experience of going beyond both arising and nonarising, then we continue to see birth as the first cause, the moment that something starts. And we will continue to create all of these different experiences of apparent objects inside our minds and consider them real.

In order to begin to transform how we live our lives, we can turn to the Buddha's life story for inspiration and encouragement. When the Buddha was still Prince Siddhartha, he grew curious and left the confines of his palace to look around. He saw the sick, the old, and the dying. This progression is our conventional life experience. We are born, we get sick, we get old, and we die. Without any spiritual practice or meditation, our life's journey stops at death.

Without spiritual practice what happens after death remains a complete mystery; we don't know anything about the dead. Even in India, a country that is a major center of religious tradition, there is still a group that is similar to modern-day Humanists who don't believe in anything before birth or after death.

The Buddha set out to pursue something greater. He could easily have spent his whole life in the palace. It is said that he had hundreds of women and attendants. All of his earthly desires were met. He could easily have stayed there indulging his senses, but he remained restless. As the story goes, the fourth time he ventured out from the palace, after witnessing the sick, the old, and the dying, he then saw a yogi. This was a very significant moment.

We can interpret this life story as a wonderful analogy for our own understanding of this doha. In order to achieve this mystical experience of going beyond both "nonarising" and "not nonarising," you have to go beyond death. The only way to go beyond death is through meditation.

The fourth appearance in the Buddha's life story—the appearance of the yogi—inspired him to look further than death. If we see death as the end of everything, then it is easy to rationalize all of our indulgent behaviors. If we think our only experience unfolds in this one lifespan between birth and death, and if we don't believe in karma or rebirth, then it is easy to focus our whole lives on pursuing happiness through trying to satisfy our senses.

But those who have not stopped at death in their inquiry, those who have gone further in their spiritual investigation, have uncovered a deeper message. As they go beyond the limiting notions of birth and death, there is a transformation of their entire experience.

In our own practice we become a spiritual person for the first time when we take refuge. By taking refuge in the Buddha, the Dharma, and one's spiritual community or Sangha, we are now letting go of our former worldly selves. In some sense it is a small death, a letting go of our old way of living, and in its place our spiritual self emerges.

After taking refuge you are a new person. You have resolved to transform yourself and to become a spiritual being. Through your meditation experience, if you have that mystical experience of the wisdom of that inner space between our thoughts, then you will understand for the first time that you are nonarising. You will understand that you were not born and will not cease.

This is what is meant when the *Heart Sutra* says, "the wisdom gone beyond, unborn and unstopped." This experience of inner space, of that wisdom, is beyond birth. Because it is beyond birth, then it is also beyond death. There is no cessation. Meditation can allow us to experience that state, which is free from both birth and death.

Now we need to ask the question: what is birth and what is death? Although in conventional life we are all born, most of us have no memory of our birth experience. We may celebrate our birthday, but we have no real connection to what the actual experience was like for us.

For those who have a mystical experience, death is not actually death. Through meditation you can experience a state of wisdom that is not subject to death or birth. In this way, the buddhas who are fully enlightened are beyond birth and death.

This begs the question: if there is no death, how are the buddhas reincarnated? What we learn from the teachings is that for us, birth is actually forced by our emotions and karma. Because of karma we are thrown back into birth and death in an endless cycle. But the buddhas choose rebirth out of compassion for the sake of all sentient beings.

Normally we have no memory of the moment of conception. Most of us don't remember when we were conceived because we also have no memory of our death. Buddhist teachings say that if you have some memory of your death, you will also be able to remember your birth.

At our level we know that we will all die. And 99 percent of us will die with tremendous physical and mental pain and anguish. I have spent time with the old and the dying, and you see in the hospitals here nearly everyone is on very intense painkillers and sedatives like morphine. Many of these drugs numb you completely, and you have absolutely no consciousness of your own death process.

Most of the time, when you are presented with unbearable pain, you choose this pain relief. But the yogis and some lamas say that even if you have intense pain, it is better to remain aware of that pain as you die instead of relying on medication. There will come a time in our own lives when we may be forced to make that choice. The stronger our meditative experience is, the more freedom we will have in making that decision.

The way our medical system is geared, most of us will die under the influence of strong painkillers, and we will not know how we die. We will be so spaced out during our death that it will be similar to a deep sleep. But even in that state of deep sleep, although you cannot remember anything, your consciousness is still continuing.

When you wake up in the morning and you're conscious again, you will still carry all the experiences you have gathered and all of the emotions you have lived with. Birth is very similar to this. We will carry all of our old habitual patterns and cravings and emotions into our next life. These desires will force our conception again and again, and we will be driven by impulses that we don't understand because we lack awareness.

With our desire we look for an object to become attached to. When something threatens that attachment, then we experience aversion. We are attached to that object in the first place because we are not awakened. Through our forced rebirth we have continued to carry all of our emotions and karmic propensities in our mental continuum.

So conception is the moment where the mind, driven by all of these desires and other emotions, becomes imprisoned in the object of your attachment, which in this case is your parents.

Out of all the objects we form attachments to, we know from our personal experience that our strongest emotions are for other human beings, especially those of the opposite gender.

This is how we have been conceived—with all of these conflicting emotions. There is no free will involved. We are forced into rebirth by our emotions, and when we act and react with those emotions, we are conceived. And from these mental activities our physical body evolves. Matter is formed from our mind and emotions. Consciousness does not arise from our physical form; it is the very basis on which the physical body first takes shape.

If we study each week of the nine months of a pregnancy, we observe how gradually our sense organs are developed. At some point we begin to see, at some point we begin to hear, at some point, because of our vision, our outer universe begins to develop through our senses. Once our consciousness can begin to operate through our sense organs, then we begin to establish that there is a universe around us.

Our emotions and karma force us to have a material form that drives us to become dependent on material things. And as we grow dependent on these objects or people, we become very attached to them.

Now when something threatens our strong attachments, we will experience anger. So if we determine that desire is the source of our birth and all of our creations, then we could also say that anger is the killer that represents our death. We see that these two forces are inseparable.

There are some Buddhist scholars and meditators who understand these subtleties and say that in the moment you are born, you have already begun to die. This is because they see death as the constantly changing nature of impermanence. So there is the big death in which our whole body changes, and there are also all of these small deaths in which our body changes from the very moment we are born.

So we see that death and birth are there simultaneously. In the same way, if we use the analogy of a river, without the collection of all of these drops of water, all of these atoms, there is no river. Death is like this river. It does not happen without all of these other moments of change along the way.

Those who have achieved the mystical experience of birthlessness and deathlessness have reached their understanding because in that one moment of change they have freed themselves from desire and anger. What they have gained is a very strong mindful awareness. With that awareness they have freed themselves from all of the afflictive emotions and ultimately even from the limitations of birth and death.

Until we have achieved that freedom, we will be forced to take rebirth. Each past moment will force the present moment in our lives. Each present moment will force the future moment. We will remain trapped in this cycle of our lives.

If we look at images of the Buddhist wheel of life, it is depicted as a circle to emphasize that it is interdependent. There is no first cause, so nothing exists independently. Every moment is dependent on another moment; every event is created by a previous event and will produce a future reaction.

The great yogis and mahasiddhas have reached a place of true independence because they've gone beyond birth and death. They are no longer trapped within this endless cycle because they have gone beyond these afflictive emotions.

Of course, we must address the obvious question of why enlightened ones like the Buddha continue to reincarnate if they have attained freedom from birth and death. The answer is simple. At the heart of that profound wisdom, there exists a deep compassion for all living beings. With this wisdom and compassion, the enlightened ones are then free to take rebirth to help others.

While it may appear to be similar to ordinary birth, the rebirth of buddhas is very different because it is not forced. Their birth is not painful, and their life is not full of suffering. They have free will. From that present moment they've attained freedom from emotions, and their objectless compassion can manifest in all of their actions.

These enlightened minds are operating in a completely different realm from the one we normally live in. In this inner wisdom of the mahamudra that Virupa is referring to in the doha, they have only their present mind. They have gone completely beyond time. They no longer have a past or a future. There is nothing compelling them toward a forced birth or death.

So returning to the Buddha's life story, the fourth time Prince Siddhartha left the palace, after seeing the sick, the old, and the dead, he finally encountered the yogi. This moment in the Buddha's life has so much importance. The yogi represents the path of meditation that is the only way to free oneself from all of these other miseries of sickness, old age, and death. The young Prince Siddhartha was so inspired by his encounter with the yogi that he abandoned everything in order to pursue a spiritual path, which ultimately led to his awakening.

Spiritual realization is found primarily through meditation and through witnessing our own experience. These realizations cannot be gained through rigorous academic studies, philosophy, or debate.

While the teachings can inspire us and give us tremendous encouragement on our path, ultimately we must discover this inner wisdom for ourselves.

Mahamudra can be understood to be that state beyond all apparent objects. It is a space free from the incessant inner chattering that our minds normally produce. The wisdom of mahamudra also frees us from the very causes of those apparent objects, causes which have their roots in what we call *sleeping emotions*. Even if we have attained a certain level of equanimity at the surface of our minds, if something can still provoke a reaction in us of desire, attachment, anger, or ignorance, then we know that we still have these emotions buried inside us. We refer to these as sleeping emotions.

Meditation is the only way to move beyond these repressed feelings and karmic imprints. Since it is not just at the level of the sense organ and sense object, meditation allows us to uproot the very sources of these sleeping emotions in consciousness itself.

According to Buddhism, death is the separation between physical matter and your mind. So it follows that after physical death, you will no longer experience these apparent objects. You will no longer have an eye organ with which to see form. You will no longer have an ear organ to experience sound. None of these sensory impressions will continue.

But while we are in these physical bodies, we are constantly barraged with sensory experiences. We can compare this to a dream. We may dream that we are eating something, and until we wake up, we are very sure that we are having a real experience. You can consume and experience everything in a dream, completely sure it is real until you wake up.

If we do not purify our inner chattering while we are alive, these constant mental dialogues of conflicting emotion will follow us right into the intermediate stage of the bardo and even into our next life.

If we read the *Tibetan Book of the Dead*, we learn that after death we enter the intermediate bardo phase. This experience is based entirely on our underlying emotional states. Anger can manifest as all of these seemingly tangible enemies. Attachment can manifest as all of these addictions. All of our sleeping emotions can create intense mental images in our bardo journey.

These emotional states will be far more overwhelming in the bardo stage because we will be unable to satisfy them. Ordinarily when we grow hungry, we are able to eat and temporarily fulfill that craving. But in the bardo state you may be hungry all the time with no way to satisfy that desire.

In the intermediate stage of the bardo, all of our experiences and the imagery that our minds create are a result of emotions we have not yet resolved. When your karma has not been completely exhausted, then all of these cravings and feelings will manifest in the bardo, just like they do in dreams. If you have completely purified your karma, however, and there is nothing left to express, then nothing will surface in the dream.

In our regular lives we dream all the time. We fantasize constantly about what we want, what we don't have, and what we wish we could change. Most of us carry this same constant stream of mental chatter right into our death.

But as I have mentioned, the experience of all of these emotions in the bardo state can be way more terrifying because we don't have any outlet to express the experience. We no longer have our sense organs with which to satisfy a craving or block an unwanted sound or smell. So all of these karmic imprints can play out in the bardo stage and reach a very frightening level of intensity if we have not resolved them in our lifetime.

For those who have done some meditation in their lives, according to their level of realization, there are ways to overcome and prevent overpowering emotional experiences. And it is said that those who've attained a high level of understanding during their physical lives and have seen the clear light of that inner space can avoid the bardo entirely at the time of death. They have attained that freedom.

Some yogis who have gone through this process have then recorded their experiences. But at our level, this memory of the experience of death is very rare. Occasionally we hear reports of people who have had near-death experiences. But it is very rare that a person can actually remember death itself.

So instead we can use sleep as an opportunity for developing insight into the experience of death. Many higher yogas like Vajrayogini practices indicate that if you want to understand your own death, then you can learn about it from sleep yoga. Even nightmares, with their sometimes-terrifying mental imagery, are a very real glimpse into the more frightening aspects of the bardo journey after death. And the experience we have when we wake up each morning is a glimpse of the experience of rebirth.

We can view sleep as a temporary death. For this reason, it can be highly informative. If we practice sleep yoga, then we can learn a lot about ourselves. Through sleep yoga we can get a sense of how our journey will go at the time of death. We can determine whether we will have a journey that leads to freedom from cyclic existence or a journey that leads to a continuation of the cycle of forced birth and death.

5

Not Beyond Mind

not the original dharmata, and also not beyond mind

IT IS IMPORTANT THAT we define this word *dharma*, because dharma has many different meanings. When it is referred to in the context of the Triple Gem of the Buddha, Dharma, and Sangha, then the word Dharma means the Buddha's teachings. And based on those teachings, Dharma also means meditation and spiritual practice.

But in the case of these mystical songs, the words *dharma* and *dharmata* have different meanings. In this case, *dharma* is defined as holding some characteristics. In the world of phenomena, everything that we come into contact with, everything that seems apparent to us, can be said to have general characteristics.

For example, one general characteristic of all phenomena in the relative world is that all conditioned things are impermanent. In addition to general characteristics, there are also unique characteristics to these apparent objects.

So we can define general characteristics as those that are shared by many objects together. And unique characteristics are particular to that one object. As humans we share many general characteristics, but each individual also has its own unique traits.

Dharma has a Sanskrit root meaning of *dharana*, which means something possessing both general and unique characteristics. Everything that we study in the phenomenal world can be said to hold certain characteristics. So we've determined the meaning of dharma here is phenomena holding both general and unique individual characteristics.

Furthermore, all of these phenomena also contain dharmata. Although we lack precise language in English, dharmata can be translated to mean "thingness," which pertains to the essential nature of something. While the term dharma addresses characteristics, dharmata refers to the basic nature or essence. In order to understand what Virupa intends when he says "not the original dharmata," we should refer again to the opening lines of the doha:

The mahamudra of samsara and nirvana
is completely pure by nature, like space.

In these lines Virupa is inferring that there is an *original nature* similar to space. Space is there all the time. It is devoid of all phenomena. It has always been there, and in this sense it is unconditioned.

Within the arena of space all things come and go. Things arise and disappear. They begin and cease. All of these conditioned things are growing and decaying, subject to constant change. But the space in which all these conditioned things unfold remains unconditioned and unaffected by this change. It is this nature of space to which Virupa compares mahamudra.

So while mahamudra is unconditioned like space, and has been in our mental continuum for all time, it is not as easy for us to realize or experience it individually. Mahamudra is obscured by all of our attachments and aversions and by our complex involvement with different objects.

If we examine how we are conducting our life, we see that we are not identifying ourselves with that inner space. Instead, we are intensely identified with conditioned things. We are bound to the objects in our lives.

More important, as individuals we are identifying either with the subject, whatever it may be, or with the object. And without this duality, we have no way of understanding our experience. We have been completely trained to interpret the world as the interaction between subject and object, self and other.

Much of how we identify ourselves and others is based on societal norms and cultural conditioning, especially if we are very extroverted and very easily influenced by others and by the outer world. Even the name we are given at birth, which comes to define us in so many ways, is not something we brought with us into this life. Our name is not inherently who we are, it was given to us by our parents or by a priest or a lama.

Quite often behind that name we see the influence of religion. We also see trends of children named after famous people or great leaders. For example, many Tibetan families have someone named Tenzin in honor of His Holiness the Dalai Lama.

So we see that from a name we can identify whether someone is a Muslim or a Christian or a Jew. We can often tell immediately what country they are from. These names have been passed down for so many hundreds of years and are imbued with meaning.

Now the name that we are given at birth does not carry any inherent truth. Someone may be named Jesus, but that doesn't automatically make that person Jesus Christ! If someone is named Buddha, it does not mean that person is already enlightened. Instead it acts to identify them with a certain community, nation, or culture.

Of all the religions, Buddhism is less community oriented. Of course we take refuge in the Sangha as part of the Triple Gem, but Buddhism has much more to do with individual experience.

When we meditate and when we talk about awakening, we are not talking about enlightenment occurring in a community or group. We are talking about individual, personal awakening.

We must examine whether this individual awakening is facilitated by cultural identifications, starting from the name we're given, starting from the family we're born into, and looking at the community we are raised in.

Beyond that, we have to look at the country we grew up in and even what part of the world. What we find is that so much of our identity is based largely on society. Our family and culture have projected so many things onto us. And we have to question the extent to which we are subjectively involved with those objects.

Often we identify ourselves with a particular class. For example, class has played a pivotal role in Indian society. Your caste is determined at the moment of birth and continues to define all of your opportunities in life. Whether you are brahmin, kshatriya, or untouchable, the limitations of your life are already predefined for you.

The Buddha was very opposed to the idea of caste. The Buddhist understanding of karma and personal awakening transcends all of these identifications. The enlightened state is beyond the duality of subject and object, rendering class meaningless.

As long as we are invested in our social status, saying, "I am brahmin," or "I am upper class," or "I am military," we are identifying ourselves subjectively with something. And as long as we are bound by this separation of subject and object, this bondage will prevent our awakening.

We have to start where we are. Virupa's teaching is saying there is no original dharmata, because we have identified ourselves so thoroughly at the subjective or objective level, and we have not gone beyond to see that inner space. So we are always identifying ourselves with something.

To awaken ourselves, to discover that inner space, we have to start where we are. Let's examine the reality of a cup, for example. At our level we cannot say that the cup has never existed. That is not our experience. We've assigned all of this meaning to the cup. Perhaps we paid a lot for it, so we really value it. Or perhaps it was a gift from someone and has real emotional importance to us. It also has the utility value of something we can drink from. For all of these reasons we become very involved with this object.

Now if we take it to the next level of inquiry, then through the cup we have to try to find the nature of the cup. For yogis or spiritual practitioners, there's a chance that through meditation they may see the thing as well as the "thingness," or the nature of this object, simultaneously.

So the dharma would be all of the characteristics of the cup, both unique and general. The dharmata would be the "thingness" or essential nature of the cup. In order to realize the nature of the cup, we have to go all the way through our understanding of it. We have to use objects we know in order to see beyond them.

If we don't have any inner realization yet, then we have not seen the nature of things. This is why Virupa says "not the original dharmata." At our level we may not understand what Virupa means when he states that mahamudra is pure like space. This is due to the fact that we are still functioning in the dualistic world of subject and object. Starting where we are, we have to inquire into the nature of each individual thing in order to start to see their nature, or dharmata.

There are some readers who may ask, "Why do Buddhists have to break everything down to the smallest atom? Why do Buddhists always reduce everything?" If you are very invested in your physical world and are attached to all of these beautiful objects, then this effort to understand dharmata may seem irrelevant or even alarming. You may wonder, what is the harm in appreciating all this beauty and pleasure in my life?

The Buddha's purpose was not to make us all anarchists. The Buddha did not intend for us to reject or destroy anything. If you can appreciate beautiful objects or experiences and transcend your attachment to them, then there is no risk.

But we can see in our lives that usually beauty and pleasure make us more and more addicted. The more pleasure we experience, the more it increases our appetite for similar pleasures until soon we are held prisoner. We can all see how this manifests in our lives, even in subtle ways, fueling our restlessness.

All of this Buddhist deconstruction and analysis is an effort to find the truth. Is there any substantial reality worthy of our attachment? Generally every object we grow attached to is subject to constant change. And when this change leads to a result that we don't like, these pleasurable objects will give us pain. This pain will give rise to aversion and anger. We can see this process constantly unfolding in our lives.

When we grow attached to something beautiful, we want that beauty to be eternal. But that is against the laws of impermanence. As long as that beautiful object exists within the conditioned world, it is going to change. And when things change, we often have a very difficult time accepting the results.

Recognizing the insubstantiality of all conditioned things and incorporating that into our spiritual practice helps us to overcome all of our destructive emotions. We must use the object in order to gain an understanding of its nature. Only through the dharma will we learn to see the dharmata.

At our level there is no "original dharmata." Instead we must use the objects of the phenomenal world, and eventually through deep meditation we can begin to see their true nature.

We can apply this method to everything. As His Holiness the Dalai Lama always says, interdependency and emptiness are like two sides of the same coin. He is referring to this same principle—the dharma and dharmata are also the two sides of this coin.

Dharma is interdependent because all these phenomenal things are arising because of the relationship between various causes and conditions. When causes and conditions come together, things appear. So that is how things are formed in interdependency.

If we look more closely within that interdependent world, we cannot find any independent existence. Everything is a result of something else. The absence of independent existence is the empty nature of phenomena. These are the two sides of the coin of dharma and dharmata.

I believe it was Nagarjuna who said in one of his texts, "Only through the relative truth will we see the ultimate truth." This is because we live in a relative world, and we must use what we know in order to transcend it.

This is one reason why we need to accumulate merit. We cannot misunderstand this idea of emptiness and turn it into a kind of nihilism.

If we think that, because everything is empty, we can just disregard the natural law of karma and indulge ourselves or kill or abandon moral conduct, we will never see the ultimate truth.

The only way for us to see the ultimate truth is through the relative truth because we live in a relative world. We don't have an inherent experience of ultimate truth. We don't have a realization of emptiness without spiritual practice and without a thorough examination of the relative truth.

The terms relative, dharma, and interdependency are all pointing to the same meaning of the truth in the conditioned world. And the words ultimate, dharmata, and independent are all referring to the unconditioned nature. We can also understand this by looking at samsara and nirvana.

We live in samsara because we live in this cycle of birth and death. But through meditation practice within samsara, there's the possibility of realizing the awakening of nirvana. So samsara is the dharma and nirvana is the dharmata.

Once you have attained nirvana, nirvana and samsara are the same—all duality is gone. Some masters say, "You don't go somewhere else to find nirvana. Nirvana already exists within samsara. You simply have to realize it."

When you know nirvana, then you will understand that nirvana and samsara are inseparable; they are the same. But if you don't achieve that level of realization, then samsara and nirvana will always appear to be two different things.

This is why we need to start where we are on the journey of our own personal awakening. This is the reason why there is no such thing as original dharmata somewhere else. We have to go through the dharma to realize the dharmata right here in the conditioned world.

not the original dharmata, and also not beyond mind

Let's examine this line "also not beyond mind." We've already established that in the context of these songs, dharma is referring to all of the objects in the relative world. This includes all of the objects of our sense organs. So we could say that the first imprisonment of the phenomenal self is in relation to the dharma, to these objects.

In addition to objects, we also have this personal self through which we have created a whole identity. We have a name, we have a car, we live here, we are from this country, and so forth. This is the powerful identification with self by which we perpetuate "I" and "my."

Our identification of ourselves is based on the five aggregates of form, feeling, ideation, formation, and consciousness. Now if we examine more closely, we find that at the subtlest level, as our life proceeds and as we grow more keenly aware of our ever-changing physical body, we become more strongly identified with our mind as the "self."

Early in our lives we may have more attachment to our physical body. When we are young, agile, and beautiful it is easy to define ourselves by our physical form. But as we age and become aware of how our body is constantly changing, we begin to see its insubstantiality.

Even those who don't engage in spiritual practice may still begin to identify themselves more strongly with their mind rather than their physical body as they age. And in Buddhism we believe that once our physical elements have dissolved in death, all that will be left will be the mind. So we can see that the mind is the more permanent subject in a person's identity.

Now although we may say that mahamudra is beyond mind, at our level we have to use the mind to know mahamudra. In the same way that we have to use the relative object of the cup to know the nature of the cup, so too we need to use our mind to get beyond it to that space of mahamudra. We have to start where we are, with the objects at hand. We have to learn to work with this complex tool of the mind.

The only way for us to glimpse the mahamudra of that inner space is by cultivating the mind through sustained meditation practice. But in the beginning, this can be extremely challenging, because the mind is filled with so many emotions. The mind is so riddled with afflictive emotions that it is nearly impossible for us to see its true nature.

This is the reason why we begin our meditative practice with shamatha concentration meditation to calm the emotions. When anger, jealousy, pride, and all of the other emotions are still strong in us, we are unable to see anything clearly.

For this reason, we begin our practice with shamatha meditation in order to subdue those emotions. And if we are doing a sadhana practice, then we do the generation visualization to calm the emotions and to cultivate more focus and clarity. When you have gained these qualities of calm attention, then you are ready to see the nature of mind itself.

Now in the beginning this may not make much logical sense to us. It's as if we are saying, "the knife should be sharpened in order to cut itself!" We may wonder why we should focus on perfecting our minds if we are actually trying to go beyond them. Why are we filling the mind with all of these images during the generation stage of the sadhana practice if the whole goal is to achieve the emptiness of that inner space?

The process doesn't work in an ordinary way. Because the mind is a composite of so many differing emotions, we must approach our training of the mind with skillful methods. Mind is not just one single entity. Mind is composed of a vast array of destructive emotions, positive emotions, and neutral emotions.

Meditation is a very effective method for calming destructive emotions. The more destructive emotions we overcome through meditation, the more positive emotions will begin to dominate our experience, and this will allow the mind to have greater freedom. These positive emotions will then help the mind to more clearly see its own nature.

In order for us to progress we cannot see mahamudra as something beyond the mind. If we have no realization, we must start where we are. We know that we are emotional beings. We possess all of these feelings. Our task is to begin to find a way to see mahamudra in the midst of anger, in the midst of attachment and confusion.

Since we cannot immediately destroy all of our destructive emotions, we need to learn how to harness them for the purposes of our own realization. We have to learn the methods that will help us to see the wisdom in even the most destructive emotions.

This process of transformation is the very purpose of the higher Vajrayana. Vajrayana practice states that there is wisdom to be found in the midst of the emotions. So when Virupa says "also not beyond mind," this is what he is implying. The wisdom of mahamudra is not to be found outside of the mind. Rather, inner space can be found by going right through the mind instead. We have to utilize what we have in order to transcend it.

So we must learn all of these methods and apply them correctly to our mind through our practice. A great Sakya lama once said, "In Buddhist meditation it is all about method. If you know the method, then you can practice enjoying everything and you will be awakened. But if you don't know the method, then even if you stay in a cave for your whole life, denying yourself everything, then still you will not gain any insight."

Method is very important. What this Sakya lama is saying is so true. If you don't know the method, then doing a retreat in a cave may be very similar to being in prison. And without proper methods, instead of transforming you, the sensory deprivation of that retreat may actually serve to increase your cravings!

I have certainly heard of people going into retreat and coming out more conflicted than they were before. When you are denied something, it is quite natural that your cravings will increase. So if you have not used the correct methods, the correct motivation and meditations, your retreat may actually provoke very neurotic behaviors. It is possible to become quite crazy as a result of this renunciation if proper methods are not applied.

On the other hand, if we study the biographies of the eighty-four mahasiddhas, we find that these great awakened masters were not necessarily retreating to caves in the Himalayas to meditate. They were living ordinary simple lives. Most of them were householders. But within that ordinary life they were able to see the extraordinary. Through these methods they achieved awakening, right in the midst of the marketplace of mundane life.

When we talk about the different vehicles of Theravada, Mahayana, and Vajrayana, in some sense we are just talking about different methods. If you have the correct method, you can achieve awakening much faster and with fewer difficulties. But without the right method, it will usually take much longer, be more challenging, and you will make more mistakes.

When Virupa says "also not beyond mind," he is including mental activities in his reference to the mind. So mind and mental activities include all emotions as well.

As humans we experience such a wealth of different emotions. If we have the correct method, then every single emotion can become an opportunity to see wisdom. We can integrate all of our worldly experiences into our practice.

This is because when you have a strong emotion, your mind has very strong energy. The intensity of this energy can become a wonderful tool in your spiritual practice. This energy created by emotion can really fuel your transformation if properly applied.

But on the other hand, if you don't have the right method, strong emotion can utterly destroy you. When you receive an initiation in Vajrayana practice, it is thought that this empowerment will lead to awakening. But if you don't apply the proper method, then this initiation has the potential to make you more destructive.

If we study Vajrayana deities, we see that on the surface they all represent different destructive emotions like anger, passion, and ignorance. Now if you don't have a solid understanding of all the methods and instructions, you may view these deities as solely representing emotion. And the mention of all these destructive emotions may only intensify your own feelings.

But with the correct method, you learn to use your emotions in order to see the wisdom within emotions. You begin to see that emotions, by their very nature, are empty. Virupa says "also not beyond mind" because we must utilize our mind and emotions to see our wisdom nature. Only by using them can we ultimately see mahamudra.

So we use the dharma to see the dharmata, the selflessness of phenomena. And we use the mind and emotions to see the selflessness of the person. It is our clinging to our idea of ourselves that also produces all of our other behaviors of clinging to objects. This is how we normally live our lives.

Due to our established sense of "I" based on the ego, we create a strong sense of attachment to all of our possessions. This sense of ownership creates a very powerful kind of attachment: "my house," "my car," "my child," "my country." Based on our development of our ego, we then feel the need to expand our property and territory. We begin extending our emotions to the whole universe.

In order to go beyond these two forms of clinging—to the self and to the object—we must use the available methods. We must use the dharma. We must use the mind and emotions to transcend such clinging. If the proper methods are applied, then ultimately one will have the realization of mahamudra.

Once you realize mahamudra, you cannot claim that it is original in the sense that it was there prior to self or object. This is because it is your own personal realization. How can we say the emptiness of a cup is there before the cup itself? This is hard to prove. It is only through the appearance of the cup that you can prove the emptiness of the cup.

This is the same with a person. Because I have a strong sense of self, I can use that in meditation to realize my selfless nature. Now if one person has the realization of that selfless nature in everything, you might wonder why he or she can't somehow produce that enlightenment in others at the same time.

Unfortunately, that is not the case. Realization is an individual path. It is not a community effort. And it's not as if by one person achieving that realization, we will all suddenly understand mahamudra. Certainly the realization of the masters, as revealed to us in texts like this doha, can be a profound source of inspiration. But ultimately the Buddhist path is focused on individual effort. It is a personal journey. You must first transform yourself in order to achieve any realization.

6

Also Not Nonbeing

also not nonbeing because being and nonbeing
cannot be expressed with the mind

THE UNION OF CLARITY and emptiness found in mahamudra
is also known as *clear light*. It is said that the moment of death is
one of the best times to realize this union of clarity and emptiness. For
great yogis who have not yet come to realize mahamudra, the time of
death can be a profound opportunity for realization.

It is said that if we have committed ourselves to meditation practice
while we are alive, then at the time of death there is a chance that we
will recognize this clear light. By this I mean that the clear light that
you have cultivated through meditation can become one with the clear
light that is always within you.

For this reason, many lamas and yogis remain in a meditative state
for days or even weeks after doctors have pronounced them clinically
dead. Although all of the vital signs have stopped according to modern
medical standards, the yogi's complexion has not changed. While they

are in this meditative state of the clear light, their bodies do not begin to decay. Their skin remains healthy, and there is a subtle warmth that can be detected at their heart center. It is almost like these yogis are only in a deep sleep.

Seeing this clear light is the realization of mahamudra. It is the highest realization. If you have reached this understanding, then there's no question of being or not being, existence or nonexistence. You have gone beyond the duality of both.

If we have not realized this clear light, then our death process will be very different. Generally, for us, because death is often quite painful, we die unconsciously. When we become conscious again following death, because of our remaining ego, we will experience the bardo. This is the intermediate state between death and rebirth.

So from the bardo to the moment of conception, and on through our entire next life, if we have ego consciousness, then we will continue to cling to the duality of existence and nonexistence. In that clear light state, however, because we have transcended the ego, we are freed from all of this dualistic thinking.

The notion of existence and nonexistence is based heavily on our belief in our own existence. In Buddhism it is said that all destructive emotions arise from the basic ignorance of not knowing who oneself truly is.

The root of this ignorance is that we still believe that our egos exist and that there is an "I" that we can locate somewhere inside ourselves. This belief in the existence of a separate self is the ignorance that prevents us from truly knowing ourselves.

Those yogis who have seen the clear light will know their true nature for the first time. But those who don't see their true nature will continue to have strong attachment to all of existence because of their ego. And if anything threatens that existence, they will experience a very strong feeling of aversion.

In this way our emotions and our ego are interrelated. As long as there is ego, there is existence and nonexistence, and all of our emotions are generated. If we have gone beyond our mind and our ego, then this question of existence will not even apply.

Let's take an inanimate object like a book as an example. To a book, there is no such thing as existence or nonexistence. But for us, when our consciousness is rooted in the ego, then we will be very attached to our own existence. And our belief in our own existence will give rise to our belief in the existence of other things. This issue of existence and nonexistence is very important because it is the source of all of our destructive emotions.

We are conceived out of the bardo state due to our conflicting emotions of attachment and aversion. Due to our attachment to one parent, we are forced into rebirth again and again. And we carry these conflicting emotions throughout lifetimes. These conflicting emotions create the duality of existence and nonexistence, desire and aversion, and drive us in all of our activities.

Because we have this physical existence in a human body, we are quite convinced of existence. How we relate to the world is based entirely on this belief in existing things. But when something decays, or when an object is used up or destroyed, we become sure of its nonexistence.

So we can see that inanimate objects, which don't have any consciousness or mind, lack awareness of existence or nonexistence. But this is also true for those who have gone beyond the mind. Those who have seen the clear light of mahamudra are completely free from these extremes.

Those meditators who have seen mahamudra have freed themselves entirely from all of the emotions generated by existence and nonexistence. But for most of us, almost everything we do is fueled by the interaction between existence and nonexistence. The conflicting feelings that this duality creates in our minds propel our actions and reactions.

It is said that yogis who remain in the clear light have gone beyond time. Time as we know is relative. Time is not an ultimate or innately existing measurement.

Although there is an experience of bliss in the clear light state, that bliss is not dependent on any object. Freed from all emotions, bliss can be found in that inner wholesome balance that is no longer interdependent in any way.

As long as there are feelings, then we still have not transcended the mind. Feeling is connected with all experiences of pain and pleasure, happiness and unhappiness. But the state of bliss is beyond feeling.

It is interesting to observe what generates the strongest reactions in our lives. For example, if we have a headache, then we will become acutely aware of that part of our head where the pain is. Let's say that the headache is causing a piercing pain in our right eye. We will be so aware of that point of pain, but we may not even think about our left eye, which is unaffected. Likewise, in our lives, we tend to focus most on the things that are bothering us and causing us more suffering, and we tend to lose awareness of everything else.

Clear light is the union of bliss and emptiness, and in that union, there is no ego. And because there's no ego, then you don't have any attachment to existing things, or any aversion when that existence is threatened. For someone in mahamudra, everything is the same, everything is equal.

For this reason, many teachings say that this is a state of equanimity in which you have equalized everything. You cannot accomplish this without going beyond all of the destructive emotions. We may be wondering whether equanimity is existent or nonexistent. Equanimity is found in the middle, freed from both the extremes of existence and nonexistence.

Those who remain in that union of clarity and emptiness are free from extremes and nonextremes. And this is the reason why, when they are in that equanimity, their experience is inexpressible.

In our regular lives we are very accustomed to expressing existence and nonexistence. But when you are in a state of equanimity, when you are in the union of bliss and emptiness, you will not be able to describe that experience.

Until we have that experience, it may seem a bit paradoxical and difficult to understand how something could be inexpressible. Generally, whatever we express is at the conceptual level and based in the mind. But when something is beyond the mind, how will you describe it?

Ordinarily we even struggle to relate the concepts we have in our own minds to others. Most of what we express has to do with our inner conditions. Even in the relative world, we cannot always express what we experience; we cannot convey our particular reality to other people.

not connected with any dualistic phenomena,
originally homogeneous.

We have established that at the relative level, the extremes of existence and nonexistence can become causes and conditions for more destructive emotions to arise in us. Because of our attachments, when something is lost or destroyed we experience so much pain and anger.

At an even more extreme level, the belief in existence and nonexistence can give rise to eternalistic and nihilistic thinking. If you are attached to something, you may become convinced that it will last forever. Initially you may find real comfort in this conviction that it is eternal. And if you misunderstand nonexistence as being devoid of all karma or moral conduct, you may become very destructive or careless.

But if we look more closely, we see that the more attached we become to something and the more convinced we are that it is permanent, the more dependent we become on it. The Buddhist understanding is that when you are dependent on so-called "permanent" objects, you will never have liberation. This is especially true when existence becomes the object of your faith.

And at the other extreme, if you become fixated on nonexistence, then you may fall into a very dangerous kind of nihilism. The risk here is that you will disregard the laws of cause and effect and the rules by which phenomena function.

It is said in the teachings that when you have developed a nihilistic view, there is a very real danger that you will disregard the natural law of karma. And if you cultivate a nihilistic view and attitude in your mind, then you may become an anarchist. If you deny how causes and conditions give rise to results, you may do very negative deeds thinking that nothing matters anyway. So these are the risks of the two extremes taken to that next level.

If you study the higher Madhyamaka texts, then through logical exploration you try to go beyond all of the extremes—not only the extremes of existence and nonexistence but also the extremes of both and neither.

You attempt to get to the point where you are no longer grasping at any concept. The moment at which you cling to an idea of existence or nonexistence, both or neither, then the grasping itself will keep you from liberation.

One of the great Sakya masters said, "If you have grasping, you do not have right view. Irrespective of whether your conclusion is eternalistic or nihilistic, if you have some grasping in your mind for any entity or object, that grasping will prevent you from attaining liberation."

This is why in Buddhist practice, after shamatha meditation, you also have to do *vipashyana* or insight meditation. And after doing generation stage practice in the context of deity yoga, then you have to do completion stage practice.

Even when you have generated yourself as a deity, you must not get attached to that image. You cannot become attached to divine pride, thinking, "Now I am Tara or I am Vajrayogini." You have to go beyond that identity in order to achieve liberation. Even in the *Heart Sutra* we find the words:

> Form is emptiness, emptiness is form. Form is not other than emptiness, emptiness is not other than form.

These four kinds of emptiness have the same meaning as the teachings of Virupa's doha. They both present methods for going beyond all of the extremes. And the purpose is to free our minds from grasping at any object. Whether the object is material or mental, a conclusion or an idea or a feeling, any grasping activity will obstruct the mind from liberation.

This is the reason why mahamudra, the clear light, is not connected with any dualistic phenomena. Ultimately the state of mahamudra is free from all possible extremes. This is the correct view.

Although the Buddha gave so many different teachings and explained so many philosophies, practices, and disciplines, there was one clear directive. For our own personal transformation, it comes down to three things: right view, meditation, and how to integrate meditation and right view into your life.

Of these three things—view, meditation, and integration—right view is the most important. In his teachings, the Buddha offered a good example. Oftentimes monks and nuns will take up to 250 vows regarding moral conduct. The Buddha said that if a practitioner is upholding all of these vows but becomes attached to their own good behavior, thinking, "I am the greatest, I am the best practitioner," then this will become an obstacle. If they esteem their discipline and allow their good deeds to feed their egos, then even those good deeds can prevent the practitioner from achieving liberation.

Another good example is that of a scholar. If a scholar masters different philosophies and thinks they are the authority on a certain topic, this can present a real challenge to their progress. Even within the Tibetan lineage sometimes there is competitive debate in which one practitioner says "Madhyamaka is best" or "this school is better than that school."

Even while the purpose of all of these methods of study and conduct are to free a person, if they are practiced without correct view, they become an obstacle. If these behaviors are fueling ego development, then they will greatly compromise the process of transformation.

This is the reason why right view is critically important. That right view must be free from all of the extremes. The aim of all study, practice, and conduct is to go beyond grasping at any state whatsoever.

In the history of Tibetan Buddhism there was once a debate. The question was whether that state of freedom from extremes was equivalent to a state of nothingness. What was concluded was that these states could not be defined in the same way.

When someone who has studied, contemplated, and meditated reaches that state of emptiness, it is very different from someone who has never studied. For someone who has never studied, that state of nothingness is just a blank mind.

So one state is completely based on ignorance, and one state is based on wisdom. That is the difference. Emptiness and nothingness may appear to be the same, but they are not. The wisdom of emptiness is realized through deep meditation and practice. The state of nothingness is a void state where the mind is just spaced out and lacking awareness. It may be free of concepts momentarily, but it has not transcended them.

Looking again at the cycle of death and rebirth, we can see how this difference plays out. Most of us experience death in a state of unconsciousness. We become very spaced out as our elements dissolve. Our minds temporarily shut down as this often fearful and painful process of dying occurs.

But as we journey through the intermediate state of the bardo after death, our consciousness begins to surface again. As it arises our ego too will come back. It's the driving energy of the go, and all of its conflicting emotions, that forces us to take rebirth again and again.

Now on the other hand, if we realize the wisdom of emptiness, if we see the clear light, then we gain complete freedom. That wisdom will not be forced by karma and defilement to be reborn again and again. Instead we will freely choose rebirth in order to benefit all sentient beings. This rebirth will then be free of all of the pain and conflicting feelings. So we can see how there is a significant difference in how nothingness and emptiness affect the life cycle.

So we have established that mahamudra is free from all of the extremes. It is free from grasping at objects and concepts, and it is free from all dualistic phenomena. Virupa refers to it as "homogenous" because it is always the same, always this unconditioned equanimity.

When you have the clear light experience then you no longer have this polarity of existence and nonexistence, attachment and aversion. Your awareness remains balanced. It is the experience of being one with everything. Once someone has the experience of the clear light, then everything becomes clear light. You are the universe, and the universe is you. Everything is pure.

But when we have not had that experience yet, there is always self and other. We experience attachment to ourselves and aversion to others, which breeds many conflicting emotions. There is so much discrimination and no equanimity.

7

Those False Horns of a Rabbit

Even the explanation of the activities of defining the essence,
equivalent with the fallacy of those false horns of a rabbit
 being sharp or dull,
all phenomena are not different from that characterization.

AT THE MOMENT WE live in a dualistic universe. Because we
believe in our subjective selves, then we interact with the universe as an object. Our universe begins with our fetal development and
eventual birth.

Although we don't have much understanding of how we are conceived, some of our sense organs are already experiencing the universe
even when we are still in utero. Even in the womb we may experience
changes in light or other sensory interactions with our surroundings.

After we are born, our character begins to develop. The family and
conditions we are born into begin to shape us. We are immediately
given a name that will become a very important way in which we identify ourselves in the world.

So a name is a good example of what Virupa means here by "characteristics." Characteristics are what we use to identify a person or an object. There are many unique ways in which we can identify a person by recognizing that person's particular attributes. And there are many general characteristics that also apply to that person.

Earlier we looked at the connotations a name carries within family tradition, culture, and geography. But if we look deeper, according to Tibetan grammar and terminology, a name is a sound. A name is based on a series of letters, and a letter is a sound. So based on these sounds and letters, we create a name. The sounds that make up that particular name can carry so much importance in our lives. If someone says something bad about that name, you can feel so hurt and so much pain. If someone compliments that name, you can suddenly feel elated.

If we look closely, how much does that name actually identify the essence of that person? Can any part of the person be found in that name? We live in a world where names are so important. People have even been willing to die in order to defend a name. But names are really only a series of sounds.

Family is also an important part of the identification process. For this reason, most cultures also include a family name or some other broader identifier in the name as well. And then through education and experience we may gain many other titles like doctor, PhD, professor, president, or CEO.

In the course of our lives we grow to be identified in many different ways. But all of these identifications are in some sense given to us by society. And within those identifications, if we look closely, how much of the essence of the person can we actually find in that name or title?

This is true of any object in the universe. This is true of all conditioned things. The Buddha taught that all conditioned things have two kinds of characteristics. All conditioned things have both unique and general characteristics.

Take fire for example. The unique characteristics of fire are that it is something that burns, something that is hot. Or the unique characteristics of air are that it is light and moving.

And then the general characteristics of both air and fire and of all conditioned things are that they are impermanent They are all constantly changing. So although all conditioned things share general characteristics, they are always identified by their unique characteristics.

Now the mystical song is saying that all of these different characteristics with which our emotions and ideas are involved are like the horns of a rabbit. All of our mental, physical, and verbal activities are all like the horns of a rabbit.

We go through our lives obsessed with characteristics, constantly speculating on the rabbit's horns. Are they long or short? Pointy or round? We are so completely preoccupied with the particular details of these horns that we have failed to remember the obvious. We have overlooked the fact that rabbits don't even have horns in the first place!

This is how the relative world is. The relative world is based entirely on characteristics. But within those characteristics, when we look more deeply, we cannot find any essence.

This also applies to our discussion of mahamudra. We have described how the realization of mahamudra is beyond words, beyond expression, and like space. But until mahamudra has become an inner experience for us, we will not have that realization. The words we use to discuss it are not mahamudra. Space is not mahamudra. These words, at their best, will only ever be a reference for us.

We often come to believe firmly that a name has some inherent existence. We are convinced that all of these objects really exist. Furthermore, we become strongly attached to them and then our emotions are involved and our ideas are formed.

This is how we interact and react. The more emotional involvement we have, the more real we make those things we are attached to. So we can see that reality is not something that exists independently in the outside world. Your particular reality exists within you and is created by you.

Now within all of these particular characteristics, if we look and look, we still cannot find any independent existence. In order to help us better understand our lives and the universe, the Buddha taught that the interdependent world created by causes and conditions is only the relative truth.

Within that world of relative truth, he taught that there are other relative truths that are imperfect. Going back to Virupa's example, if we say that a rabbit has horns, this is an *imperfect relative truth*.

Normally we have a karmic consensus and most humans will share certain sensory experiences. For instance, most people can agree that snow is something white. But if someone is jaundiced and is seeing snow as yellow, then that yellow snow is an imperfect relative truth. It is imperfect because the majority of human eyes, due to our karma, see snow as only white.

One of the masters said, "If you keep telling a lie again and again, then even that lie can start to seem true." This is the same with relative truth. We have lived in a world of relative truth for so long that our identifications, emotions, and ideas are completely wrapped up in that relative truth. The relative truth seems so real to us. And this is why we have so many feelings of pain and pleasure in reference to the relative world.

Many of those relative truths and our ensuing feelings are based on societal projections. So your personal feelings are constantly being affected by cultural conditions. Society is very powerful.

Some of this societal influence has positive effects like laws that protect us and keep large groups of people living harmoniously together in cities. But society expects you to behave in a certain way, whether it is real or not, whether it's ethical or not. And that's where the danger lies. As history shows us, society can influence an entire population to ignore their basic morality.

So based on a consensus, when the majority agrees on something, that is known as a *perfect relative truth*. And based on the natural karmic law, when we share the same karma, we have a similar experience.

For instance, because of our shared karma, the majority of us agree on our experience of color. But if our karma is such that we are color blind, then we will have a very different experience.

So back to our example of snow. Snow is not inherently white. If the color white is in the snow, then snow should appear white to everyone. No one, no matter what their karmic vision, should see snow as yellow or any other color.

So we see that how we experience the universe has much more to do with our own inner conditions than it does with some inherently existing universe. Whether the universe becomes agreeable or disagreeable to you has much more to do with your own predispositions and perceptions.

One day the sun might be shining. Some people love the sun, and they consider this great weather. Other people who cannot be in the sunlight too long because they are prone to sunburn or because of some ailment might consider it a bad day.

This is true of all of our experiences. And our reactions to the same exact things are also changing over time. Some rich food that you used to love and could digest easily may now become the cause of sickness. The food itself has not changed, but your system has changed.

Your system has changed because your karma has changed. It is due to the karma. That's why we call this "karmic vision." And when the majority share the same vision, like agreeing that snow appears white, then that is the perfect relative truth.

There is an old Indian story. One time in a particular kingdom there was a very polluted rainfall, and all the poor people could not afford to cover their source of water. Only the king who had enough resources managed to cover his well. So when the poor townsfolk drank that polluted water, they all became crazy. Only the king was unaffected. But soon the crazy people began pointing at the king, saying he was the crazy one because he was not behaving like them. Eventually even the king became suspicious of himself and began to wonder if he really was mad! That's the power of the majority.

When there is consensus based on a majority, then there is a perfect relative truth. And based on that perfect relative truth, we agree to project some meaning onto an object. This is how we communicate.

All letters and languages are based on agreements made within perfect relative truths. Language is not created naturally or by some superpower. Language is composed of man-made agreements. We concur that if we write this letter, then it should be R, and it should sound a certain way. Or if we write this shape, it will be O. This is how language evolves and we learn to agree and communicate with each other.

We learn to use these sounds to refer to different objects. When a baby is given a name at birth, the child will always be known by that name. This is the same with all of our other communications.

Because of that shared agreement about meaning, language can function, and communication of ideas can occur. But it only works for those who keep the agreement and share the karma to experience that reality, that meaning.

There are thousands of different names for sugar. Even just in India there are many dialects. For this one object, sugar, there are so many possible names.

Only those people who share the same dialect will understand a reference to a given object. Perhaps the same word in a different dialect actually refers to something else instead of sugar, in which case the speakers of these two dialects will not be able to communicate well.

In this way, if we examine the relative interdependent world, which is created by causes and conditions, some things are perfect, and some things are just projections.

So, for example, maybe even in interdependency we can see that from a mango seed, under the right conditions, a tree can grow. But if we look at our two hands, the idea of a right or left hand is all imperfect projection.

This is called "right," and I'm attached to the idea of it being my right hand. But it is only right because of the left. Left has not produced the right hand, and the right hand has not produced the left. Right and left are just relative concepts, they don't have any essential meaning.

In this way, if we examine how we are interacting with objects, we will find that we encounter many objects of perfect relative truth. This truth is based on our karmic vision and our shared consensus about those objects—the perfect relative truth that snow is white, for example. We will also encounter some objects or experiences that fall into the category of imperfect relative truth, imperfect relative truth being something that even in the relative world is not the agreed-upon perception that the majority has adopted. So yellow snow would be an imperfect relative truth that only someone with particular karma to have their vision affected in a certain way would perceive.

Now relative truth is not universal truth. But the problem with us is that we are constantly trying to find universal truth through relative truth. We are always eager to establish some ultimate truth, but we are trapped within our relative world. It is only through meditation and practice that we can move beyond the constraints of relative truth.

The limits of the relative world are constantly posing problems for us in our daily lives. Because we believe that our truth must somehow be ultimate or universal, we are always involved in arguments and miscommunications with other people. We become so frustrated when someone cannot see our point of view because we are so convinced that we have the truth. These communication gaps happen constantly, not only in our regular lives but also when it comes to larger issues like that of religion. All of the "isms" are a tremendous source of disagreement in the world.

Now on the other hand, as the great masters show us, through meditation it is possible to have profound mystical experiences. In that state of wisdom in mahamudra, it is possible to become one with ultimate truth.

The ultimate truth also has a perfect and an imperfect aspect. Everything we learn in Buddhist texts and in the great philosophical books are just imperfect ultimate truths. They are imperfect because they are based on somebody's word and because they are knowledge you are acquiring, not personal experience. There is no way to carbon copy the ultimate truth and gain that understanding through study alone. The truth can only be experienced through practice and meditation.

Of course, you have to learn from the gurus. These great teachers can give you blessings, they can give you empowerments, and they can introduce you to the truth. But their introduction is not the ultimate truth.

Teachers can also show you the path. As the Buddha said, "I will show you the path, but you have to walk." The gurus can guide you and give you reference points, but you have to practice, and you have to experience this through meditation. Your own personal experience is most important.

The more personal experience you have, the more wisdom you will gain. Experience must arise from within you. If you merely copy from someone else, you will never gain the necessary experience.

It's almost like cheating on your homework. If you simply copy someone else's work, then you rarely learn the material. Only when you study hard and pass the exams based on your personal effort and experience will you have actually learned something.

So the perfect ultimate truth is your own personal experience. No one else can share this with you or create it for you. But the imperfect ultimate truth can be shared and studied.

All of the profound teachings on emptiness, on mahamudra, on enlightenment are all just imperfect ultimate truths. These texts are just for reference. These teachings can serve to guide you to your own personal experience of that perfect ultimate truth. But that perfect ultimate truth can be experienced only by you.

When you have experienced that perfect ultimate truth, then it is known in Buddhism as *awakening* or *enlightenment*. There are many names for it. But this awakening can be described as the moment when, for the first time, you know yourself completely.

Until that moment of awakening to your true nature, you will be living in the realm of imperfect ultimate truth, perfect relative truth, and imperfect relative truth. Our lives in these truths are controlled by our inner conditions—inner conditions that are based on destructive emotions and based on our karma.

We project these inner conditions and karma into the universe through actions. Because these actions are based on afflictive emotions, they produce even more karma, and we experience so many different feelings and emotional turbulence.

In the *Four Limitless Prayers*, ultimate peace is referred to as "equanimity." That equanimity can become bliss only when you know yourself completely and realize your true nature. You must discover this wisdom inside you.

As long as we are living in the imperfect ultimate truth or the two relative truths, we will continue to have destructive emotions. We will continue to act upon and create all kinds of karma. This is the reason why imperfect ultimate truth at our level is based on isms.

If we look around at our ordinary experience, we see that every creature is propelled by feeling. We see how the simple feeling of hunger compels animals to go out and eat. Even at this basic level, animals are pursuing this feeling of satisfaction and pleasure. Due to the limits of their intelligence, animals cannot go around creating wars or fighting over religion, but they are still very driven by feelings.

We find in more intelligent creatures, like humans, that we base much of our truth on isms. We become deeply invested in the truth of our particular religion. We talk about our Gods as if they were a universal ultimate truth for everyone.

This ultimate truth that religions have found cannot possibly be a perfect or universal ultimate truth. If it were universal, then we would not be fighting wars in the name of our faith. If it were universal, we would all naturally agree on one truth instead of killing each other to try to prove that we are correct. The ultimate truth can be only one conclusion; there cannot be many different and conflicting ultimate truths.

It is clear that these ultimate truths of the isms are not a perfect ultimate truth. They are varied and imperfect. We need only look at history to see how many brutal wars have been fought in the name of these isms. More people have been killed defending their religions, more battles waged over conflicting views of the truth, than over any other cause.

Personal feeling is strong but operates at a lower level. Isms function at a much higher level and are far more pervasive. Isms are harder to renounce. Personal feelings can be met and satisfied, and you may be able to move beyond them. But isms may remain a driving force in you for as long as you have a mind, for as long as you have knowledge.

If religion remains only at the knowledge level and does not reach the level of personal experience, there will be no inner transformation. Any knowledge based on some imperfect ultimate truth or based on a relative truth like capitalism or communism cannot become wisdom.

This is not to say that the people who create these systems are not intelligent. Those who create these isms are often highly intelligent, and the level of intellectual conclusion they have reached reinforces their beliefs. Once you esteem these leaders and become attached to these conclusions, your emotional investment in these ideas can become very powerful. Powerful because you have determined that these isms contain some kind of ultimate truth which you are now dedicated to.

Your devotion to this truth may now become so strong that you are even willing to sacrifice yourself to a cause. Meanwhile, however, the conflict these beliefs create in you, and between you and the universe, can become the cause of tremendous suffering.

Irrespective of how the world is functioning and running, and in spite of how we are trained to function in it, the most important work we can do is inside ourselves. For our own sake, and for the sake of others, we have to transform. We have to discover the wisdom within us.

If we have not experienced the perfect ultimate truth through our meditation, there is a grave risk. There is a real danger that we may become lost in that imperfect ultimate truth. Discovering the truth inside us can take so much practice and contemplation. It is easy for people to give up and quickly adopt the truth they learn in books or in classes. It is easy for people to latch on to intellectual knowledge as the hallmark of truth.

All of the isms, especially the religious isms, are part of that imperfect ultimate truth. Instead of religion becoming a salvation or a vehicle for enlightenment, religion becomes a method for conflict. Conflict between oneself and others and the universe.

For those who have seen the perfect ultimate truth through meditation, any conflict of self and other is completely dissolved. In that perfect ultimate truth, you cannot find an ego. Once you cannot find the ego, you cannot find any self or other. You have gone beyond both subject and object.

This is the reason why meditation is so important. Meditation is the only method to discover that perfect ultimate truth within oneself. It is only through meditation that we can join knowledge with wisdom.

Otherwise, without meditation, all our education and even our religious studies will remain just knowledge. Knowledge in the sense that it will merely be another collection of information in our brain. But that brain will not be joining with our heart.

Only through meditation is there a possibility of joining the heart with the brain. And when the two are joined, you will become a wiser and more wholesome person. This is what the Buddha is referring to by the union of compassion and wisdom. The compassion in the heart merges with the intelligence and wisdom of the mind. When they become one, you have realized the perfect ultimate nature within yourself.

> The relative phenomena of the world, however they appear,
> are without essence, mere names, mere sounds, mere
>   designations.
> Not the slightest bit of difference between names and mean-
>   ings exists.

As we discussed earlier, we think that all of these apparent objects in the relative world really exist. We use our sense organs to interact with these objects, and we use this interaction as proof of the object's existence. When our eyes see something, we believe that it's real. When we hear something, we establish that sound exists. When we can smell something, then that is proof that what we smell exists. The same can be applied to the other sensory perceptions of taste and touch.

So if objects are apparent to our sense organs, we use this as proof of their existence. But Virupa's teaching is saying, between those objects appearing to our organs and the names we give them, there's no difference. Both are relative and not inherently existent.

Only yogis who have meditated and transformed their karma can understand this teaching easily. For most of us who live with apparent objects without any insight or realization, it may be a little bit challenging.

In some Buddhist texts it is said that water can be many different things to different beings. As humans we experience water as something to drink, something to bathe in, something we can use to clean things with. Water has all of this utility for us. But the same water can be very different for beings in the ocean. For fish and other beings in the ocean, water may be more like a home.

Furthermore, the Buddha taught that the same water can be very different for beings in different realms. Those who have insatiable hunger may see water as pus and blood, while those who have a lot of anger may see it as molten lava.

So what this means is that objects are not inherently existent. Objects exist in dependence upon your sense organs and inner conditions. As the saying goes, "Beauty lies in the eye of beholder." The perception lies in the viewer, not in the object itself.

The more we examine, the more we study, the more we can prove this. This is the reason why Virupa says that all of the names, sounds, and designations that we project onto an object and even the object itself are only relative truth. There is no ultimate truth in any of them. Based on our societal interactions as humans, and based on our karmic experience, we have agreed on certain truths. Other than that agreement, ultimately both name and object have no independent existence.

What this is saying is that all these values, all these names and meanings, are only our own projections. We have projected all these ideas onto the object based on our karma and our emotions. But we cannot find the perfect ultimate truth in either the names or the objects that the names designate.

Once we have experienced perfect ultimate truth through meditation, we will achieve freedom. Otherwise we are always emotionally involved. Otherwise our karma, our ideas, and our conflicting feelings will always dominate our lives.

Some philosophers have theorized that humans are born free. The Buddhist view is that we are not born free. But even if we all agreed that we were born free, look how quickly we lose that freedom as we become chained to society. We may have been born free, but everywhere we are in chains. We don't feel any sense of freedom. Even in a country like the United States where the culture is built on the notion of independence, if we look honestly within ourselves, we will realize we are not free.

If we look within, we realize we cannot find any inner space. We realize we rarely ever feel at peace. We're always restless. We're always stressed. We're always being given the message that we should be doing more, achieving more accolades, earning more money. We are even being held prisoner by the idea that we should be having more fun! We are perpetually being marketed objects that will supposedly make us happier, but all they ever do is increase our desires and cravings. They bring us less and less peace and comfort.

How is this possible? Why do we feel more insecure even though we are the world's most secure, wealthy, and powerful country? Even though we have every kind of insurance possible and massive military strength, why do we feel so incredibly vulnerable?

What we find is that there's something inside us that has a lot to do with how we experience our life in the outside world. Only enlightenment or the realization of ultimate truth can bring that inner space where we have complete freedom. And within that freedom, we have bliss and joy. That's why meditation is the only way to achieve such inner joy.

8

Innate from the Beginning, Not to Be Sought Elsewhere

MAHASIDDHA VIRUPA WAS ONE of the most important Indian masters. If we were to count the most accomplished masters—including the Buddha—on just our fingers, Virupa would be among them. When we study and practice what he taught, and when we realize all of the transmissions that we received from him, it is clear that he is far more than just a scholar.

However, Virupa was indeed a great scholar and an esteemed professor at Nalanda University. During his life, Nalanda University was one of the biggest universities in India and really an international center of learning. Many students from China and other countries traveled there to study.

After the time of the Buddha, the Dharma teachings were preserved in several ways. The first was through the scholars who were called *panditas*. Panditas were scholars who had knowledge of all ten of the different sciences through their studies. These sciences included the medicinal arts, logic, poetry and more. Dharma was the only inner science among those ten.

Some panditas, in order to continuously preserve Buddhist scholarship, devoted their entire lives to teaching. It was through their role as teachers and scholars that they served the Dharma in their work.

The Buddha defined three ways to serve the Dharma. The first is through your own practice, which is the most important. The second is through teaching the Dharma. The third way to be of service is to assist other meditators and scholars.

There have been many fine scholars of the Dharma, and many learned teachers. For this reason, Buddhism has a very strong tradition of learning.

As we all know, if you want to learn, you can dedicate your whole life to gathering knowledge. Yet each new thing you learn will lead you to see that there is even more to learn This is the risk of scholarship without meditation or practice: if you are not cultivating inner wisdom through practice, the more you learn, the more dissatisfied you may feel.

Another way that the Dharma was preserved after the Buddha's lifetime involved panditas who, in addition to teaching, cultivated their own spiritual practice. When their meditation led to transformation and realization, they were called mahasiddhas, which means "great accomplished ones."

If we study Virupa's biography, we learn of all the mystical powers that he achieved. Virupa was very rare in the sense that he was a pandita as well as a mystical person. It is very rare to encounter masters who have gained great accomplishment through both methods.

One of the benefits of a scholar who then also becomes a meditator is that they can bring a certainty to their meditation experiences due to their knowledge. Their scholarship can affirm whatever they are discovering through their own practice.

If scholars have studied the concept of emptiness intellectually and have come to conclusions based on logic, then when those conclusions become a foundation for their meditation, there is real confirmation of what they are experiencing.

If you don't have that scholarly training, then it is possible while meditating to confuse an experience of nothingness with an experience of emptiness. Because these states may manifest in similar ways, if you don't have that base of knowledge, it may be easy to misunderstand your meditation experiences. Due to this confusion, we find that emptiness can easily fall into any extremes. But with some certainty from your studies, your practice can be significantly strengthened.

Take the communists for example. They are atheists and do not believe in a creator God of any kind. Now we see at the higher level of Buddhist philosophy that we also go beyond any theistic beliefs. So, from the outside perhaps, we could say they are both atheists. But communism has not cultivated a thorough spiritual science through reason or logic to prove nonexistence. Furthermore, they have not practiced any meditation that would allow them to go beyond mundane concerns. So their beliefs are based on a lack of knowledge, not on inquiry.

Their main proof that there is no God is that they cannot see one. Their ism is based on this life, with no sense of rebirth. So in many ways their atheism is a result of blindness or ignorance, not a result of rigorous logical examination and not a result of having transcended religion through meditation.

Buddhist scholars and meditators on the other hand, based on logic and meditation experience, have gone beyond theistic models. So communists and Buddhists may both say that they are atheists, but there is a big difference. One conclusion is based on knowledge and transformation, and the other is purely based on ignorance and has not been reached through examination.

Scholars can be served very well by the knowledge they've acquired if they become meditators. But knowledge can also create real obstacles. This is partially due to the fact that scholarship is very entertaining and rewarding on a certain level. The more you learn, the hungrier you can become for information. In this way, scholarship can keep you busy for your entire life.

Virupa became a mahasiddha through tantric practice. His experience did not stem purely from mind-based meditation but rather the physical energies that are harnessed in tantric practice. This is a critical reason why he was able to achieve such high realization in so short a period of time.

In comparison, if you only ever practice shamatha meditation, then at some point you may become very attached to that peaceful experience of calm abiding. That peace may actually be misleading in the sense that you will want to remain in that state for a long period of time because it is so relaxing.

Although it is peaceful, shamatha meditation is mostly neutral. It does not have very strong transformative power. The only real transformation in shamatha is that the peace you are cultivating helps you to overcome your active destructive emotions. You are not necessarily developing any strong insight, and you are not purifying your karma or addressing any sleeping emotions.

In Virupa's case, he attained deep insight to the point where the realization in his mind had the power to overcome all physical distractions. He was also able to transform all inner destructive forces. Due to these powers, he became the most powerful yogi. This was actually his other title. He is well known as "the most powerful yogi."

Most other meditators became powerful only through meditation. By meditations based on the physical energies, they gained control over all of the four material elements and became very powerful.

In Virupa's case, not only did he overcome the inner elements through his practices of inner heat, breath retention, and all of these various practices, but he also overcame the basic feminine and masculine energy within himself.

This is why he is one of the most powerful yogis in the Buddhist lineage and even among other Indian traditions. In some sense, his yogic powers, tradition, and transmissions are older than Hindu hatha yoga.

This is why when we study his mystical songs, we can sense that these are coming from a very profound level of meditation experience. These are not scholarly expositions of some tenets or philosophy; they are coming from his deep inner mystical experiences.

> The relative phenomena of the world, however they appear,
> are without essence mere names, mere sounds, mere
>   designations.
> Not the slightest bit of difference between names and mean-
>   ings exists.

Most of the time our experience of the world is relative. We live in an interdependent universe, and because we have all of these sense organs, we experience the phenomenal world.

Our current experience occurs due to interactions between the mind and emotions and between our sense organs and their sense objects. Because of these interdependencies, our universe is one of relative phenomena. It is a relative world. Relative in the sense that these factors must come together interdependently in order for us to have any of these experiences.

All of these apparent objects of our sense organs—what we see, what we hear, what we smell, and so forth—appear to exist because of the interdependency. Now the question is how real and perfect they are. How ultimate are they? These questions have to be addressed.

In our philosophical studies, we are trying to understand whether these experiences are independent or interdependent. Most Buddhist philosophical studies focus on whether we can determine any independent existence within this interdependency. Is there any independent existence at the object level, the organ level, or at the emotional level? If we can prove that there is something that exists independently, then we have gone beyond relativity.

Within Buddhist philosophical teachings, we have four levels of conclusions. One major difference between Buddhism and theistic religions is that theistic religions cannot accept interdependency because they believe in the first cause, namely, a creator God.

But within Buddhism, all four different philosophical schools accept the idea of interdependency. The difference, however, lies in the interpretation. Although all four schools of Buddhism believe in interdependency, the resulting conclusions differ significantly.

If you look at the conclusions of the lower schools from the perspective of the higher schools, you see that, despite their claims, they still haven't truly accepted or proven interdependency. Although the lower schools appear to conclude that phenomena are relative and interdependent, still we see the lower schools' conclusions falling into one extreme or another, existence or nonexistence.

The first Buddhist philosophical conclusion is materialist or realist. Buddhist realists can reduce any object into pieces and conclude that at the ultimate reduction of, say, a cup, there is one indivisible atom in that cup that is independent. Because they claim that one cannot reduce that atom any further, then that atom is the building block of all material things. So while the realists believe in the interdependency of the cup, they still conclude that reduced to its smallest atom, there will be something that exists independently.

From the viewpoint of the highest Buddhist philosophy, the conclusions of the realist school are still not ultimate because the realists believe in the independent existence of atoms. When the higher philosophical schools examine that atom, they find that even that atom doesn't exist independently. This is either because you can still find many subatomic particles within that one atom, or because you cannot find any independent particles at all.

In this way, if we study all of the different levels of Buddhist philosophy, then from the highest level of the Madhyamaka school, we recognize that all of the other conclusions are still relative. Whether the conclusion is that of the independently existing atom or of the mindonly school's conclusion of the mind, they are all only relative. There is no true independent conclusion in all of the three lower Buddhist philosophies because they still fall into the extremes of existence or nonexistence.

The purpose of studying philosophy is to come to that conclusion. As an accomplished scholar, Mahasiddha Virupa studied all of this philosophy. But the power of his mystical songs lies in the fact that they are based on his meditation experience.

In meditation you do not necessarily rely on logic. Deep in a meditative state, when you have the experience of inner space, whatever is false will simply dissolve. In that space between thoughts in your mental continuum, whatever is real will remain.

This is why Mahasiddha Virupa is saying that all relative phenomena, however they appear, are without essence. Whatever the apparent objects we experience may be, they will dissolve in that deep meditation of the inner space. In that profound emptiness of the inner space, all of the apparent objects will dissipate.

In that inner space it will become clear that there is no essence. These objects are all merely names or sounds, merely concepts void of any inherent existence. Whether it's the sense organs or the apparent objects for the different senses, everything else is mere designation, just a projection of our own emotions.

When we have strong emotions, our emotions are expressed through our senses and then to the object. So the object is the mere designation of our projection. All the value we place on that object, all of the emotional involvement we bring to it, are merely a projection of our inner conditions.

Whether we call something a bell or call something else a cup is due to the meaning our inner conditions have assigned to those objects. This is the reason why these same objects are often perceived in dramatically different ways for individual sentient beings. Even people may look at the same bell and see something different. There is no universal cup and no universal bell.

When Virupa says "not the slightest bit of difference between names and objects exists," he is concluding that neither the name of the object nor the object itself has any inherent existence. For this reason, there is no difference between them.

A name, as we know, is a reference we use to identify a given object. This is how we try to communicate based on these elaborate systems of names we've agreed upon. And as we have explored in an earlier teaching, even our birth name does not refer to some intrinsic nature of our person. Names are only for the purpose of identification. We have given a name to that object in relative terms, and that's how we have come to identify it.

If we look more closely into the object and try to determine what the object itself is, we cannot locate any essence. So although both name and object are different on the relative level, ultimately they are the same because they lack any essence.

We've established that relative phenomena are just projections. All values are projected. They are just designations. All of our experiences of relative apparent objects are based on our own inner conditions. Whether the object will bring us pain or pleasure is wholly dependent on the inner conditions with which we interact with that object.

If we contact the outer object with desire and attachment, then the outer object can seem more agreeable. If we successfully obtain it, it may temporarily give us more pleasure and happiness. But if we relate to that same object with anger, it may suddenly become a source of pain and suffering.

For us human beings, the driving force in our lives is *feeling*. How we experience a given feeling has much more to do with the inner condition of our emotions than it does with the outer object itself. We all know very well that one object can be both a source of pain and pleasure and a cause of suffering and also happiness. Although it is the same object, our inner conditions can create all kinds of reactions to it.

So we see how the phenomenal world and our inner conditions are interdependent. That interdependence gives rise to all our experiences. This is how we can understand our emotions. The strength of our experience relative to any object has a direct correlation with how strongly our emotions are involved with that object or activity.

The more involved we become with that object, the stronger our feelings grow. And as long as we have intense feelings, we will not see the object in a clear light. We will be unable to see the object as it really is.

This is the reason why the relative world is never perfect. It's always imperfect because our inner emotions are imperfect. In some sense inner emotions are blind. When we relate blindly to the world, our interactions generate even more emotions, which further obscure our vision. This is why we are unable to see the true nature of the object, to experience the object as it really is.

At our level, object, feeling, and emotion are completely interdependent. Due to our feelings, our emotions are increased in this perpetual chain reaction. The more our feelings are involved, the more obscurity there will be at the level of the object. In the world of relative phenomena, we cannot see any ultimate essence or truth.

Innate from the beginning, not to be sought elsewhere,
the nature of the mind, without a name, mahamudra
free from proliferation

It is important to clarify that mind, and the nature of mind, are two completely different things. At our level we still experience mind in the same way we experience a cup. As we have discussed, we must go through the cup if we are to find the true nature of the cup.

Right now, we cannot see the nature of the cup; we see it only as a physical object. This is similar to how we perceive our own mind. For us, our mind is experienced as drops of thoughts, rushing one after another. These thoughts occur so rapidly that they form a steady stream, a constant river of thoughts. The nature of the mind is completely obscured in that swift current.

This brings us back to the river example. Although the river is made up of tiny drops of water, when there is speed to that flow, it appears to be a steady continuum. Although the whole river is made up of individual drops, we cannot see them due to this constant rush of water.

Likewise, at our level we are often unable to see even one individual thought. Instead we have continuous thoughts that arise one after another in this steady stream.

When we meditate, we become aware for the first time of how many thoughts we have in our mind. Through meditation, the pace of our thought process will begin to slow, and we will start to see more clearly the possible space between the individual drops of thought.

Still using the river analogy, as we proceed in our meditation, we may reach the point of seeing different atoms within a single drop. We may reach a level where we see four different elements within those atoms. But even in this reduction, we still have not seen emptiness, so we don't yet know the nature of the water.

It is the same with our mind. Although the pace of our thoughts gradually slows, we still don't see a gap between them. As long as we don't see the space between our thoughts, and as long as we don't see the gap between two drops in a river, their true nature will be obscured. We will not see ultimate truth.

Back to the example of the cup. If we investigate the cup more and more, eventually we will no longer find it. If we break it down and reduce it to the smallest atoms, then where is the actual cup? Now this forces us to question which is ultimately true: the cup that we see, or the realization that if we reduce it, the cup does not actually exist? Which conclusion is more accurate?

Ordinarily, according to our conditions, we see this cup as completely real. But if this cup is real, then it should be the same for everyone. We all know this is not the case. Even among humans, some may see this as a cup, and some may see this as something else depending on their conditions. A child may see it as a toy. Someone from another culture may find some other use for it entirely.

So we see that the nature of the object is different from the object we generally experience. Likewise, the nature of the mind and the mind are very different. Mind is what we normally experience. Nature is within the mind, but we have to use the mind to go beyond itself. Only then will we know its true nature.

The further we delve into the mind, the harder it will be to find. This is why in the sutras it is said that if you look within the mind through meditation, you will not find it. What you will find is clear light. The nature of the mind is clear light.

Although we are trying to describe this truth through words, it can only really be discovered through personal experience. For now, we are relying on Virupa's mystical experience, but whether this will become our own personal understanding or not depends on our meditation.

Until we personally experience this, we will remain dependent on something else. Virupa's realization of the nature of mind may not necessarily become our realization. If we don't meditate, then any truth we adopt from studying these songs will be like a carbon copy. It will not be the original experience.

The experience of the nature of mind is not something that can be duplicated. It cannot be created by someone for another person. This is something very personal and original, which you have to discover independently. And while the process of discovery is very personal, once you truly see the mind's nature, then that ultimate truth is no longer individual. The ultimate truth transcends the personal.

Virupa says "innate from the beginning" because that nature is not something artificially fabricated. It has no beginning. It has no first cause. It is free from all causes and conditions.

When the song says "not to be sought elsewhere," it means that in order to find the nature of the cup, you must examine the cup. You don't look to a bell to find the nature of a cup. Because we are operating from a relative world, we must go directly through the relative object itself. But once you realize the nature of the cup, it is possible that you will also see the nature of the bell.

What Buddhists have realized is that apparent objects are limitless. All of the objects and our sensory perceptions of them are limitless.

If we want to find the nature of all of these objects individually, then there will be no end to our examination.

So instead of trying futilely to see the nature of every single object, we use meditation to see the nature of the mind. Once you see the nature of the mind, then that understanding can be integrated into your experience of all apparent objects. Your entire outlook will be completely changed.

So while meditation is very introspective, ultimately by seeing the nature of the mind, your experience can turn outward and allow you to see the nature of everything.

> the nature of the mind, without a name, mahamudra
> free from proliferation

As we have discussed, *maha* means "great" and *mudra* means "seal." Once you have seen the nature of the mind, it is like a great seal that can impress that seeing onto all the other objects.

When we put a seal on something, then we are certifying it. What we are certifying here is that by seeing the nature of the mind, and by integrating it into all objects, we are in effect certifying the nature of the whole phenomenal world.

"Free from proliferation" means that in the state of mahamudra all proliferations disappear. In that inner space, all of the extremes of existence, nonexistence, both, and neither fall away. All of these proliferations are extremes.

When you are in that ultimate state that is the union of clarity and emptiness, although you are empty of all emotions, what remains in that emptiness is wisdom. That inner space between the drops of thoughts is free from all extremes.

In this way it is equivalent to the nature of space, without a name from the beginning. Outer space can become a mirror with which to know inner space. In some sense outer space is a reflection of inner space. So because enlightened buddhas have seen that inner space, all phenomena have become pure for them. They have seen the purity inside their minds, and therefore everything is pure.

We must ask, between all the apparent objects and the space in which all of these apparent objects arise, which is more real? Which is more lasting, the space or the object? Which is ultimate?

> equivalent with the nature of space, without a name,
> from the beginning

Outer space is unconditioned. It is not created by any causes and conditions. There is no beginning and there will be no end. This same space provides the sphere in which everything else arises.

All of the elements including earth, air, water, and fire as well as all objects arise within this space. The universe unfolds, and all planetary systems emerge. But all of these apparent objects come and go because they are all conditioned. They begin and cease. Space, however, is unconditioned, and therefore it is beginningless and also endless.

This is the same as the nature of our minds. That space between our thoughts is beginningless and endless. When mind becomes one with that inner space, that is enlightenment. That is the mahamudra, the clear light, the union of clarity and emptiness.

Outer space can inform our realization of inner space. Both outer and inner space are unconditioned. They have never begun, and they will never cease. As long as there's mind, then in the mind there is emptiness.

We cannot yet see the drops in the river. But yogis can see the drops, and within the drops they can see atoms. Within the atoms they can go further until they see emptiness.

It is the same with the mind. Yogis can see emptiness in all thoughts, all emotions, and all activities in the mental stream. In that sense outer space and outer objects and the inner nature of the mind become unified at the ultimate level. They become unified in the sense that the nature of both object and subject is the same; it is the union of clarity and emptiness.

With this realization, the order in which you relate to the object will change. First you will see emptiness, and then you will see the cup. In this way, your connection to the cup will be completely altered. You will no longer interact with that apparent object based on all of your emotions. It will no longer illicit more emotions in you.

The buddhas see the nature of the cup as well as the object and are freed from interdependence. All relative phenomena and apparent objects are an opportunity for the practitioner to discover the true nature of the mind. And when the true nature of the mind is realized, the nature of the entire phenomenal world can be understood.

9

Empty Throughout All Time and Always Selfless

IN ALL OF OUR sitting meditations our goal is to see the space between two thoughts. But just seeing that space during shamatha meditation is not necessarily seeing the nature of mind. That's why we also need to practice insight meditation.

Within insight meditation we have four different kinds of mindfulness. Mindfulness of impermanence, mindfulness of suffering, mindfulness of insubstantiality, and mindfulness of seeing emptiness.

This fourth insight involves pointing to the partial nature of mind. The mind is partial because in order to see its nature in mahamudra, we must realize not only its empty nature but also its awareness.

Mahamudra is the union of both emptiness and clarity. We are introduced to mahamudra during Vajrayana empowerments where, for the first time, we are shown that the true nature of mind is clear light.

This clear light refers to awareness. In this context it is that self-awareness of seeing the mind—the mind seeing its own true nature. In that realization the mind dissolves, and what you are left with is awareness itself, which is wisdom.

The union of clarity and emptiness, when it becomes personal experience, is the wisdom of awareness. This is true self-awareness. In the *Heart Sutra* it says, "self-awareness, like space." That is another way of referring to mahamudra.

Mahamudra is best cultivated through Vajrayana practice. Shamatha and insight meditation are cultivated to achieve the foundation upon which mahamudra can then be experienced.

This is why we refer to Vajrayana practices as *taking the result into the path*. The results from Theravada or Mahayana practice become the cause and the path to carry that result into the Vajrayana. These all refer to that experience of the nature of mind or mahamudra.

nonarisen by nature, free from the proliferation of signs

Signs here refer to those characteristics of interdependency where there is birth. Because we have been conceived and are born, we are now living. But one day we will die. None of us escape this cycle. These three phases of birth, life, and death are in a state of constant change from moment to moment.

Depending on whether mind and body are together or not, Buddhists have assigned different names for these stages. According to the Buddhist understanding, mind is there already. Our mental continuum is already there. But during conception and birth, one's consciousness and physical elements come together. From that meeting, the physical body begins to evolve and the fetus begins to form. When we are born, our physical body continues to develop.

Some say the moment we are born is the moment we begin to die. Even while the body is developing in the early years, we have already begun moving closer to its degeneration. Moment by moment we are aging—we are moving toward our death.

Birth and death go hand in hand because all of life is impermanent. When the mind and body are eventually separated again, when our consciousness leaves the body, then that is known as the moment of death.

We can see all three of these different signs in sentient beings as well as inanimate objects. As long as something is conditioned, it will be subject to those signs and stages. There is a creation where things appear, a time where they remain, and a time of decay when they disappear. This is how we have different experiences with apparent objects moment to moment.

What if we try to see these signs in the nature of mind? In the nature of the mind we cannot find birth. This is why Virupa says "nonarisen by nature." Because we cannot find birth, we also cannot find remaining. And because we cannot find remaining, we also cannot find death in the nature of the mind. When we discover our true nature, then we are free from birth, free from remaining, and free also from death.

Now on the other hand, for all interdependent things, we will always be able find all three stages. In interdependency, in the relative world, everything is conditioned. And conditioned nature is based on this cycle of birth, remaining, and death.

all-pervading, unmoving, and unchanging like space

This line refers to that gap between two thoughts that we have been describing. That gap is like space in that it is unconditioned. Like space, the nature of mind is free from obstructions, free from moving, and free from change. The nature of mind is all-pervading like space.

Until we see that space between our thoughts, our meditation experience will be very different. Early in our shamatha meditation, at the first two levels of practice, our thoughts are still rushing. These first two stages of shamatha meditation are known as "the waterfall" and "the river" because at this point in our practice our thoughts are still rushing rapidly in a steady stream.

In a waterfall we cannot see any space between the drops. What we see is water rushing past at great speed and volume. There is no ability to see the separate drops. In a similar way, our first experience of shamatha can be very overwhelming. Thoughts are coming one after another. There is constant movement. In fact, it may move so fast that it seems almost permanent and unchanging. As a massive waterfall almost appears to be a permanent fixture, so too the drops of our thoughts may rush so fast that we don't even see them changing.

This is something we all notice early in our meditation practice. For the first time we begin to become aware of all these patterns. Thoughts are moving very fast, and thoughts are changing very fast, but we also begin to see that thoughts are separate.

What we realize is that these thoughts are not all the same. If they were all the same, then if we had one angry thought, that angry state should become constant for us. But that is not the case. We have anger, then the anger passes. We have pain, then the pain resolves. We have joy, then it is lost. These patterns are always shifting. We see that thoughts are not "all-pervading." Thoughts are moving and changing constantly.

On the other hand, for those who remain in that space between thoughts, the experience is very different. Even if you have not seen the inner space, if your shamatha meditation proceeds to the third level called "the pond with streams," and then the fourth level called "ocean with waves," then you may begin to experience a tremendous calm. Your thoughts are no longer moving and changing rapidly. You no longer have many individual thoughts. There is more peace. Finally, the fifth level of shamatha practice, "the ocean without waves," is a state of profound calm in which the mind does not fall into any distractions whatsoever.

Our progress in shamatha meditation aids our ability to gain wisdom through insight meditation. Returning to the four kinds of mindfulness in insight meditation that we discussed earlier, if you reach the fourth level, then you will experience emptiness directly. And this will be the experience of all-pervading inner space, unmoving and unchanging. This space will be the nature of your mind.

If we simply study these words without connecting them to our meditation experience, then our understanding will only ever be intellectual. But since this is a mystical song, if we bring this into our own practice, then every line has something profound to reflect on in our own meditation.

empty throughout all time and always selfless

Inner space is also beyond time. Time is relative. When we talk about this moment, the present exists only in reference to the past and to the future. Other than how it relates to past and future, there is no way to prove that the present is occurring.

A timeline will exist as long as we have thoughts and as long as we have a mind. But if we go beyond the mind to the nature of the mind, then we've gone beyond the timeline. We've transcended the relative constraints of time.

When you are in that inner space, where is the person? The person, self, and ego are there as long as we have mind and thoughts. As we discussed, all of the inner emotions and inner thoughts we have project a sense of self and other. If there is other, there must be self. If there is object, there must be subject.

We can see that within a society, there are many things we project onto that society, and many things that society projects back onto us. Our identification is so dualistic because of these constant projections that reinforce the dynamic of self and other.

Whatever family and culture have placed on us and whatever we have accumulated as a way to identify ourselves in the world is based on names, concepts, and time. But something that is beyond time cannot be identified. This is because most of the identifications in the relative world are based on either measurement of quantity on the timeline or measurement of a material object.

For this reason, when we have seen that profound inner space, then everything that is relative, everything that has been conditionally created, will be dissolved. And whatever is true will remain.

This is why in the deepest meditation, yogis can remain utterly at peace. They are free from all the conflicts of the conditioned world. They are free from the duality of self and other, which has created so much tension and unrest.

Someone who is in that deep meditation not only experiences peace but doesn't even use that much energy. No karma is created because there are no thoughts. Mental activity burns the most energy for us. The more thoughts we think, the more karma we generate. And the more karma we have, the more stress we produce, which uses so much of our energy.

See, karma is also based on a timeline. If something has gone beyond time, then there is no more karma. Karma is cause and result, and cause and result only work on a timeline. All karma created at the mental, physical, and verbal levels is relative, because it is based on a timeline.

When something has gone beyond time and beyond mind, there is no creator of karma. That's why in the nature of the mind there is no karma. There is freedom from cause and result—freedom from all mental activity.

Another way to understand it is that karma is created by the ego and the self. If we reach a selfless, egoless state, then who is the creator of karma? Since there is no creation of karma, then we are at peace.

On the other hand, the more ego-based mental activity there is, the more emotions we generate, and the more karma we create. This can be a rather vicious cycle, breeding more and more suffering and dissatisfaction.

When we reflect on karma, the Buddhist understanding is that as long as you generate more karma, then you will be trapped in this perpetual chain reaction. Karma creates, the creation acts, and then action becomes reaction. This reaction creates more karma, which fuels the whole cycle again.

But when the creator, ego, and self are gone, when they are dissolved into space, then you are free from all karma. You are free in that natural state of the mind.

not the characteristic of concept, like a mirage of a river

When causes and conditions come together, our experiences can be likened to a mirage of water. But the water in a mirage is not real and can never quench our thirst. When causes and conditions come together, all of our conditioned experiences unfold. All of these experiences are based on concepts and characteristics.

As we have already explored, there are both unique and general characteristics that can be applied to any object. The unique characteristics are specific only to that one object; the general characteristics are shared by all conditioned things.

General characteristics include change and impermanence. Since all conditioned things are created by causes and conditions, they are all subject to impermanence. The unique characteristics are a way to identify all of these impermanent things.

How can we differentiate humans from animals? How can we differentiate each individual person from other humans? We rely on unique characteristics to determine these differences. Characteristics operate solely on a relative level.

At the ultimate level we cannot find characteristics. So all characteristics can be compared to a mirage; they have no ultimate existence. Yet look at how easily we are fooled in our conditioned world! We are always chasing after these countless mirages, thinking they have some ultimate truth, hoping to satisfy our thirst.

Even in a river there are general characteristics that we identify as a river. But when yogis see drops of water within the river, in the drop the river cannot be found. And if you go further to the atomic level, in the subatomic particle you cannot find the drop. And at the subatomic level, if you can find air, water, fire, and earth elements, then this indicates that you cannot find one separate element in an atom. Because even the subatomic particles are composed of the other elements. So at this level, where is the river?

The river is an illusion formed when causes and conditions come together. And when these factors move at a certain speed, then we think that there is a river. But if we go deeper and deeper, we cannot find any river. This is how our relative world is.

This is why Hindus and Buddhists say this world is *maya*. It's an illusion. It's a mirage. On the surface it may seem as though everything is real, everything is working. We may experience the illusion of all of these experiences. But as our philosophical understanding and meditation grow deeper, all of our outer experiences change.

Now this begs the question: are all of the experiences we have dependent on outer objects? Are these experiences stemming more from outer objects or from our sense organs? Or is the mind the most powerful part of our experience?

We must examine this through meditation. Meditation is a very introverted practice. We remove ourselves from the whole universe and try to focus on only one thing. So if we are focusing on our breathing, all our sense organs must be attentive to that one point. Our eye is focused on the breath, our ear is on the breath, and all the sense organs are now paying attention to the breath.

When our focus becomes very strong, then we can turn that focus to investigate the mind itself. That's how we find self-awareness. We remove ourselves from the whole universe to see what is inside us.

At a sense organ level, the outer experience is perhaps more powerful, but when we go deeper in our meditation, we find that it is our consciousness that has the most power. We learn that the consciousness has the most influence over how we experience everything.

This is why in the teachings and in the accounts of great yogis we hear that all of these outer experiences are dependent on our inner conditions. Based on our inner conditions, we then experience all outer objects. The very same object, depending on our inner conditions, can give many different experiences at different times or places in our lives. It is still the same object, but the way we experience it may be radically different.

If an object had all the power to produce our experience of it, then that object would give us the same experience every time. But that is not the case. We know from experience that our relationship to objects is always changing. One moment we love something, the next moment we hate it. One moment we are so attached to some object, and the next day we want to get rid of it.

Whether the mirage of water will be just a mirage or will be real water depends entirely on what's inside us. Our perception of the whole outer world is a result of our inner conditions and karmic propensities.

Since these dohas are coming from a mystical yogi, he has already realized that all our experiences stem from the mind. Although we may firmly believe that the apparent objects that we experience are somehow inherently existing, what the great meditators see is that they are all a result of the inner conditions of our minds.

As we have discussed earlier, imagine that today I meet someone for the first time. In this first encounter with that person I have no information. After the meeting, however, I carry an idea and image in my mind of who that person is.

So although the person is gone, I have already formed an idea of who that person is based on our interactions and the person's physical appearance. These impressions create a narrative in my mind of who the person is, which I build on with more and more thoughts after our first meeting.

Are the thoughts and images that I carry with me after the person has left real? Who has actually created these images? I have made all sorts of judgments based on my feelings and projections. I bring all of these conclusions into my next interaction with this person, and my inner narrative will have a strong impact on how I see the person now.

Where is the reality of that person? How much is simply my own projection? This is how we interact with all of the people and objects in the relative world. We assume that our impression is the reality of that object, when really it has far more to do with our own inner creation.

The great yogis have shared the realization that all apparent objects that we perceive with our senses are first stored in our mind. Then they become part of our emotions and thoughts and are the source of all of our projections.

Virupa is saying that these projections are like a mirage. We think that they are real, but the truth is that everything we experience in the relative world has far more to do with our own ideas, feelings, affinities, and karmic propensities.

Now if we look deeper and deeper into our thought processes through meditation, we conclude that these mental formations are due to interdependency—that is, the interdependency between an object and our ideas, emotions, and karmic projections. If we separate these into parts, we cannot find any reality in them.

So what is appearing inside the mind is not something we can actually find. What is appearing in the mind is not true. It is all an illusion. We cannot find any substantial evidence of inherent existence within these projections.

What we learn is that the true nature of everything is emptiness. Whether we are examining objects in the outer world or examining our own inner concept of them, there is no reality in either. We see that the empty nature is true at the subjective level as well as at the objective level.

not bound, not liberated, having never moved from
the original state.

In samsara, our life cycle is based on destructive emotions and karma, which propel us to be born again and again. We experience all three kinds of suffering in samsara. Bound by our emotions and the accumulation of karma, we do not experience any freedom. We are forced to be reborn repeatedly.

We engage in spiritual practice in order to gain liberation from the wheel of life. We refer to this liberation as "nirvana." We are under the impression that since we are in samsara, we will have to find nirvana somewhere else, somewhere outside of samsaric existence. But this duality is also an illusion.

When Virupa says "not bound, not liberated, having never moved from the original state," what he is saying is that nirvana is not to be found somewhere else. As we have said before, nirvana and samsara are two sides of the same coin. If you remain in the middle, then you are free from both.

These dohas are coming from a highly realized master who has seen mahamudra. In that union of clarity and emptiness, even nirvana is seen as an extreme. When you have achieved mahamudra, you are free from both samsara and nirvana. You are free from existence and also free from nonexistence.

The original state Virupa refers to is that inner space that is the true nature of your mind. That inner space is always free from samsara and nirvana. So even though the nature of mind is the union of clarity and emptiness, if you become attached either to the clarity or the emptiness, you will fall into an extreme.

Only practice and meditation provide the potentiality for you to realize the union of awareness and emptiness. That realization of union has the power to go beyond both. It is free from all extremes, free from what is binding, and even free from liberation! You have gone beyond this duality of nirvana and samsara to see true freedom.

The original state is like space. Within space all these clouds come and go, but they are all circumstantial. Space is clear and it is never bound and never liberated. Our ordinary human experience is that when clouds come, space is obscured, and we think that this is samsara. And if clouds are gone, we think space is liberated.

But the truth is that the clouds have never conditioned space. The nature of space is always the same, only the clouds have changed. So the clouds coming together is samsara. The clouds going away is nirvana. This is our limited understanding. But the original state of space, the original state of the nature of mind, is unconditioned. This is why Virupa says "having never moved from the original state."

10

The Play of Mahamudra, the Original Dharmata

All sentient beings are emanations of mahamudra.
The essence of those emanations is the forever nonarising
dharmadhatu.

T HESE LINES PRESENT A very profound teaching. Philosoph-
ically this is the same as what is said in Madhyamaka, "Where
there is emptiness, there is everything."

As we have discussed, outer space is unconditioned and is there
from beginningless time. Within this space all of the planetary systems come and go. All these stars and planets are not permanent.
There are limitless galaxies, and they are always changing because they
are conditioned. Space is what gives room for all of these planetary
systems to occur.

Where have all of the sentient beings inhabiting these planets come
from? We think we are conceived and come from our mother and
father. We think humans have evolved from a common ancestor we

share with apes. We have all of these explanations for our existence. But for a mystical person, there is a far more profound explanation.

Virupa says, "All sentient beings are emanations of mahamudra." So the Sakya masters, as we know, have defined mahamudra as the union of clarity and emptiness. This union of clarity and emptiness is also the union of compassion and wisdom. We must ask, then, what is the potentiality of mahamudra within the mother's womb?

In tantric practice, we find all the inner anatomy related with the four elements. The essence of the four elements is the white and red elements we have received from our father and mother.

These red and white elements have the potentialities of wisdom and compassion. When we have not realized wisdom and compassion, then the red and white elements are the condition to increase our ignorance and all of our attachment and aversion.

Ordinarily the mixture of the red and white elements with which we are conceived actually imprisons our consciousness. Our consciousness becomes trapped between these elements, and we develop all of these conflicting emotions of attachment and aversion.

Depending on our gender, one element will become the condition for attachment, and one element will become the condition for aversion. Then they manifest in feminine and masculine energy and are the cause for all the organs and all the sense objects to appear. Without wisdom and compassion, we operate in this constant tension between attachment and aversion.

So when the doha says "all sentient beings are emanations of mahamudra," in essence Virupa is stating that all sentient beings come from that wisdom and compassion, the union of which is the mahamudra.

Until we see this, however, what we will experience is a life driven by attachment and aversion. Our unconscious mind will be ruled by the ignorance of not knowing our true nature. Without this understanding, all sentient beings will be conceived by and imprisoned in the conflicting emotions of the red and white elements.

In some sense this explanation is approaching the issue from a reversion. Our current experience is one of evolution. We learn that we are first conceived, our fetus develops, we are born, and we grow. Our understanding is based entirely on this timeline and on our physical experience.

If we don't meditate, we will never have the experience of maha-mudra. Until we meditate, we will not see that the union of wisdom and compassion can also be found in these masculine and feminine elements and in these essential natures.

All of the tantric practices—the generation and the completion stages—are a method to reverse and free the consciousness that has been trapped between those two elements. So this is another gateway through which we can know what is inside us.

Once we see that our true nature is the union of wisdom and compassion, then every sentient being is just an emanation. When we realize the ultimate truth of mahamudra, then we understand that everything we perceive in the relative and interdependent world is only an emanation.

For those who have seen the mahamudra of wisdom and compassion, the ultimate is the Buddha. In the Buddha there is no sentient being. Sentient beings are those who have not experienced awakening yet and are still filled with afflictive emotions that cause suffering. This is why the Sakya theory of the three visions states, "for sentient beings with afflictive emotions there is suffering."

This is the impure vision of our ordinary life experience. As sentient beings, we are shaped by afflictive emotions that result in suffering—the suffering of pain and unhappiness and the suffering of pleasure and happiness.

When we look closely, we see that even happiness and pleasure are not lasting, and they eventually lead to even greater unhappiness because we are so attached to those pleasurable feelings. Even the neutral feelings are rooted in ignorance and are a form of suffering.

But yogis have the vision of experience. Out of pain and suffering, they can cultivate compassion. Out of pleasure and happiness, they can cultivate loving-kindness. Out of neutrality, they can cultivate equanimity. This is the experience of the masters. And when these yogis continue meditating, they have the realization of pure vision. This pure vision is the awakened state, the vision of mahamudra.

Virupa is speaking from that realization of pure vision. This is the purity with which the buddhas see us. But what we see with our impure vision is sentient beings who don't have any experience of awakening or buddha nature yet. The great insight is that we all have these potentialities of pure vision within us.

The essence of the nature of all limitless sentient beings is the union of compassion and wisdom. This union is nonarising. It is the clarity and emptiness, which has always been the nature of our mind from beginningless time.

This is also how we explain the continuum or tantra. That continuum is referring to the clarity and emptiness that is always in the mind. It does not arise or cease. It is beyond all of these conditions.

> Also all characteristics of dualistic appearances, happiness,
>   suffering and so on,
> are the play of mahamudra, the original dharmata.

Because we have not seen the nature of the mind, because we have not realized mahamudra, we are conceived from ignorance. Ignorance gives rise to attachment, aversion, and all conflicting feelings. These emotions and feelings are rooted in the ego. So we see that as long as we have ego, we will have all these feelings. All our feelings are a result of the karma that is created by those three destructive emotions.

Any karma created by these three destructive emotions of desire, anger, and ignorance will have a direct correlation with resulting feelings. These feelings are pain and pleasure, happiness and unhappiness, and neutral feelings. If we want to study feelings in great depth, the Abhidharma teachings provide a thorough examination.

While feelings are experienced at the physical and mental level, we still include all feelings into those three categories. In order to understand why pleasure and happiness are listed as a form of suffering, we have to look to the source of all feelings.

The Buddha saw that all feelings are rooted in the ego, and this is why they are also part of our suffering. Pleasure is suffering and happiness is suffering because they both cause destructive emotions. Every pleasure and every happiness has the condition to increase our pain and suffering.

At our level, all these feelings are based on the dualistic appearance of self and other. Thus all of our actions and reactions are based on our emotions and the interplay of subject and object.

If our karma or action is based on desire and attachment, then if that desire is fulfilled, we have temporary happiness and pleasure. If our karmic reaction is pain due to which we have anger, then we experience suffering. And whenever we don't have any tangible reaction, these are still considered neutral feelings. Neutral feelings qualify as a form of suffering because they are still in some way rooted in our sleeping emotions and in our ignorance.

Until we see mahamudra, any feelings we have are a sign that deep down in our mental continuum we still possess sleeping emotions. Whether we are eating in a neutral state or are even in a neutral state of deep sleep, we are still filled with sleeping emotions. We know this because the minute we wake, our feelings resume. The destructive emotions have not been eradicated by that neutral state in any way; they are there in the mind all the time.

Although in a neutral state our feelings are not actively being expressed, they are still repressed somewhere deep in our minds. This is what modern psychologists might refer to as intuition or the unconscious mind. But Buddhists define these as the sleeping emotions. Many of our actions and intuitions don't have much rational support because they are based on those unconscious feelings. But those unconscious feelings are often the driving force behind all of our decision making.

If we look honestly at our lives, we see that most of our decisions are not exactly rational, especially those decisions based on our desire to feel good, to feel happy. This is nowhere more obvious than in our social relationships.

What makes us fall in love with another person is often based primarily on our sleeping emotions. This is why we see over and over again that people end up in relationships with people who are not even good for them. Yet these sleeping emotions have taken precedence over any rational thought.

So although the emotions are sleeping, they still have a great deal of power over our decisions. We tend to refer to strong feelings of pain or pleasure as our understanding of what feeling is. But really, most of the time, we are feeling the suffering of neutrality without even recognizing it.

Even in our sleep we are experiencing the suffering of impermanence. Although we may not be taking any action, our bodies are changing. We don't want to be changed. We are desperately clinging to the idea that we are somehow permanent. But the emotions and karma are the cause for all the changes to occur.

When Virupa refers to "the play of mahamudra," we don't understand because for us it is not just a play! For us these feelings are intensely real. Whatever we do in our lives, feelings dominate our experience of ourselves and the world. Feelings are what drive us to seek things, to accumulate things, and to create identities.

But for those who have some experience of mahamudra, even these feelings are just play. Play in the sense that they are just like theater playing out on the great stage of emptiness. Those feelings and characters are not our true nature. They are just roles that have been assigned by our karma, by our actions and reactions. In that theater we are destroyed and elated, anguished and delighted daily. But those who have seen mahamudra know that none of it is real.

Early in our meditation practice, one of the main obstacles is that we are haunted by past feelings. Even the pleasurable memories plague us because we are still so attached to those people or experiences or objects as they were. The fact that we have lost them somehow, or that they have changed or grown, brings us so much nostalgia or sorrow.

If our ego has been wounded, that pain is impressed very deeply in our minds. This is why it can take so long to heal. Our memory of that pain can be the source of so much perpetual anger, which destroys our present moment.

Pleasure also makes a strong impression that we cling to. As that temporary pleasure fades, we feel fear. We desperately want the pleasure to be permanent. Pleasurable memories also become the measure of our current experience and create our expectations for the future. Good memories often leave us feeling restless and discontent when they cannot be recreated.

So we can see this is not play for us! This is our reality. But for those who have some meditation experience, even the extremes of pain and pleasure are just play in the sense that they are not permanent. Those with meditation experience do not get wrapped up in feelings. They can let go very easily because they see the true nature.

Our experience is completely dependent on the level of our meditation. The deeper our meditation is, the more our perspective changes. We will see the insubstantiality of all our feelings. Those who have the experience of mahamudra are no longer acting and reacting to create more feelings.

For yogis, everything is play, and the true nature is dharmata. Even feeling has the true nature of wisdom. All ideas have the nature of wisdom. When we see mahamudra, we see the emptiness and clarity in everything.

> Because there is no truth and nothing on which to rely
>   in play itself,
> reality never transcends the seal of emptiness.

Those awakened ones who see their true nature come to the conclusion that everything that is interdependent—everything in the relative world—is unreliable. It is unreliable in the sense that it is never independent.

If something is not independent or ultimate, how much can you depend on it? Everything interdependent will keep on changing. Even if one thing appears to be permanent, because it is interdependent, something else will change to affect it. In interdependency and relativity, everything is subject to change and to decay. In the relative world, everything is an object of suffering.

If our goal is to achieve complete independence and freedom, then relativity is not a reliable object. This is not to say that we should not work through relativity. As we have discussed, we must work with the relative world to get beyond it. We have to start where we are.

Another side of relativity is karma. We have to work according to karma while bearing in mind that this cause and result are not ultimate. We live under the laws of karma, and we must use karma to go beyond it to something ultimate, something reliable, which is the true nature.

> Some are completely tortured with empowerment rites,
> some always count their rosary saying *hum phat*,
> some consume shit, piss, blood, semen, and meat,
> some meditate in the yoga of *nadi* and *vayu*, but all are
>   deluded.

Another way to understand this is that if you have reached the top of the Himalayas, then you no longer need all the methods that allowed you to climb. Likewise, if you have crossed the bridge and reached the other side, you no longer need the bridge.

What purpose does an empowerment serve for those who have already seen the union of compassion and wisdom? They no longer need an introduction to the nature of their minds if they have already realized mahamudra. Not only do they not need empowerment, they no longer need to engage in spiritual practice. They don't need to work on that bridge or practice their climbing skills. They have gone beyond the method.

When the doha says "some always count their rosary saying *hum phat*, some consume shit, piss, blood, semen, and meat," this refers to the fact that when someone achieves mahamudra, they have gone beyond what is dirty and what is pure. There is no longer any distinction to be made between what is good and what is bad.

Whether shit and piss are dirty or not is all in our minds. If you are the Buddha, you have gone beyond what is clean or unclean. But until you have gone beyond, then according to your inner conditions, concepts, and emotions, you will project different things.

The purpose of mentioning this is to demonstrate that someone who has realized mahamudra has gone beyond the way ordinary people judge experience. Whether something is clean or dirty, pure or impure, is all relative. But mahamudra is referring to the perfection that is beyond all judgments and discrimination.

In the state of mahamudra, not only have you gone beyond distinctions of pure or impure, you also have gone beyond your attachment to what is pure and your aversion to what is impure. One reason Vajrayogini practitioners taste the nectar in their practice is to go beyond those attachments. Our life and society are driven by consumption. And our consumption is based largely on our attachment and our wish to acquire what is good and pleasing.

The ritual tasting of nectar in the sadhana is to go beyond those perceptions, feelings, and emotions. We are training our mind to see that all food we are eating is only to support our body so that we can practice. We are trying to move beyond consumption based on desire and pleasure.

Virupa is also referring to yogic practices related with the four elements, including nadi yoga of the chakra systems and vayu yoga of the air practices. And what the doha is saying is that none of these methods are necessary for someone who has gone beyond. Those who have achieved mahamudra don't need to rely on these completion stage practices. The consumption of these impure substances refers to the nectar-tasting yogas found in practices like Vajrayogini practice.

We don't need any of these yogas. Even the eleven yogas of Vajrayogini are unnecessary. The purpose of yoga is to transform our ordinary activities into the extraordinary awakening conduct of a buddha.

So if you have become a buddha and are enlightened, then you are already transformed.

As we know from Virupa's life story, he was already transformed and awakened. He said, and others have certified, that he reached the sixth bhumi and achieved mahamudra. He no longer needed these yogas. All of these practices were now useless to Virupa because he had gone beyond them.

11

Connected with the Sublime Guru

E ma ho!

THERE IS A SANSKRIT word *evam*, which you can find in many sadhanas and other Sanskrit tantric texts. *Evam* means wisdom and compassion. The *e* here in the doha represents *evam*. *Evam* also has the meaning of "suchness" or "thatness," which is that experience of the union of wisdom and compassion.

The experience of inner space, where you have even gone beyond feelings, is represented here by the word *ma*. *Ma* means *mahasukha*, or great bliss. So the experience of suchness, due to the union of wisdom and compassion, is an experience of great bliss. When you are introduced to the union of wisdom and compassion within you, through the blessings of the guru, you will know the greatest bliss you have ever experienced. *Ho* means the wonder and amazement related to that great bliss experience.

Now we must not misinterpret bliss as a feeling. Feelings are still in the realm of the ego, and they are related to destructive emotions. This experience of great bliss has gone beyond all destructive emotions, as well as beyond karma and feeling. In the experience of inner space, you discover complete peace within yourself, and therefore complete peace with the universe.

There is no longer any distinction to be made between inner or outer space at this point; you are one with the cosmic universe. Because you and the universe have dissolved into the realm of empty space, there is no longer any self or other. As a result of this dissolution of self and other, there is no longer any conflict.

Until you have experienced this high level of realization, these words may be very difficult to understand. But the more you practice and meditate, the more you will begin to have a glimpse of that space.

Having been connected with a sublime guru,
one should realize as follows:
because there is some kind of delusion,
true realization does not exist.

The word *guru* in Sanskrit means "heaviness." The guru is said to be heavy with teachings, transmissions, and realizations. The guru has received many profound transmissions and is endowed with a wealth of knowledge, as well as realizations based on these trainings.

Teaching is very important. It is said that the greatest compassionate act of the Buddha is the Dharma teachings. Only through knowledge will you be inspired to apply yourself to your practice. And only through practice will you discover inner wisdom.

It is knowledge and practice that have the power to free us from the root causes of our suffering. When the guru shows us the path and shares the teachings with us, this is the greatest act of compassion. It is the deepest form of compassion because it has the potential to bring us ultimate freedom.

If you are in the midst of suffering, you may not feel that the guru's teaching is a very sympathetic act. You may wish for the teacher to show more empathy in the way that you are accustomed to receiving support from friends or family. You may wish to solve the immediate problem at hand.

But teachings have the great potential to transform knowledge into wisdom. If you achieve wisdom, then you can free yourself not only from your current suffering but also from all pain and conflict. The teacher addresses the root causes of suffering, and this is a profoundly compassionate act.

Since we don't have the fortune to receive teachings directly from the Buddha, we must rely on gurus to carry these pure teachings down through the lineage to us. It is important to point out that the guru is often very misunderstood. This may be especially true in the West where people carry very different cultural expectations and project many other roles onto the teacher. But in general, regardless of the culture, we can often detect a certain amount of delusion and misconception in the spiritual practitioner with regard to the guru.

The guru is here to help us go beyond. Most of the time, however, we see the student becoming very dependent on the teacher. There is a Buddhist story that describes this dynamic well. Let's say someone is pointing a finger to show you the moon. If, instead of looking up, you look at this person's finger, then you will never see the moon!

This story of the moon illustrates the misconception the student has often had about the guru. This confusion is not just endemic in the contemporary Western world; it has occurred throughout the centuries in the East as well. This mistaken projection extends not only to the guru but also to our dependence on the Buddha, Dharma, and Sangha. If we become completely dependent on the Triple Gem, we will never get beyond the finger to see the moon.

Until we see the guru within us, until we see our own buddha nature and integrate the Dharma and Sangha into our beings, we will be caught up in our outer projections. Even the guru can be a mere projection of our own emotions. The Triple Gem can be misused to actually reinforce our ego, our inner conditions, and our karma.

If we become too emotionally dependent on the guru and the Triple Gem as outer manifestations, then our destructive emotions of attachment will be magnified, and our expectations raised. If we reach a moment of conflict where the guru or Triple Gem are not comforting to us, are not supporting our emotional reality, then we will face many challenges and bitter disappointments.

So Virupa is cautioning us to reflect on our delusions. Each of us must ask the question, who is our guru? How much is that guru helping us to go beyond? Is our understanding of Buddha, Dharma, and Sangha freeing us or merely forming more attachments and dependencies?

Let's revisit the bridge analogy. Imagine we are using a bridge to cross a deep river. What happens if we become very attached to how beautiful the bridge is with its striking architecture? What happens if we discover one particular view of the water that we love, and we want to linger on the bridge every day to see it?

In this way, if we become very attached to the bridge and never actually use it to cross to the other side, then the very object that was there to assist us will become a real obstacle in our spiritual growth. We will never reach the other shore.

From the very beginning we need to know that the bridge and the guru are only vehicles, only methods of crossing over. All refuge objects are methods. All rituals are exercises to train ourselves to go beyond. In this way, the outer objects are relative. We must go through them in order to see the ultimate objects within us.

Because we bring all of these projections, habitual patterns, and expectations to our relationship with the guru, some level of delusion persists. As long as there is delusion, we will never see what our true nature is. We will never go beyond the bridge. We will never see the moon. We will just be staring at the finger that points to the moon, endlessly discussing the qualities of the moon, but failing to look up.

True realization cannot exist if we are too caught up in our intellectual understanding and too dependent on our guides and objects of practice. We could look at the finger and talk about the moon for many lifetimes without gaining any real experience. All of this is to say that we must be careful that we are not so busy studying and discussing the Dharma that we miss the message.

Earlier in the doha, Virupa said that even empowerment is deluded. All practices are deluded. All of these different conducts are deluded. Virupa is saying this because he has gone beyond all of the props. He is writing from his mystical experience of mahamudra, wherein he realized the ultimate freedom from all of these delusions.

Now at our level we may find Virupa's statements very confusing. They may even inspire some doubt or fear in us We have taken refuge in these objects, and now he is saying they are a delusion! People have coined the term "crazy wisdom" for this behavior. This is when a realized teacher seems a bit crazy according to our relative sensibilities and beliefs.

When you have seen the guru within yourself, then you don't need to rely on the outer guru. When you have seen who the true guru is, you will not be trapped in your dependency on an outer teacher. Likewise, once you have gone beyond the bridge, you will no longer need it.

If the bridge is later washed away or broken, it will not matter. If we lose the guru as a physical being, we will not lose our meditation experience and wisdom. If we have transcended all of our emotional attachment to the guru, then we will have abandoned all of the emotional games and our need for recognition, praise, support, guidance, and even love. When we have gone beyond, there will no longer be any conflict, because one's guru and oneself are the same. Subject and object will be dissolved.

Any situation can be used to benefit our spiritual growth if our ego is not invested in an outcome. But most of the time we don't see the perfection. What we see at our relative level is always black and white. Based on our ego we are always discriminating between what is good and what is bad.

As long as something feeds our ego, we decide it's good for us. If it doesn't feed our ego anymore, we decide it's bad. It's our enemy. If it makes us feel happy, then it's our friend. If it causes us pain, then we despise it. But ultimately how can we define goodness?

When we achieve perfection, we have gone beyond ego. Therefore we have abandoned these limited ideas of good or bad. But until we reach that realization, we still will react based on our ego. If our ego is not fulfilled, all of our destructive emotions will arise. We may become irate that someone has let us down or insulted us, but in reality, we are only failing ourselves with this reaction.

In order to grow, we must learn to use every situation in the relative world as a method for transformation. When relatively we project something as good, then we should use that goodness to go beyond goodness. Whenever we project something as bad, we must also use that negative experience as a cause for transformation.

Look at medicine for example. Often it is only the proportions, only the dose, that determines whether a substance is a medicine or a poison. Medicine can become poison. Poison can become medicine. It all depends upon the prescription and your attitude and ability to properly digest that substance.

This is why the tantric teachings are very challenging and very powerful. One must have a proper understanding of the base, path, and result. If you look back at the base and path from the perspective of the result, you will know that base and path are only relative. They are not a perfection. Only the result is the perfection. If you are too immersed in the base and path, thinking that those experiences are ultimate, then you will miss the true perfection.

At the moment our experience is a human one, based on the five aggregates and our senses. We don't yet see the wisdom in these aggregates of matter, feeling, ideation, formation, or consciousness. Early in our practice we cannot see the whole path of how things are transformed. This is why we may find Virupa's teachings quite challenging.

But if we have a complete understanding, or even perhaps a glimpse of that inner space, then we will receive some blessings from these dohas. We will understand the ways in which Mahasiddha Virupa is helping us toward realization. We will see how Virupa is trying to free us from all of the emotional games that bind us to the relative world.

Free from any extremes of partiality or bias,
since there is nothing to realize and no realization,

the homogeneous original state is neither
with nor without extremes.

So in your meditation, when you have a glimpse of that ultimate
state of mahamudra, you will have a brief vision of that freedom. You
will see the potential freedom from any conflict. You will understand
freedom from any extremes.

Now although these observations are coming from a highly realized
mystical person, we can actually see how neuroscience and quantum
physics are beginning to prove some of these ancient Buddhist realizations. Science is beginning to prove, at the relative level, what the yogis
have known for thousands of years.

Buddhism spoke of *shunyata* or "emptiness" some 2500 years ago.
Now scientists are discussing the quantum vacuum, which is similar
to the realizations of the Vaibhashika school of Buddhist philosophy.
Physicists are discovering that, at the quantum vacuum level, they can-
not prove that matter exists. Matter is just moving energy—a process.
It has no static material component.

Science is beginning to agree with Buddhism that we are all interconnected. What we do, what we say, what we think—everything
affects others and therefore the universe. Some leading scientists and
doctors are now turning to the wisdom traditions and finding many
parallels between scientific and spiritual discoveries.

Science has long focused on exploring conditioned things. But the
closer scientists look, and the deeper they investigate, the more they are
realizing this unconditioned emptiness in which all conditioned things
must occur.

So whether it is called a quantum vacuum or shunyata, we still must
be careful, as researchers and practitioners, not to let this emptiness
become an extreme. It is important that this realization be experienced
within us. Only when emptiness becomes an inner experience will
there be any real transformation.

Regardless of our intellect and knowledge, if we are focused solely
on exploring outer space, there will be no inner growth. We will not

know the union of method and wisdom or the resulting bliss. Only when shunyata becomes our personal realization through meditation will we gain an understanding of mahamudra.

If our understanding remains at the object level, then it will still just be our mind perceiving shunyata. This mental grasping will not be a kind of realization. Knowledge can obscure the experience of the ultimate because the mind is still busily involved with all of its concepts and ideas.

The "homogeneous original state" that Virupa refers to is not the quantum vacuum or outer emptiness; it is the integration of the emptiness within you. This integration, this space, is mahamudra. The original state that Virupa is talking about is neither with nor without extremes. It is free from all possible extremes of existence, nonexistence, both, and neither. As we have reiterated many times here, mahamudra is the ultimate state.

If one realizes in this way,
there is definitely no one else to ask.

Let's go back to our discussion of the role of the guru. When you have reached this state of union, you have no need for an outer guru. You don't need to ask anyone to guide you. You don't need anyone to point out the moon, and you no longer need any refuge objects. There is no more merit or wisdom to accumulate through practice.

Until you reach that realization, of course you need to rely on the guru, the Triple Gem, and the practices. You rely on them, but you cannot become dependent upon them. The work must be within yourself.

This is one very important message that the mystical songs of the dohas are bringing to us. Because we are not at that high level of realization, we need to rely on refuge objects, but that reliance must be temporary. It cannot become something permanent that we cling to in our lives. It is only a method for going beyond.

The refuge objects are the scaffolding we depend on while building our experience. When we have reached a certain level of realization, the scaffolding is unnecessary. If we are too dependent on the scaffolding, we will never be free.

If we see the Buddha as someone to rely on permanently, then we are treating him like a god. We are becoming theistic and projecting an outer hero figure to worship and depend on. However, that is not the purpose of the Buddhist path. The purpose of the path is to transform ourselves until we are completely free of all dependence.

> Since diversity appears as the dharmakaya,
> a mind that accepts and rejects never arises.

As we have already established, we see all the apparent objects in our lives based on our inner conditions and on our mental and emotional projections. All day long we are rejecting and accepting things. Our lives are characterized by this constant process of discriminating between apparent objects, between people, and among experiences. This discrimination is based on our perception that these objects are all different from each other and that our decisions will create various results.

But if we see the dharmakaya, the true nature within all of these diverse objects, then we realize that there is nothing to reject and nothing to accept. Until we see the dharmakaya, our ego-based mind will continue to categorize every single thing we interact with in the relative world. But when we see the dharmakaya nature in every object, the environment itself becomes our teacher. We no longer need the teachings to help us discriminate between right and wrong karma. There is no such thing as good or bad karma anymore because we have gone beyond both. There is no longer anything to accept or to reject. We have transcended all of those emotions and actions.

> There is nothing to meditate or not meditate,
> and nothing is covered with characteristics.

If someone has realized the union of clarity and emptiness, then that person has even gone beyond the need for meditation. Meditation is just another method. Meditation is another form of scaffolding, which is vital to the process, yet unnecessary to the final result.

Meditation is vital because we have to break through all of these emotional involvements with the characteristics. We have identified each and every object in our lives by certain unique characteristics, depending on its utility to us and our emotional involvement with it. These characteristics that we've established determine how we relate to each thing, each person, and each experience.

As we have discussed, there are unique characteristics for each object. These are based on identifying that object according to the projection of utility. At a personal level, we see characteristics according to our attachment, aversion, or indifference to each object. We have also defined the general characteristics, such as impermanence, which apply to all conditioned things.

In either case, both general and unique characteristics are there because we are caught up with the ego and still trapped in the conditioned mind. Someone in the state of ultimate mahamudra has gone beyond all of these conditions. Everything is now the same for them. All characteristics, unique and general, have dissolved.

> One should never depend on apparent
> and nonapparent objects.

At this point in our lives, because of our sense organs and our emotions, we are constantly dependent on objects. We create our whole reality based on how we experience those apparent objects through our sense organs. Above all else, it is our emotions that make us dependent on these objects.

However, in the state of mahamudra, we are free from all emotions. We become a witness to the conditioned world. We are still aware of all objects, but we are no longer emotionally involved or dependent upon these objects in any way.

Without the realization of mahamudra, our entire experience in life is more or less based on our emotional involvements. Even the subtlest feelings are all still based on the three main emotions of desire, anger, and ignorance. These three core emotions give rise to all of our varied feelings of attachment, aversion, and indifference.

If we have desire, then it follows that we will also have objects to which we become attached. If we have anger, then there will be objects to which we have a strong aversion. If we have ignorance, then we will have objects of indifference. As long as any of these emotions are present and affecting our engagement with the objects, there will be no freedom.

Apparent objects can be defined as those objects that have a direct connection to our sense organs. These are the objects that we see, smell, taste, etc.

Nonapparent objects have more to do with our mental activities. Nonapparent objects are even more pervasive and challenging because they create a wandering mind. A mind that is caught in conceptualizations of the past, attached to memories, or busy imagining future plans, will never be present.

With apparent objects, although our emotions are still involved and we are not seeing those objects with wisdom, at least there are no active concepts. But with nonapparent objects, all the thoughts of past and future are in the mind. Even when we close all our senses, these thoughts will come up.

We know this because these nonapparent objects surface in our dreams every night. Our dream life is a good indication of how our intermediate-state experience of the bardo will be after we die.

We carry these nonapparent objects in our mental continuum even through death. Even though they are not apparent to the senses, and even when the senses and physical body are no longer even there, these nonapparent objects remain in the mind.

There have been some very interesting scientific studies of people's mental activity after they've had a stroke. There is a lot to learn about how different parts of the brain affect different mental abilities.

We have to ask ourselves where the memory we have of someone is actually stored. We have a mental image of that person in our brain, but no one can actually detect it. Despite all of the advancements in imaging technology, there is still no way for scientists to capture an image we hold of someone by subjecting us to an MRI or any other scan. If these pictures we hold in our memory cannot be detected by any scientific measurement, where do these images actually reside?

According to Buddhism, when we examine the mind in the bardo, the brain is already gone. The brain has died, and the body has been cremated, yet it is said that in the bardo we will continue to carry those mental pictures we've created.

These beliefs may be very challenging for scientists to prove or disprove. Since the brain is gone, what is left to measure? Scientific methods cannot examine the immaterial mind. This is another frontier that Buddhists and scientists will converge at in the future.

Will we ever be able to locate where our mental pictures are actually residing? Will scientists accept Buddhism's experience of the intermediate bardo state after death, which is so filled with mental imagery? If science and Buddhism can reach a shared perspective on emptiness, then it is very possible that we may also one day share an understanding of nonapparent objects.

A mind with action and agent does not exist,
free from all objects.

Our mind is always working. We are burning so much energy with our mental activities that we often grow exhausted and stressed. The mind is always thinking, and those thoughts are both agent and action. The thinker is the agent, and the thinking is the action. We are constantly thinking, and that's why we are creating karma all the time.

Karma starts with thoughts in the mind. The more we think, the more karma we create. This is the reason why we are aging. Karma happens on a timeline. As long as we are thinking, then we are aging and changing, and at the mental level we will not achieve any freedom.

At the mental level, thinking is all related with mental objects. But when one has realized the inner space of mahamudra, there is no longer any thinker, and there are no longer any thoughts to have in that union of clarity and emptiness.

Right now, we don't have that empty space. We need only sit down for meditation to see how quickly our thoughts are rushing one after the other! This may be especially true for people who are naturally more mentally active. These quick thinkers are often prone to more emotion because their thoughts have more speed and take them rapidly through a range of feelings. The result can be very unsettling and can create a lot of restlessness.

Until there is a gap between our thoughts, we will be stuck in this interplay between the agent, who is the thinker, and the action, which is the thinking. As long as these two exist, we will not have gone beyond the mind to achieve the freedom.

12

Since One Is Free from All Attachment

VIRUPA WAS BORN IN a very high class, in a king's family. Like the Buddha, he grew up to renounce his kingdom and that life of opulence. As we have discussed, Indian society was divided into four classes or *varnas*. This caste system included the brahmin or priestly caste, the kshatriya or ruling class, the vaishya or merchants, and then the untouchables, who were the very poor shudra class.

In India a person's caste was determined at the time of birth. It was not like here in America where upper class and lower class are based largely on your income or net worth. In India it was just determined by the family you were born into. If you were born a brahmin, then you were in the brahmin caste for your whole life. If you were born to the noble families of the kshatriya caste, then you were nobility for your whole life.

To some extent the entire Hindu religion is based on this caste system. The Buddha was remarkably progressive given his time period because he saw beyond these classes. Many modern thinkers see the

Buddha as a social reformer because his sangha or spiritual community was open to everyone, regardless of caste. In the Buddha's eyes, once you were following the Dharma, everyone was equal. There was no discrimination to be made among spiritual seekers.

There are some who have questioned gender equality in Buddhism. If we examine Buddhist practices, we see that discrimination was only made between monks or nuns to benefit their meditation and spiritual practice. Nuns stayed at the nunnery and monks stayed at the monastery. That much separation was necessary. But if we look at all of the other religions stemming from India, we will find Buddhism to be the least discriminating among them. Buddhism broke through those barriers of class struggle.

Now as we learn from the Buddha's life story, sometimes being born into a noble family can actually be of real benefit to one's spiritual path. Once the wealthy and powerful renounce their kingdom, they have the potential to become very good meditators. Since they have known the life of luxury and comfort, and realized it is still filled with mental suffering, then all of their curiosity for that lifestyle has been abandoned.

If you have grown up in extreme poverty, on the other hand, struggling among the lower classes, there are fewer things to renounce. And even if you devote yourself to your spiritual path, you may still harbor some deep craving, some dream of wealth and comfort. Until you have fully experienced power and seen that it also brings sorrow and dissatisfaction, it may be more challenging to completely let go of some ideal you hold.

The nobility have experienced all of the material pleasures of the kingdom and all of the emotional power of control, but those who have renounced this life have come to recognize the suffering and anguish that exists despite all of that luxury.

When the Buddha was still a prince, he had hundreds of attendants. He was surrounded by beautiful women. He had great power and wealth and all of the advantages so many of us only dream of having.

But what the Buddha discovered is that when those dreams become one's reality, there is still unhappiness, there is still restlessness. Even when you are given every material comfort imaginable, there is still dissatisfaction. This is what drove the young prince to leave the walls of his kingdom and to wander through the streets.

As we described earlier, this was where the Buddha first encountered the suffering of the sick, the old, and the dying. This was a great learning process for him. It occurred to him that he too could become sick, that he too would grow old and die. He realized that he was not immune to this impermanence regardless of his power and wealth.

The fourth time the young prince ventured from his kingdom to walk the streets, he saw a yogi, a meditator. This was the profound moment of change for the Buddha. He realized that there was another way to live. He gained hope that there was a spiritual life that would transcend this suffering of impermanence. For the first time, he had hope that there was something beyond death.

Only meditators and spiritual seekers will understand this. For those without a spiritual understanding, life extends only from birth to death. For those without spiritual experience, death is the end of everything.

On that fourth journey from the palace, when the Buddha saw the meditator, he developed hope that there was something larger and more important to work toward. All of the accumulation of wealth and power no longer interested him.

As we know, the world is filled with intelligent people who accumulate so much prestige and knowledge, but none of that will allow them to cultivate this spiritual insight. It is only through renouncing worldly priorities and meditating that one will achieve realization.

According to Buddhist legend, Shakyamuni Buddha is the fourth buddha. In Buddhist mythology, it is said that the buddhas before Shakyamuni were also from noble families. So we see that having a whole kingdom to renounce makes the act of renunciation even more powerful, and the story shows us that these princes have discovered something far greater and more valuable than all their worldly pleasures.

So, much like the Buddha, Virupa also renounced his kingdom. He pursued the spiritual path and studied with many different masters.

He became a renowned scholar and was the abbot and professor at the famed Nalanda University in India for many years.

During the day, Virupa was teaching the Dharma, but at night he would do tantric meditation. When he was older, he grew very discouraged because he was not seeing any signs of realization. He was almost at the breaking point, ready to completely give up tantric practice.

That very night he had a vision of the tantric deity Nairatmya yogini. She appeared to him with encouraging words. She said that what he was doing was not fruitless. She assured him that he had already made great progress and that if he continued, he would achieve full realization.

After Nairatmya yogini visited him, Virupa meditated very diligently. Just as she had predicted, he soon reached a very high level of realization. At that point Virupa left Nalanda University and became a wandering yogi.

What Virupa had seen for the first time was his own true nature, the ultimate truth within himself. In some sense he had gone so far into his own mind that he had gone beyond himself. He had also gone beyond any discrimination between right and wrong.

In this way, Virupa had transcended all conventions of physical and verbal activity. All of his actions were now based on his awakening. If you study his biography, there are many episodes where his life seems very unconventional to us. In fact, we may misinterpret many of Virupa's actions based on our limited understanding.

For an enlightened person, every action is an expression of transcendence. The rest of Virupa's life was an expression of his compassion and wisdom, which had transcended even our limited understanding of what is right and wrong.

In our lives, we orient our judgments based on the self and ego. If something agrees with our ego or self, then we deem it to be good. If it disagrees with us, then we call it bad. If we experience pleasure, then something must be good, and if something causes us pain, then it must be bad.

All of the eighty-four mahasiddhas have gone beyond the self and ego, but our limited projections may cloud how we judge the actions of these enlightened masters. This is where our faith is tested, our devotion is tested, and our compassion is tested.

Until all of our faith, devotion, and compassion become wisdom, we may find the manifestations of these great yogis quite challenging. We are judging them from our experience here in the relative world, but these great masters are living and performing deeds from a state of ultimate truth.

At our level of understanding, there is a conflict for us between relative truth and ultimate truth. For these realized masters, however, there is nothing to accept and reject. It is all the same, and every situation itself can become a teacher.

Now for us, on the other hand, we are constantly accepting and rejecting experiences. We do this all day long. We divide everything into likes and dislikes. All of our interactions are based on the strength of our ego. As long as our self is the driving force in our decisions, we will have many emotions.

Virupa's mystical songs are not like regular Dharma teachings or philosophical texts. They are coming from that ultimate wisdom that has transcended all of these dualities. Only through our own meditation practice will these songs resonate in us or come to make perfect sense.

A mind with hope and fear does not exist,
turned away from all attachments,
if one realizes the original reality shown by the guru.

Until we have gained the experience of seeing our own true nature, we must rely on teachers. This is the whole purpose of tantric empowerments and initiations. The purpose of these rituals is to be introduced to our true nature through the guru. And that true nature, which we meet in the course of the empowerment, can then be carried into all our tantric meditation practice.

Meditation is not necessarily just sitting on a cushion and then having all kinds of experiences. People may report all sorts of visions or hallucinations in their practice. They can talk about all of these thoughts, but really these experiences are just manifestations of their own inner chattering, much like dreams.

Really, meditation practice is for continuing to cultivate whatever was introduced during the empowerment. This is the reason why we do all of these sadhana practices: to carry on this glimpse of our true nature, which we were shown during the initiation.

If you have seen your true nature, you will know it as the most peaceful experience you have had in your whole life. It cannot even be categorized as a feeling because it is peaceful to the point where you don't feel anything.

Normally, we become most aware of our feelings when they are unpleasant. If something is a cause of stress, we will suddenly become completely focused on it. If there is physical pain in any part of our body, then wherever that pain is, we will feel that area more intensely than the rest of the body. If we have a toothache, then suddenly that one area in our mouth will dominate our entire physical and mental experience.

So if you don't have any pain, or for that matter any pleasure, then how do you experience your body in this profound meditative state? It is not like forgetting your body, and it is certainly not a feeling of numbness. Instead you are so completely at peace with your body, so at ease within that awareness, that you don't feel anything. There is no longer any conflict between attachment and aversion, pain or pleasure.

When you have had a glimpse of that deep meditation, you will have an understanding of this possible equanimity. You are not ignoring your body, or mind, or the universe, but your awareness has become so deep that you are beyond conflict. You are beyond the duality that gives rise to so much attachment and aversion.

In that state of peace, there is no pain or pleasure. In the deepest meditation experience, you no longer feel yourself. When you are in that zone, you are not self-conscious and you don't feel yourself, so you also don't have any expectations. Without expectations you will no longer have any fear.

See, whenever we have expectations, we also have fear. We are afraid of what will happen if our expectations are not fulfilled. We have expectations because we are attached to something that we want. It could be an attachment to outer objects, to other people, or to various sensory experiences. Often our expectations are based on an attachment to something within us. In each case, we see that as long as we have attachment, then naturally it will give rise to expectation. And as long as there is expectation, then our hopes will also breed fear.

For people who have had a deep meditation experience, when they reflect on it afterwards, they know that in that deep state there were no emotions. There were no sensations, and because of that it was profoundly peaceful. Only when you remain in your original nature will you know this peace.

Tibetan lamas will often use the analogy of water when they describe meditation. If dirty water is placed in a container, then the more you shake the container, the more dirt will be stirred up in that water. But if you let the water sit still, eventually all the dirt will settle, and the water will become clean and pure again.

Meditation is this same process of allowing all of the impurities and afflictive emotions to settle. When all these emotions of attachment, expectation, and fear calm down, the mind is at peace.

The nature of your mind is like that pure water, but along the way, all of these other impurities were mixed into that water. The more karma we create, the more we are stirring that container of the mind with our afflictive emotions. And the more we stir, the muddier the water will become.

When the mind is disturbed with emotions, then we are never relaxed or truly at peace. Even when we are enjoying ourselves immensely, there is always underlying fear and stress. In fact, feelings of pleasure and happiness can create tremendous expectations. We want these feelings to last, and we are afraid they will not, so we have this underlying sense of fear. This fear gives rise to even more emotions of attachment and aversion, and the whole cycle feeds itself. We are never free in this cycle.

So meditation is a method to go beyond all of these expectations and fears. Only the great meditators can do this because they have also gone beyond the ego. They have gone beyond the self. As long as we have self and ego, then we have the emotions. And as long as we have emotions, then we will have expectations and fear.

This is the reason why our lives are so filled with anxiety. The more we get what we think we want, the more anxious we become. The irony is that the higher we go, the more frightened we grow of losing that status. Whether it's financial success, fame, or physical accomplishment, the more we succeed, the more we have an underlying fear of failing.

We feel insecure because if we have accomplished something great, we will have much further to fall when we lose it. If we are famous briefly, and then our popularity wanes, we may experience way more hurt and pain than if we'd never been famous to begin with.

So that's how the ego is playing with our life. Our self is directing our life. This is the reason why many of these great mahasiddhas became wandering yogis. They wanted not only to free themselves on the inside, but they also wanted to be free on the outside.

These yogis learned that one of the greatest ways to achieve security is by living in total physical insecurity. They realized that the less they had to cling to, the freer and more peaceful they felt.

In our lives, however, we are still under the impression that physical security will make us feel very secure. But really, if we look closely, it is quite the opposite. The more financial security, the more insurance, the more safety we have in our lives, the more insecure we often feel because we are constantly aware of what we could lose.

By nature, life cannot be completely secure because it is conditioned. We are born, we get old, and we die. None of us can avoid this process, no matter how much money we have. No matter how physically secure we've made our existence, we will still be subject to the laws of impermanence.

Yogis have realized this and have chosen to wander, free of all possessions. The more they have accepted that insecurity, the more freedom they have achieved. And that new freedom actually creates a profound sense of security.

These yogis have seen that birth, old age, and death are only a change of clothing. The body will come and go, but these realized ones have seen that there is something to rely on beyond death.

This is what the Buddha realized the fourth time he ventured out of the kingdom and saw the meditator there on the street. That is when he was introduced to the idea of something greater than his current existence.

For the Buddha and for Mahasiddha Virupa, death is not the end of their journey. Their great journey really begins with death. So that's why the fourth episode in the Buddha's life story was so important. That was the moment when he realized that only meditation could bring true security and happiness. He realized that practicing for this greater spiritual journey was the only way to abandon all expectation and fear.

The diversity of recollection and awareness
automatically dissolves into the dharmadhatu.

Once you have that deep meditation experience, everything is dissolved. Only the part of you that is true will remain. In your meditation, it doesn't matter whether you are a famous person, a doctor, or a scholar. Whatever titles have been given to you by society will no longer matter. Whatever you have gained and achieved in your relative life will be dissolved.

The word *dharmadhatu* here refers to our true nature. Through meditation we realize how we have been chasing our dreams for much of our life. We have been actively pursuing all of these outer accomplishments, but in reality, they are just projections. They are just dreams. When we are in that deep meditation, they all will dissolve.

Consciousness does not remain on an object,
since one is free from all attachment and grasping.

For those who are very experienced practitioners, there is no longer any separation between meditation and life. For the masters, it doesn't matter whether they look out or look in, they are always in a meditative state.

But when we are beginners and first learning to meditate, we have to practice focusing on one object. This is a way to train us to cultivate our concentration in order to overcome many distractions.

Normally, meditation is challenging in the beginning because our sense organs are accustomed to grasping at all of the sense objects in our daily life. We always seem to need something to look at. We always need something to listen to. We always need something to smell. All our sense organs need to be constantly engaged or consuming sensual objects. We are led to believe that we must consume sensual objects in order for our lives to be fulfilling.

But if we look closely, we realize that the more we consume, the more restless we become. This is how we've been operating since we were born. Our senses are hungry. From the moment we come into this life, we are looking, we are listening, we are tasting, and we are chasing after objects with all of our emotions.

Now when we meditate, our focus changes. Instead of pursuing outer objects, we become introverted. That's why the first lesson in meditation is to choose one object. Often we start with focusing on the breath, or on a blue flower. We try to bring all of our senses to concentrate on one single object.

We know that whenever we first try to do this, instead of focusing on the object, our mind is wandering all over. And the more wandering we do, the less happy we become. There even has been research to prove that when our mind is distracted, we are the least happy. But when our mind is completely present, we are the most at peace.

There are countless things in the universe for us to grasp at. There are billions of people. There are so many different sensory experiences. There are so many objects. We divide the whole universe into three categories: objects of attachment, objects of aversion, and objects of ignorance.

We pursue certain objects because we are attached to them. We reject other objects because we have some aversion or indifference to them. So it is clear that our sense organs and our corresponding sense consciousnesses are driven by emotions to grasp at objects and to classify them immediately.

Meditators who remain in the present and look into an object without emotions actually see the object much more clearly. When we look with strong emotions at something our vision will be obscured. We have been looking at things since the moment of our birth without ever seeing them completely. What we see instead is based entirely on our emotions.

In order to truly see something, we have to view it without emotion. When our eye organ sees an object without emotion, then we will see it more clearly than we ever have before.

When you see with attachment, you are already deluded. What you are seeing instead is merely a projection of your inner attachments. Due to this misperception, you completely miss the truth of that object.

Until you meditate, you won't really know an object. No one wants pain and suffering; everyone wants happiness. But this blind pursuit of objects only increases our pain and restlessness. It only fuels our hunger for more sensory satisfaction.

All phenomena are liberated in the uncontrived original state.

When your meditation is deep enough to see the true nature of your mind, you will achieve ultimate freedom. Then you will no longer be bound by your emotions. Not only will you be free from your emotions, you will also be free from all of your emotional projections to the outer world. You will have transcended dualism; you will have moved beyond self and other. And without self, there is no longer any ego in us to project things.

As we can all observe, we have a very strong attachment to the self. As a result, we then form strong attachments to the concept of "mine." The concepts of "I" and "my," which the ego produces, are an expression of our attachment to the universe. This is what compels us to extend our egotistical territory. The stronger our identification with "I" and "my," the more need we will feel to extend our territory, to accumulate more property, to devour more objects. The result is that instead of seeing our true nature, we are going further and further away from our true self.

But when we meditate and see the true nature of our minds, we find there is no such thing as self or ego. Self and other are the same, and there is no more conflict. That original state that Virupa is referring to is the nature of mind. The nature of mind is selfless. It is egoless. When we can remain in that state, then that is original freedom.

If one is not attached to anything,
free from the stain of pride and so on,
devoted, totally connected with the sublime ones,
and free from mental activity of any kind,
there is no doubt one will be immaculate.

Depending on where you are and whether you have a lot of attachment, this may be very challenging. We have to change our priorities. Instead of getting attached to the negative things, we need to begin this transition by growing attached to positive things.

In the original state, there is no attachment in the mind. If there is no attachment, then there will be no aversion. There will also be no other mental imbalances. Most of the mental disorders come from an excess of attachment and aversion, which is rooted in not knowing oneself.

Although there are very real physiological and environmental causes to acknowledge with regard to mental illness, there are also very strong mental factors to become aware of. And the level to which we are able to recognize and respond to an imbalance will greatly determine the course of our mental health. Both physical and mental tendencies are, of course, rooted in our karma. Therefore, increasing our positive behavior can greatly change these negative propensities.

If we know that we are prone to strong attachments, for example, we can begin by changing our objects of desire. Instead of grasping at outer objects, we can start by developing an attachment to our spiritual practice. We can begin modifying our behavior by growing focused on the Dharma. We can alter the pattern of our desires by cultivating an attachment to the Triple Gem of the Buddha, Dharma, and Sangha. This is what Virupa is referring to when he speaks of "sublime ones."

These sublime ones are those objects that inspire your faith and devotion. This faith, in turn, makes your connection to them closer. Ultimately these connections can help you slowly transform until you can even go beyond these faith objects. But if your faith and devotion are dedicated to negative objects or habits, then the more connected you become to those negative tendencies, the more unsettled you will feel.

If you have a lot of attachments and defilements, then the first antidote is to bring more devotion and faith to the sublime objects, the Buddha, Dharma, and Sangha. The more devoted you become to the positive objects, the more power they will have to transform you.

Your devotion to the Buddha will inspire you to study more Dharma teachings, and it will strengthen your meditation. The sublime Sangha will further inspire and support your cultivation of positive tendencies. And as you are transformed, you will gradually begin to see tangible changes inside of you.

When Virupa uses the word "immaculate," he is indicating the point at which you are beyond both positive and negative. But for us, we cannot go beyond the positive because our negative habitual patterns are so strong.

The only way to decrease our negative habits is to increase our positive ones. So all of the spiritual practices that we are doing are increasing our positive karma. The more good karma and merit we cultivate, the more we begin to experience free will and liberation. And then eventually we go beyond the dualism of both positive and negative, both attachment and aversion, and we achieve freedom.

Because one is purified of a knower and objects of knowledge,
the direct perception of dharmata will arise.

Here Virupa is referring to going beyond both subject and object. This is only possible once you have gone beyond even the positive by seeing your true nature. That true nature in you, and in all of the objects in the universe, is the same. That ultimate truth is the dharmata, the suchness of all phenomenal objects.

The dharmata of outer objects and people and the suchness of yourself are not separate. By seeing your own true nature, you will be able to see the suchness or dharmata in all things.

When you see the true nature of all things, then wisdom will arise in you. In that wisdom there is no such thing as subject or object. They are all the same in the sense that your true nature is emptiness, and the true nature of the object is also emptiness. And realizing that empty nature of all phenomena is wisdom.

This wisdom, this union of clarity and emptiness, is the highest level of the experience of meditation. Although we have many different meditation practices, starting from shamatha, the ultimate goal of all meditation is seeing that wisdom of knowing the ultimate nature of yourself.

Once you know that true nature, then you know the nature of the whole world and the universe. That is the purpose of meditation, and that is what these great mahasiddhas have seen. That is the wisdom Virupa is sharing with us through these dohas, or mystical songs. They are not a philosophical teaching. They are the direct experience of a highly realized meditator.

13

Thoughts Arise in the Mind
Like a Stream

If one has not realized original mahamudra,
since one is always attached to everything
because of the power of dualistic grasping

MAHAMUDRA IS A VERY technical term that is loaded with
many interpretations and meanings. As we have discussed in an
earlier chapter, *maha* in Sanskrit means great, and *mudra* means seal. A
seal is used to certify the original truth of something, as in ancient times
when a king would authorize a letter by stamping it with his seal.

What Virupa is saying here is that when you have a realization of
ultimate truth, then that realization can be sealed onto, or applied to,
the subject as well as all outer objects. For this reason, mahamudra has
a meaning of union. Through meditation practice, you see beyond the
appearance of the object to the clarity or the reality of that object's
nature.

That reality is what we call emptiness. And when you see appearance and emptiness together, then that is union. The realization of that union in all things must start from recognizing it within yourself.

For people who have not had that realization, when they see something visual, they will see shapes, colors, and all such characteristics. Not only are they seeing visual objects through the sense organ of their eyes, but the objects are also immediately shaded by their inner conditions of attachment and aversion.

This is why we immediately make a judgment of whether something is attractive or repulsive. Our inner conditions make all of these projections, which determine whether something appears beautiful or ugly to us. We don't see the object as it really is.

So we could say that the whole purpose of meditation is to see things as they really are. This is what we are aspiring to do through our shamatha meditation, insight meditation, sadhana practice, and all of our spiritual activities.

For those on the Vajrayana path, the purpose of the visualization practices of the generation stage is to go beyond attachment to the ordinary perception of the personal self. And the purpose of the completion practice is to go beyond attachment to the divine deity. When we go beyond both the generation and the completion stages, that is mahamudra. That is clarity and emptiness.

Returning to the cup analogy, mahamudra is when you not only see the cup, but you also see the true empty nature of that cup. Those who can simultaneously see both the appearance and the reality of the emptiness of that appearance have seen mahamudra.

This is easy to say, but it takes deep meditation to overcome our inner conditions, thoughts, and emotional involvement with that object. We rarely see the reality of the object. Most of the time we are attached to the utility or projected value of the object. Most of the time we are caught up in our emotional involvement with that object.

Mahamudra is a very popular subject of study for scholars. Scholars throughout the centuries in India and Tibet have discussed mahamudra in great detail. Even now, we have significant debates between different schools of Buddhism regarding the meaning of mahamudra. These arguments seem to cultivate personal conclusions, which scholars then become so attached to that it obstructs any possibility of them seeing mahamudra within themselves.

As a consequence, instead of mahamudra being a state of liberation within oneself, the idea of mahamudra can become a source of intense pride and defensiveness as scholars debate the presumed "right view." If one school thinks that their definition of mahamudra is superior to another school's conclusion, then this whole conflict of self and other and this whole attachment to the ego will only increase!

So mahamudra is a great subject, which has been discussed at length among the three new schools of Sakya, Kagyu, and Geluk. This warrants further study, and it is very interesting and worthwhile to understand all of these points of view.

In the context of our study of Virupa's mystical songs, however, we are exploring mahamudra based on the beliefs of the Sakya school of Tibetan Buddhism. The Sakyas believe that mahamudra can be found only in the highest tantric practices of Vajrayana Buddhism.

So the Sakyas don't believe that there is mahamudra in kriya, charya, or yoga tantra. The Sakyas believe that one can realize mahamudra only through the highest tantric sadhana practices like Vajrayogini, Hevajra, or Chakrasamvara. The Sakyas believe that through practicing the generation and completion stage practices, one will have the resulting realization of mahamudra. Only the highest level of tantra includes the methods to go beyond both appearance and emptiness to realize mahamudra, the union of clarity and emptiness.

If you are attached to one, then you remain attached to extremes. If you are attached to the appearance of the cup, then you are still not liberated. But if you destroy the cup and are clinging to that emptiness, then that is also a form of attachment.

As we have established many times here, mahamudra goes beyond both. Going beyond both can happen only in union. That union has the meaning of Madhyamaka, the middle way, which avoids falling into any extremes.

If we have not had that realization of union, then as scholars we may have a lot of discussions and debates. The Kagyus and the Geluks think there is mahamudra in tantra and in the sutras. But the Sakyas, especially Sakya Pandita, who based his conclusions on Indian masters, conclude that mahamudra is found only in the highest tantric practices.

As long as we have emotions arising in reference to any object, then we are not free from the objects or emotions of the subjective mind or mental activities. Even remembering something of the past can be considered an object. So even if we are attached to one memory or one future dream, we will not be liberated.

When Virupa refers to the power of dualistic grasping, he is talking about these inner conditions that we bring to all of the objects in our lives. All our emotions feed our inner conditions, and when conditions such as attachment and desire become strong, then we project them onto the object, which creates even more emotions.

This clinging to things based on our inner conditions is why we have such complex and codependent relationships with the phenomenal world. We are attached to our houses, to our cars, to all of the utilities we depend on. There is a practical reason why we are attached to many of these things. We need a roof over our heads, and we need to eat in order to live.

But we need to bear in mind that as long as we have attachment to any of these things, even things we need for our survival, then we will also have aversion. And these attachments and aversions will cause us much pain and suffering.

To reiterate what we've discussed, pain and suffering are rooted in attachments and aversions that stem from our inner conditions. And those inner conditions are there because we have not seen mahamudra in the mind.

The universe is full of countless objects. If we examine objects in the desire realm, between the animate and inanimate, we will observe that we have a much stronger attraction to our fellow humans. We all know this very well. And among humans, we have far more attachment to the people we are romantically attracted to, most commonly the opposite sex.

These attachments can give us great pleasure, but they can also create in us tremendous pain. They have equal potential to bring happiness and unhappiness. If the same object can bring us both pain and pleasure, that is an indication that our inner emotions are projected onto that object. This projection is what gives rise to all of these intense feelings.

The more emotions we have, the more feelings we generate. The more feelings we create, the more likely we will be to act on them. We see this cycle repeated over and over again in our lives. So many feelings are generated between subject and object, which then become the cause for so many actions. This is how our lives are constantly propelled, through this chain of action and reaction.

> thoughts arise in the mind like a stream
> of the variety of blurred vision.
> Not abiding in the nonerroneous ultimate,
> one cycles and wanders in samsara.

If we reflect on our lives, we see that although we may change our objects constantly, our root emotions, our core projection of our emotions, is never changing. We get tired of an old object or an old relationship, so we make a change. Then we may initially get very excited and more attached to the new object or the new relationship. But when the new object grows old as well, we are equally disenchanted and unhappy, and we go searching for a replacement yet again.

Meanwhile, we have not yet learned that we cannot outrun our emotions by changing outer objects or circumstances. The inner conditions of attachment and desire will always be looking to grow attached to the next best thing. They will always compel us to try to replace one pleasurable object with another when our feelings about that original object change. These inner conditions will always control us until we look inside ourselves.

Meals are a good example. We eat breakfast and are satisfied for a few hours. Then suddenly we are so hungry again, and we are desperate to eat lunch! There is temporary pleasure with a full stomach, but again by dinner time we desire yet another meal.

Of course, we all know that we need to eat for survival. But at the same time, through eating we are fueling a cycle. A cycle in the sense that hunger and consumption go together. So fulfilling our desires actually produces more restlessness.

As long as we are fulfilled, we are restful, relaxed, and happy. But when we are deprived, we grow very restless. So this cycle is perpetuated in all of our worldly activities and interactions. Until we are in that state of mahamudra, our mind will always be wandering after various objects. The mind will always be trying to replace one unpleasant sensation with another more pleasurable one, perpetuating an endless cycle.

If we use Virupa's analogy of blurred vision, we know that if our vision is compromised, we will always see things incorrectly. The edges may be unclear, there may be spots in our field of vision, or we may have no depth perception.

Now, in our mental eye, thoughts are arising all the time. As we know, the mind is nothing other than a series of thoughts. Both the thought and the thinker are the mind. So as long as we have a thought, it means we still have a thinker in that mind as well. In that condition of thinker and thought, we generate continuous inner chatter. Meditation is the best test of this fact, for we see immediately how much inner dialogue we create between thought and thinker in our own minds.

Normally when we are preoccupied with all our sense organs and distracted by our daily lives, we don't observe those thoughts, and we don't notice the thinker. But when we start to sit, and we focus our mind on the breath, then for the first time we see how many thoughts there are. We notice the thinking and begin to become aware of the thinker as well.

What we will observe is that the mind is continuously thinking about something. The mind is wandering all the time, and as a result, we don't have any present moment. Because of that, we are not happy.

The more thoughts we have, the more miserable we are. This may sound like an exaggeration because some of our thoughts may be pleasurable, but still they keep us from being here in the moment, and still they generate more feelings.

Most of our thoughts are related to past incidents. We bring past misery and happiness into our present thoughts, and in the process we actually destroy the present. When the present is destroyed by memories, we also unwittingly destroy the future. All three times, past, present, and future, are only a continuation of our thoughts. We have lost our ability to reside freely in the present.

This is what Virupa means when he says "one cycles and wanders in samsara." Samsara is rooted in that inner chattering, and until we see the ultimate, we will always be trapped. In samsara, mind, emotions, and actions are interdependent and feed off of each other.

Due to the past, we have the present. Then from the present we continue into the future. This is interdependency. It is dependent because it relies on the three times; it is dependent on the timeline.

This is also the life cycle or wheel of life called samsara. It is a wheel because you cannot find a first cause in this interdependency. That's why the cycle of life is beginningless. We cycle infinitely unless we can realize mahamudra within us, and thereby free ourselves.

Because of attachment and grasping
to all the fame and offerings

Here Virupa is cautioning us to check our motivations and even to examine why we are meditating. Why are we engaging in all of this spiritual practice? What is our intention?

and the arising of great hearing,
reflection, and intellectual comprehension,
good experience, siddhis, blessings, and the signs of power,
the contrived path is ultimately a stain.
The wise do not entrust their minds to those.

We must constantly investigate our motivations. Doing spiritual practice will not necessarily make us a spiritual person. Whether we become a spiritual person or not is determined by whether we look within ourselves and ask why we are doing all of these practices in the first place.

"Of great hearing," in this context, refers to study, to hearing the teachings and reflecting upon them. Based on this learning and contemplation, even if you achieve some great siddhis, blessings, or power, if you are pursuing the spiritual path based on your motivation to achieve more power or fame, then these accomplishments are called "worldly Dharmas."

This is why yogis always have to carefully examine whether Dharma is worldly Dharma or holy Dharma. Holy Dharma is when you practice meditation to go beyond, to liberate yourself. Worldly Dharma is when you practice meditation so that you become famous, so that you become powerful, so that you will have a lot of offerings and wealth.

Whenever you have this grasping and attachment to these worldly things, then even if you appear to be doing great spiritual practice, you are really only using these spiritual methods to achieve the same goals that worldly beings are striving toward. In this sense, you are no different from any ordinary person who is trying to gain more property, more status, and more renown.

In ordinary life, it seems the purpose of everything is to become more famous, more powerful, more secure, richer, or more respected. These are key incentives in worldly life. Due to these conditioned incentives, we work very hard. We want to be someone in the world. We want to achieve some accolades. And we want to be loved and desired.

These motivations are fine as long as we want to remain in samsara and as long as our aspiration is simply to have a prosperous life. Even if we look closely at our altruistic behaviors in an ordinary context, we may find that underneath these actions, there is still some underlying pride in our generosity or an underlying need for recognition of our good deeds.

If we want to achieve liberation, we have to find it within us. For yogis, the holy Dharma is important because many of those yogis have already achieved wealth. As we discussed, the Buddha and many of the great mahasiddhas were born into noble families. They became famous. But still they found that they were miserable. They were not happy. They had so much suffering in the midst of that luxury, and this inspired them to look more deeply into their lives for meaning.

We are always looking to achieve something. Often the goal is wealth and power. But if you've achieved these worldly goals already, or if you have been born into them, then many times you no longer find these pleasures satisfying. But here Virupa is warning us that those who are pursuing spiritual practice with the wrong motivation will have a spiritual path that is stained or corrupted. So those who are seeking enlightenment must not entrust their minds to these false paths.

> If one is interested in those things
> and falls into the two extremes,
> because it is the root of cycling in the cycle of samsara,
> look, what is the mountain of the mind that is the root
> of everything?

If your spiritual path does not have the right view or insight, then it easily falls into either the extreme of nihilism or that of eternalism. This is why we see that most of the theistic religions are eternalistic. Whatever you call that eternal presence, whether it is God or Allah, it may be of real benefit to you. Even in Buddhist tantra, in kriya tantra, when you have a lot of pain and suffering, having someone to whom you can pray provides real comfort.

But on the other hand, if you become completely dependent on that faith object, then that attachment to your object will prevent your liberation. So we can see that eternalistic faith has benefits, but it also has risks. That's why the aim of highest tantra is to go beyond both nihilism and eternalism to the state of mahamudra.

Eternalism doesn't apply only to projections of some outer God. Even within Buddhism, you will see that many people go to the temple and pray to accumulate merit. But if you ask why they do these things, it is because they want to have a good life and a higher rebirth. So their motivation is also eternalistic. It also falls into an extreme.

Now nihilism, on the other hand, is when you misunderstand emptiness. When you do not have wisdom, emptiness can easily turn nihilistic. You may think that the truth—emptiness—is like blank space, like nothingness.

If our spiritual practice is falling into either extreme, then we have to look inside ourselves. In order to correct this, we have to examine whether we have the right view, the right training and methods. We must ask ourselves: who is the meditator? Who is it that is following the discipline? If you look and look, you may think that it is all due to the mind. But if you look into the mind, where can it be found?

> If one becomes free from the mind
> because it is not seen when looking,
> liberation is certain.

When we look into the mind and see its true nature, we have found mahamudra. In all the high teachings it is said that if we look deeply into the mind and the emotions through meditation, we will not find them. So if you look deeply enough, you come to the realization that the nature of the mind is emptiness and clarity.

In this way, once we realize the nature of mind, mind will no longer exist. We will have seen mahamudra, the union of clarity and emptiness, and the thoughts and thinker will have dissolved.

What remains is the awareness that sees that emptiness. When you realize this, then for the first time you will be free from your mind. Once you're free from your mind, then you are free from the thinker, you are free from the thoughts, you simply become the awareness. You are aware not only of all objects but also aware of their true nature. Your mind has become mahamudra, which allows you also to see mahamudra in all outer objects because the nature of your mind and the nature of the object is the same. This is how you will be liberated from dualism.

You will be free from subject and object, free from thoughts and thinker, and free from all related emotions. How much freedom we can achieve has less to do with outer objects and much more to do with our own inner conditions and with how much inner freedom we have achieved through seeing the nature of our mind. All our highest tantric meditations, where we visualize deities and do all of these completion practices, are all an exercise in seeing the true nature of our minds. Once we have seen this true nature, we are free.

14

Rest in the Undistracted State

Since the mind does not indicate "the dharmadhatu is this,"
both meditation and an object of meditation do not exist in that.
Rest in the undistracted state without any concepts
of existence and nonexistence.

W HEN WE ARE PRACTICING meditation there are three interdependent factors. There is the meditator, who is the person
practicing. Within that person there is the mind, which is the part that
is concentrating. And there is also the object of meditation, which is
what the mind is focusing on.

As we know, in Buddhist understanding, the mind and physical
body are two different things. Mind cannot become body, and body
cannot become mind. This is true because the physical body is made
up of matter, and matter cannot become mind. Mind cannot become
matter.

Now as living beings we function psychosomatically. We have physical components as well as consciousness and mind. So although we

have physical postures that aid our meditation, like the seven-pointed posture of Vairocana, meditation is primarily a practice of the mind.

When Virupa says "since the mind does not indicate 'the dharma-dhatu is this,' " what he is saying is that in the state of mahamudra, even the mind has dissolved. So the mind is no longer there to point out the dharmadhatu as some separate experience.

As long as it is the mind that is doing the meditating, then it will not see its true nature. This may be a challenging paradox to understand, but when the mind is meditating, there is still meditation and there is still an object of meditation.

So as long as the mind is still "doing" meditation, then it means there must still be a meditator, a mind, and an object of concentration. So one is still operating within this interdependency and has not yet reached the stage of seeing one's own true nature.

When we are doing shamatha meditation, for example, we become very aware of the mind. For the first time, we observe all of our wandering thoughts. And then in order to begin training that mind, we turn our focus to an object of meditation, like the breath, or a blue flower. So the goal of shamatha is to bring some focus to our mind and to bring some intentional cooperation between the meditator, mind, and meditation object.

Ordinarily our mind is in constant motion, filled with wandering thoughts. We create an inner world that is a projection of our own mind. As long as we have this inner world, with all its rapidly firing thoughts and emotions, we rarely have any genuine meditation experiences.

We may pretend to be meditating, we may perfect our posture and appear calm on the outside, but if those thoughts are still wandering, then we are not actually meditating. The goal of shamatha is to bring some focus into that mind which is so accustomed to grasping at ideas, memories, and sensory experiences.

This is the reason why Buddhist meditation practice always begins with an object of meditation. To bring that concentration onto the object, you need a method, which is meditation practice. This can take many forms, like shamatha meditation, insight meditation, or sadhana practice.

We can observe that when we are meditating, there is always the person who is the meditator. Within that person, the mind is doing the meditating. And depending on our method of practice, we will also have a particular meditation object.

The object of meditation will change according to different methods, and it will also change according to our own realization. But as long as we have these three separate factors of meditator, mind, and object, we don't have any true meditation experience.

True meditation experience involves going beyond all three. When we go beyond the mind, beyond the meditator, and beyond the object of meditation, then we will achieve deep realization.

Since most of us have never gone beyond the mind, there's no way to accurately describe that experience. This is why Virupa says, "since the mind does not indicate 'the dharmadhatu is this.'" Dharmadhatu is that experience of going beyond all three factors of meditation. For someone at this level of deep experience, there is no mind remaining with which to name or indicate anything. Subject and object have dissolved, and there is a union of all three factors in that emptiness and awareness.

As we defined it earlier, *dharma* here is referring to objects, and *dhatu* means nature. So the state of dharmadhatu is the experience of knowing the true nature of all things. But if you have never gone beyond, how can you articulate something that is beyond your knowledge, experience, and thought? And if you have gone beyond, there will also be no real way to convey your experience.

This may all seem very paradoxical to us at our current level of understanding. The contradiction is there because between the ultimate and the relative there is a real conflict. Between the mind and the nature of the mind there is a negation. As long as mind, meditation, and the object of meditation are there, then you are not really resting in realization.

Through introductory meditations like shamatha, however, you may experience an increased feeling of peace. At some point, when your concentration becomes heightened, then you will also experience some physical bliss.

With that physical bliss comes a very alert and heightened clarity in the mind. But if we have never experienced that, then I don't think we have known that restful mind yet. Until we reach that preliminary experience of calm-abiding, we are still struggling mentally. We are still trying to focus on the object, but our mind is rebelling. Our mind is still wandering after many other objects.

For this reason, some meditation manuals say that when the mind is rebelling and you are struggling to control it, then sometimes the best antidote is actually to relax. Sometimes, instead of increasing our discipline and effort, it is more effective to soften our mental state. By exerting less willpower, we may actually free ourselves from the struggle of this prior mental rebellion. Sometimes the thoughts will very naturally subside when we loosen our control.

As we have discussed, if you take a pool of dirty water and stir it all up, the clarity of the water will be completely obscured. On the other hand, if you just sit still and let the water remain undisturbed, slowly all of the impurities will sink to the bottom of the pool, leaving the water clear. This is the effect that relaxing our mind in meditation can have. As we relax, the pace of our thoughts naturally slows, and the muddier elements begin to settle down again.

If we look at our lives, we see that we are most relaxed when the mind is focused on one thing. If we are distracted by a movie or engaged in athletics, then when all of our attention is placed on one activity, we often find the most mental relief.

This is why these activities and forms of entertainment are so effective and popular. Distraction can temporarily mimic some of the effects that concentration has on our nervous system and on our mental states. For a few hours, we may even forget about ourselves. As we know, however, even healthy distractions like practicing sports won't settle the underlying causes of stress and tension. These activities will give us only temporary relief. Concentration, on the other hand, has the potential to calm those waters in a more lasting way.

The difference between meditation and distraction is that in meditation the object is more neutral. If we are focusing on our breathing, it does not make us angrier, more attached, or more desirous.

Dramas and action movies, on the other hand, engage us because they speak to our inner conditions and to our sleeping emotions. Often the reason we focus on a film is because there is something of ourselves that we see mirrored on the screen.

If we study all of the most popular films, we recognize components of our afflictive emotions in them. In successful movies, there is usually at least one major destructive emotion driving the plot. And often we only consider it a good film if all three major emotions of desire, anger, and ignorance are represented, although we don't realize this is our criteria.

Violent films are very popular because they speak to our rage and anger. We may not even be aware of it in ourselves, but when we see it on the screen, we may feel very drawn to it. This is also true of all of the dramas that explore different aspects of attachment. We see our own latent desires played out in other people's stories, and we are completely engaged by that experience. We are also drawn to films where there are mysterious elements, or where major mistakes and misunderstandings are made. This type of theme speaks to the elements of ignorance and confusion in us.

These three primal destructive emotions become the measure of whether we find something interesting. Whatever form of distraction we find relaxing in some sense mirrors some or all of these three destructive emotions of anger, desire, and ignorance.

When these primary emotions are heightened, they will make us feel either overstimulated or very relaxed. So while these same elements are recognized in the process of meditation, the difference is that the experienced meditator can see the emptiness in all of these destructive emotions.

The similarity is that both distracting activities and meditative practices bring a focus to the wandering mind, but only one has the potential to see the root emptiness. When distracting elements end, we are immediately hungry for the next distraction, so we can feel that relief. But the peace and relaxation that is cultivated through meditation can have a much more stable effect on us and give rise to all of the other positive qualities.

The calm abiding that is cultivated through shamatha meditation will heighten our awareness. This heightened awareness will give us greater insight. We can then apply that insight to see the nature of the object of meditation. In fact, we can begin to apply that insight to all aspects of our lives. Our daily life can become a living meditation.

So even if we go to the cinema, we can use a movie as a teaching on impermanence. Instead of going to the movie for the sake of pure distraction, we can use the film to help us contemplate how everything is always changing, moment to moment. We can use the film to understand the suffering nature of samsara and the insubstantiality of those projections on the screen in front of us.

Movies can become a wonderful contemplation on interdependency. There is a projector, a projection, and a screen, and within the interplay of these three elements, all of the actions and reactions unfold. But if you see the empty nature in these elements, then you have some experience of insight meditation.

In our insight meditation we can ask ourselves, where is the person, what is the movie, where is the object of meditation? When you are in that state of insubstantiality and emptiness, then you have gone beyond the screen, the projector, and the projection.

At the different levels of insight meditation, when you become aware that everything is always changing, then you can begin to recognize that change as a source of constant suffering. And then you can go another step to realize that this suffering is insubstantial. And when this insubstantiality is experienced, then you will know emptiness. If you are fully aware in this state of emptiness, you will no longer have any concepts of existence or nonexistence; you will have gone beyond both.

One problem we face is that even if we close our senses to what is happening externally, we still manage to carry all of these experiences in our minds. So renouncing external existence still doesn't solve the problem of all of those things existing inside of us.

In this way, the whole outer universe can become part of our inner world. Existence and nonexistence are experienced first in our minds and then we project those visions to all of the objects in the outside world. In order to experience the true meditative state, we must go beyond both existence and nonexistence. Only when we have transcended all extremes will we reach an indescribable bliss and peace.

All of these worldly distractions and forms of entertainment can certainly provide a brief reprieve from our suffering. But that rest is not based on going beyond the causes of suffering. That rest is still dependent on our emotions. We are essentially indulging our senses and emotions in different objects in order to be entertained or in order to externalize our inner conflicts and thereby achieve momentary relief.

But when we go beyond, our mind can experience the dharma-dhatu. This is when we see our own true nature for the first time. Only through seeing our true nature will we come to the realization that there is no mind.

If you have never experienced this, you cannot explain it. And if you have seen your own true nature, then that will be equally hard to express. So when you have gone beyond both, that awakening will be indescribable. And although we attempt to refer to it by many names, most importantly it is an experience of the union of clarity and emptiness. It is an experience of profound peace.

As we have discussed, early in our practice there is still a meditator, a meditation, and an object of meditation. Only at the fourth level of insight meditation will we be able to go beyond the object of meditation and perhaps even the meditation and meditator. But even at this fourth level we have not realized limitless bliss and compassion.

It is only the highest tantric meditations that provide a path to that realization of mahamudra. All the tantric sadhana practices, all of the completion practices, are methods for cultivating limitless joy and compassion out of that emptiness.

This bliss and compassion is limitless because it is not coming from an ego. When we have realized selflessness, then that inner wisdom can give rise to these limitless experiences. So although at our level we may still think of these states of joy or bliss as feelings, they are not based on the self or emotions. Therefore they have limitless power.

But until we have achieved that emptiness, everything will still be based on the mind and ego. That's why at our level we always ricochet between contradictory emotions. We alternate constantly between love and hate, compassion and passion, confusion and relaxation. We are trapped in this play of opposites because we have not achieved that ultimate reality.

> If one intellectualizes emptiness, nonarising, beyond mind,
> freedom from extremes, and so on in any way,
> not dwelling in actual reality, one will be very distracted.

These words can come only from the deep experience of a meditator. A scholar will not write this because it is the role of scholars and philosophers to intellectualize everything, including emptiness!

Philosophers and scholars study all of the great texts at universities. They learn about the Buddha and about the experiences of all of the mahasiddhas and great Indian scholars. Ultimately they deduce the truth based on their examination of all of this knowledge and education. Since they don't have the realization of wisdom, they merely collect all the information from every possible external source and draw conclusions based on others' experiences.

Virupa is cautioning us yet again. He is saying that if we are so busy with ideas and academic study, we will remain distracted from actual reality. We even have this stereotype in our culture of the absent-minded professor. So we have noticed that these great scholars are often so caught up in their intellectual studies that they forget to be in the present moment.

If you spend your life intellectualizing and studying these dense philosophy books, you will remain very busy. In some sense you will actually be going farther and farther away from reality. The most important truth is knowing about yourself and your mind. But instead of knowing the nature of your own mind, you will be studying the minds of others. The more you study, and the harder you investigate the outer world, the less you will learn about your own true nature.

If we study emptiness as an intellectual concept, then if we are very good scholars, we may even become nihilistic. If we are not developing compassion and clarity along with that emptiness, then we may think of that emptiness as nothingness or as a negation of everything. If we read the words of the *Heart Sutra*, it says, "No eye, no ear, no nose, no tongue, etc. . . ." These negations may be very destabilizing at the intellectual level without any insight from meditation.

There is also the opposite risk that, without meditation practice, we may intellectualize the truth to be something eternal and nonarising. We may mistake unconditioned emptiness as almost godlike. And if we become attached to those nonarising eternal entities, we will also find ourselves further and further away from actual reality and from the truth of our own nature.

God can be interpreted in many different ways. Sometimes eternal deities seem to be created out of our own fear. When we experience fear, then we are desperate for some comfort. So in reaction to this fear, we create deities for our protection and reassurance.

If it is our innate nature to want to live forever, then it follows that we would want to create an immortal God to revere. If our biggest dream is immortality, then it figures that we would want to imbue some external projection with this power. So based on our mental situation, we will come up with any number of outer manifestations.

Even if we are studying Buddhist psychology, we still will be exploring ideas in our heads. Often this sort of knowledge serves to trap us in our thoughts. We can see that there are still so many arguments about extremes in Buddhist philosophy. Even among the Tibetan schools there is a lot of debate.

The more skeptical you become as an intellectual and the more doubts you have, the less peace you will find in your mind. To some extent scholarship thrives on arguing. The classroom is designed for questioning and doubt. But the more doubts we have, the more of a skeptic we may become. This will produce even more thoughts, until our mind is teeming with ideas. We may excel in the academic environment, but we will discover that this actually brings less and less peace.

Scholarship leads to strong opinions that actually reinforce our egos. Even within Tibetan monasteries we find that scholars are always locked in some debate. It's one thing if you conduct this questioning for the sake of clarifying your meditation experience, but often these philosophical arguments actually cultivate more pride and arrogance in the student.

We can see through experience that meditators usually die very peacefully. Scholars, on the other hand, have a much harder time letting go. Our experience at death is proof of whether or not our spiritual or scholarly pursuits have enhanced our life and transformed us.

There is a Tibetan saying that whether your practice has transformed you or not is completely proven at the time of death. The nature of our deaths is a great measure, a great test of our peace of mind. Most beings who leave some signs of realization at the time of death are yogis, meditators, and spiritual people.

Meditation is important, but we need to know the correct motivation and methods. We also need to know the object of meditation. That's why we need to receive good instruction on shamatha, insight meditation, sadhana practice, and all of these methods. Once we are properly instructed, meditation should become the focus of our lives.

> Rest in a relaxed state, disregarding empty or not empty.
> Letting go in the state of independence
> without meditating or not meditating,
> be just like a zombie without a mind that accepts or rejects.

Now the word "zombie" may have particular connotations in pop culture, but for lack of a better English translation, we will use it here. What Virupa is actually describing, though, is a state where we become a witness, much like the state of *shavasana* or "corpse pose" in yoga practice. We are no longer engaged in anything. We are no longer reacting.

Normally in our lives, we think that if we don't react, if we don't have feelings, that maybe there is something wrong with us! We might perceive this witness attitude as apathy. We are under the impression that being a living person means being reactionary. We mistakenly think that a full life requires emotional intensity. We believe that the more feelings we experience and express based on anger or attachment, the more vital and alive we will feel.

There are so many cultural conditions that increase our belief that feelings and reactions are what constitute a fulfilling and successful life. There are very few people, however, who realize that to become witness to everything going on around you without reacting to it is a profound achievement.

Only someone who has done some meditation in a past life or who has achieved some understanding in this life will know this zombie-like calm observer state, which is free of engagement, free of action and reaction.

You can only become a witness when you have a certain level of mental relaxation. This can only be found once you have fewer emotions inside you. If you are still filled with emotions, you will not have much inner peace, and you will not understand this "calm observer" approach.

So becoming that calm observer takes a lot of practice! And we cannot simply pretend on the outside that we have reached this calm remove. If we are only adopting this attitude externally, then at some point we will be tested by a difficult situation, and we will fail.

This is why we must do a lot of meditating first in order to cultivate this inner relaxation. Shamatha meditation—also known as calm abiding meditation—is a very good method for developing this peaceful mental state. Once you are in this peaceful state, meditation becomes so natural that it no longer takes effort. This is what Virupa means by "letting go in the state of independence without meditating or not meditating." There is no longer any need to force the concentration.

When your inner mental world is still busy, meditation can be very challenging. It can be the most difficult thing you've ever attempted. All of these concepts, memories, and feelings inside you can be relentless and can make relaxing the mind incredibly difficult.

We can see from experience that when we are relaxed in our lives, anything is easy. We can accomplish so many tasks effortlessly when we are not exhausting ourselves with stress. Whether we will feel relaxed or not depends on how busy our minds are. The speedier our thoughts and concepts and emotions are, the more inner turmoil we will feel. As long as these ideas and feelings are rushing and gushing like a waterfall, we will not experience peace.

Once we have experienced a certain level of relaxation through shamatha meditation, we are ready to practice insight meditation. Through insight meditation, we can contemplate the nature of impermanence, suffering, insubstantiality, and ultimately emptiness.

Insight means seeing more; it means knowing the impermanent nature of all conditioned things. And in that impermanence, we then realize the suffering nature of things. In that suffering nature, we can see the insubstantiality. And in that insubstantiality, we come to the realization of emptiness. These are the four levels of insight meditation.

We can apply these four levels to all of the outer objects, including our breathing. But we can also apply these levels to any thoughts arising within us. Any thoughts can be examined through these four insights until we realize their inherent emptiness.

Once you have completely seen the fourth level of insight, the realization of emptiness, then there is a degree of letting go. When you have seen the empty nature of things, then both the mind and its object can surrender and you can transcend this duality. You can let go in the sense that you go beyond these distinctions.

It is when this letting go occurs that you will become a witness. You will be free of reaction. See, reaction is a part of karma. When you react to something, it inspires more action in you. With this action you are then creating a further reaction, which will cause you to act again. And on it goes in this endless cycle. Action and reaction are part of karma.

When there's no more volition stemming from these mental formations, from this karma, then you stop reacting. There's nothing to accept because there's no longer any object to be attached to; and there's nothing to reject because there is no object of aversion.

When you become a witness, your mind has now achieved complete equanimity. This equanimity is free from attachment and aversion. When we say the *Four Limitless Prayers*, it includes loving-kindness, compassion, joy, and equanimity. And among these four, equanimity is the highest realization because it is based on wisdom.

Only when you have achieved wisdom by seeing the nature of emptiness both in your mind and in the outer object will you become a witness. You will no longer react because now you have achieved equanimity. Equanimity has the power to equalize the nature of emptiness in you and in others to the point where everything is the same.

This equanimity can go beyond the dualism of subject and object. At our level, the subject is always the self and ego, and the rest of the world is always the object or the other. Because of this dualism, there is always a conflict between ourselves and the world, and this is a constant source of pain.

But when this dualism has dissolved into equanimity, then we will have a universal condition where we are at peace all the time. With that peace, all our reactions have ceased, and according to other people's perceptions, we may appear to become disengaged or almost dead! But within us, the witness will be very much alive, and wisdom and equanimity will remain.

Some meditators joke that the result of meditation is to be reborn. Of course this is not a literal death and rebirth, but through meditation, the ego has been killed, and now you have been reborn in an egoless and mindless state. In this sense you are new again.

> If one dwells in my state through knowing reality as it is,
> the traces of the characteristics of dualistic appearances
> will quickly be destroyed.

These lines are very profound. What is our current state? We are so attached to thinking that we are so and so, but what is our true state? Who are we really? That is the fundamental question that we can truly answer only through our meditation.

Even extensive studies of philosophy and psychology will not answer this question fully. These systems of inquiry constantly attempt to answer the question, but the intellectual answer is not perfected. Only through meditation, when you come to recognize and dwell in your true nature, only then "the traces of the characteristics of dualistic appearance will quickly be destroyed." This is when our entire outlook will change. Instead of a personal outlook, we now will have a universal outlook.

At the moment, everything we do is based on the self and ego. And this self or ego automatically project everything else in the world to be the "other." And between this self and other, we generate endless emotions.

If we look closely at all three root destructive emotions of attachment, aversion, and ignorance, we see that they are all rooted in the ego. And based on these afflictive emotions, all of the traces of the characteristics are also formed.

If we do not know our own true nature, how will we ever know others? Only when we transcend the ego will our outlook become universal and will we truly know the nature of objects. Until then, we are trapped in the karmic play of action and reaction, and we are dependent on emotions. Only when we transcend the self to achieve that freedom will our suffering truly cease.

15

Though It Seems a Particle
Is in the Eye

A S WE HAVE DISCUSSED, *doha* is a Sanskrit word meaning "mystical songs." It is important to differentiate mystical songs from shastra. *Shastra* is a Sanskrit word for commentaries composed by panditas and scholars. Those commentaries are not coming from the direct experience of meditators.

As we know, scholarship is based on knowledge and inquiry. Knowledge consists of all of the information that we have collected from others and from our examination of outer phenomena. Knowledge gained from teachers, from texts, and even from the words of the Buddha is based on external sources of information.

According to the intellectual levels of masters or scholars, all of this logic is applied to come to some conclusion. Most philosophical texts employ logic to prove some truth. It is very rare, however, that you will find logical reasoning that can prove the ultimate truth. Most of the time, all of these knowledge-based texts and philosophical works end up proving a relative truth.

But these dohas have less to do with theory and logic. They are not based on external research or on quoting other sources. You can see from the songs that they are experiential and original. They are not a carbon copy from some other teacher or acharya. They are based solely on meditative experience.

In these dohas, Mahasiddha Virupa is sharing his meditation experience with others. The connection we have with these lines depends entirely on how much meditation we've done and on how much realization we have. If we have achieved some degree of mindfulness and insight, then these songs will resonate deeply with what we have experienced.

On the other hand, if we don't have any experience, then these songs may sound confusing and paradoxical. They may be outside of our paradigm and beyond our senses. These words may escape our reflections or even appear to contradict our knowledge.

Dohas essentially reflect direct meditative experience. Although Virupa is trying to share his mystical experience with us, transmission will happen only if we are at a certain level in our understanding. Our practice must be strong in order to make us receptive to such profound communication.

Even if these lines are beyond our current comprehension, what we can gain from them is the awareness that there is another perspective. Becoming aware of another view of the nature of reality, entirely separate from our current understanding, may plant some seeds of future realization in us. So even if we find the dohas confusing, we may still gain some benefit.

Between the perceptions that ordinary people have and the perception of reality that the mystics have, the understanding of an object will vary greatly. What the mystic will see and what we will see in that same object will be very different. This is why, for us, there appear to be many contradictions between our reality and Virupa's vision.

These kinds of mystical songs are shared with us in order to encourage our practice. They are not necessarily to encourage our studies, and they are not intended to feed our intellect. Instead, the masters have shared them with us to encourage us to transform ourselves.

When there is positive inner transformation, we will see the true benefit of any spiritual practice. Without this transformation, even if we have become a great theologian who is very learned in the scriptures, we will not necessarily become a spiritual person. At most, we will become a great scholar and thinker.

As we discussed in an earlier chapter, it is inevitable that our translation may lose some of the original meaning of these songs. This is why it is especially important to examine further Virupa's verses through discussion. English is not a very advanced spiritual language, and what spiritual terminology there is in English is mostly Judeo-Christian. So when we translate these dohas from Sanskrit and Tibetan, we are limited, and as a result, the translation loses some of its subtler meaning.

> If one is distracted by characteristics
> without dwelling in the state of realization,
> one will not be able to avert the traces
> of the characteristics of dualistic appearances.

As we explored earlier, characteristics are what we use to identify everything in the universe. This is how we discriminate and identify all of these millions of things from each other. We say, "this is a tree," "this is water," "this is a human being," and we differentiate all of these objects from one another through their unique characteristics.

So not only do we differentiate humans from other beings, but we also differentiate human beings from each other based on unique characteristics. And if we go further, we see that these unique characteristics are not an ultimate truth but are a projection of our inner conditions.

This is why all of the characteristics we have used to identify the universe do not necessarily reflect the truth of that universe. For example, human beings can identify other human beings, but not all sentient beings will have the same perception of what a human is. We cannot say, for instance, that a fish will know we are human and will see those same unique characteristics that we use to define humans.

We are functioning and projecting based on our inner conditions. As humans, we want to make our own experience a universal experience. We want to extend our reality to encompass the truth of all existence. We want to assume that if we see color, then a cat will also see that same color. We want to assume that water will be the same to a fish as it is to us. But we know this is not the case.

So the question remains: how much can we actually rely on our experience? Is our personal experience true in any way? Or is our individual truth only relative? This is what this stanza of the doha is asking.

These characteristics we use to identify any object are dependent on whether we are human. And among humans, each individual has their own very personal way of identifying things. We project all of these characteristics based on our inner conditions, and this is how we interact with the universe.

A simple example of this is to look at various experiences of vision. What significance will the visual effects of the universe have for a blind person? How will unique characteristics be altered if we are color blind? How will our perceptions be affected if we have cataracts?

Are the characteristics that we experience in the universe coming from the objects themselves? Or are we projecting our own vision onto those objects? This is what we have to investigate.

So here the teaching is saying that if we are not in that state of realization, if we are not in samadhi, then all our experiences are still projections. They are actually still just distractions.

Why are they distractions? Because they have no inherent reality. They exist only relative to our inner conditions. Even now, our mode of interaction with the universe is through our sense organs. Because I can see with my eyes, I can determine if an object is visual. Because I can hear, I can identify these other experiences as sounds. Because I can smell, I can differentiate scents. Because I can taste, I can recognize different flavors. And because I can touch, I can say these are tangibles. These objects must exist in the way that I experience them.

We interact with the universe based on these assumptions of reality. But if we are blind, deaf, or if any of our other senses are not functioning, then how will the universe be altered? Imagine the universe for a being who lacked any senses. This would be almost like being dead. How would people experience the universe if they did not have inner conditions projecting sense objects via their sense organs?

How we experience the universe is dependent on these sense organs. And what we perceive through our sense organs is also largely dependent on our inner conditions. At one stage of our life, we may be in love with someone and see them as being so beautiful. But later if we fall out of love, or if they become angry with us, then we may see that same person as being very ugly! In this case, the person is the same, our eye organ is the same, but our inner conditions have been altered. This person may appear beautiful one day and ugly the next, so we must ask, how has the object actually changed?

The object has changed because our inner conditions have been altered. When you meditate, you realize that whether you see something as ugly or beautiful is based entirely on your inner conditions of karma and emotions.

If you have a karmic affinity, then you will experience a real pull toward someone or something. There will be an inner magnet that will pull you closer and closer. Not only will you be pulled closer, but any associated objects will appear nicer and more agreeable to you.

How does this process happen? If we study the inner psychology and inner conditions of this, we will see more clearly how something can become agreeable or disagreeable to our senses. Furthermore, we can become aware of how many different emotions these inner states produce.

When we are happy, the universe will actually appear more beautiful and more pleasing to our senses. When we are angry, we will actually feel the universe to be uglier and more aggressive. What we project onto the world has much to do with our inner experience.

If you are never in a mindful and meditative state, then whatever happens in your mind will always be mixed with emotions. Based on those emotions, you will produce mental actions. Those mental states like anger, attachment, ignorance, and jealousy will then be projected onto objects.

Due to these primary emotions, we classify the entire universe into three groups. Things we love, things we dislike, and things we just ignore.

How much karma and how many emotions are created based on these dualistic appearances? Because others exist, we believe that we too must exist. And since we exist, then others also must exist. These are the two relativities through which we interact with each other and create more and more actions and emotions.

Right now, our reality is dualistic. There is no unity. There is no union because we have such strong attachment to the self. Whenever that self is threatened, then we have aversion to whatever is attacking our ego. All of this attachment to the self along with our anger and aversion to others stems from not yet knowing our true nature.

This is why the Buddha said that this whole universe—all of samsara—comes from not knowing who we truly are. Suffering comes from that basic ignorance. We think we know ourselves, but most of that knowledge is actually based on what others tell us we are, and how society shapes us. We don't have any original personal understanding of ourselves. Therefore we just habitually repeat behaviors based on who we think we are, and we become emotional when anything contradictory is projected onto us by others.

This is why we turn to others in order to learn about ourselves instead of engaging in meditation. But how will others know something about our true nature if we haven't even recognized it yet? For this reason, it will be very hard to actually gain any real self-knowledge from others.

This root ignorance of not knowing ourselves is the beginning of all emotions. Meditation is the process of coming back to know who we truly are. Once we know ourselves, then that knowing will help us to know others. And then there is a great chance that we will be able to go beyond dualism.

All of the great mystics, buddhas, and yogis have gone beyond dualism to see that union of self and universe. They have become one with the universe because they finally know themselves. If you are in a state of deep meditation, then you may have that experience too—the sameness of self and others.

But if we are completely consumed by our emotions, there is no chance of experiencing this unity. In our emotional reality, we are still trapped in a dualistic experience of the world. Our emotions determine all of our interactions with the universe.

Now Mahasiddha Virupa meditated continuously for many, many years. As we have discussed, he was a great scholar by day, teaching monks at Nalanda University, but at night he was engaged in tantric practice. After many years, without any realization, he grew discouraged. He was on the verge of giving up when a vision of the female buddha Nairatmya appeared to him.

There are many mystics throughout India and Tibet who have had great visions. But these visions are not dualistic appearances. When you become one with the universe, these visions appear, but they are not separate from you. Only when you have transcended dualism, then, as a sign, will you see a vision.

This is why in tantric Buddhism we do a lot of yantra yoga based on the practices of air and different energy practices. This is to free ourselves from the conditions of our conception.

See, we are conceived with emotions, and then born with the ignorance of not knowing ourselves. We are born in ignorance because we have died with an unconscious mind. When we come out of that unconsciousness into a conscious world, then according to our habitual patterns, we will continue acting and reacting. When we are attracted to someone, we will experience desire. When we are threatened, we may have anger.

We are conceived with these three primary afflictive emotions of ignorance, attachment, and anger. And from that emotion, our blood, veins, chakras, air, and all other components of our human form are developed in that fetus. The nature of our conception is the reason we are living a life of conflicting emotions. Our energies are still trapped in these afflictive emotions, and this is how we experience the universe.

Tantric practitioners have developed methods for using all of these energies to purify themselves. When, through their practice, all of the energies, channels, veins, chakras, and other components become purified, then as a sign of their progress, they may see the buddhas. These buddha visions are not dualistic appearances existing outside of these yogis but rather the experience of inner purity.

Right now, everything that we experience is impure. Every sensory contact that we have with the universe—even things that at first seem pleasurable—have the potential to bring us more suffering.

This is why the Buddha taught the first noble truth of suffering. He said that the nature of our life is suffering. From the moment of conception, we have evolved in this way, formed by afflictive emotions.

Meditation is the method for reversing that process. And when we are successful, we will have pure vision. Then we will see the universe in a very different light. There will no longer be conflict between ourselves and the world, and there will no longer be the causes of suffering. Instead, everything will become blissful; everything will become like light in nature. That is what is known as pure vision, when all of your energies have been purified through meditation practice.

When your energies are not purified, then you have impure vision. In impure vision, you have dualistic appearances and you have karma. And everything that you do has the potential to bring you more pain and suffering.

This is a fact: we are conceived and born with ignorance and will die with ignorance if we make no effort to reverse this process. Since we are conceived with ignorance, we do not remember our conception. And if we make no progress to alter our awareness, we will also die with ignorance because we will be unconscious at the time of death. This is why the Buddha said that life starts from ignorance.

Now this does not mean that ignorance is the beginning of our lives, but rather that ignorance is the basis of our lives. Ignorance gives rise to the desire and attachment with which we are conceived. And along with this desire comes anger. So these three root destructive emotions of desire, anger, and ignorance feed each other and are the source of all of our feelings and karmic actions.

These traces of characteristics that Virupa is referring to are the traces of emotions inside us. All of these actions based on the emotions are the traces. These traces are not found in our eyes. These traces are not found in the object. These traces are the habitual patterns we carry from moment to moment, from one life to the next inside our mind and consciousness.

As long as we have these traces in our mental continuum, no matter how much we clean our eyes, no matter how much we purify our objects, our vision will still be impure. This is why we must purify the very source of these traces, the inner conditions, which give rise to all our afflictive emotions.

If we do not approach these traces at their source, we will not be able to purify our vision. If we are only trying to solve our impure vision at the level of the sense organ or sense object, then eventually this approach will not be maintainable. At some point, the object will become ugly or old, no matter how beautiful we try to make it. At some point our eyes will also age and give us problems, and then we will experience more pain and suffering.

> Though it seems a particle is in the eye of one with
>   ophthalmia,
> the ophthalmic appearance cannot be repaired
> without curing the eye disease.

For example, if "floaters" that appear as lines or spots are affecting our vision, then these spots we see will go away only if we treat the underlying disease.

Ayurvedic and Tibetan medicine say that if you are very angry, or if you have a blood disease, then everything will be shaded red. If you have bile disease, then you will see things in a more yellow color—even the snow may appear yellow.

So these examples are used to point out that what we see is not necessarily very reliable. Although at our level we base our reality so completely on our sensory experiences, until we have a very deep meditative awakening, none of our experiences will be reliable. Until that awakening, all our experiences will be grounded in our emotions and the karma based on those emotions.

Another good example is that if we are very sick with a fever, everything around us will appear different. Any illness can affect our inner conditions, which will then change what our sense organs perceive. Our whole experience of the universe can be altered in this way, based on our changing inner conditions.

Our experience of life is shaded by attachment, anger, and ignorance. That's what we are projecting onto the universe, and that's how we are creating more karma.

Until we cure our eyes from disease, other objects will be obscured. Likewise, until we purify ignorance through the realization of wisdom, purify desire through the practice of discipline, and purify anger through the practice of meditation, then we will still be at the mercy of these destructive emotions.

The Buddha gave us the three trainings of wisdom, discipline, and meditation as antidotes to the three root afflictive emotions. The antidotes serve to complement and balance each other. Among all three trainings, however, wisdom is the most important. Meditation and discipline without wisdom are still blind. Without wisdom, the other two trainings still won't give you a reliable experience. So to cure the root disease, we must have the realization of wisdom, which will overcome ignorance.

The final purpose of all meditation is to see that wisdom. Once we are in that state of wisdom, then how we interact with others and the universe will be completely different from our current experience.

When Mahasiddha Virupa saw the yogini Nairatmya, he was seeing that inner wisdom. That wisdom vision is not dualistic, so in essence he was seeing his own awakening. And because he saw that wisdom, he could integrate it with everything around him and with the whole universe. For Virupa, everything became wisdom.

At our level, wisdom is always obstructed. We interact with others based on our emotional projections of who they are to us. We need to develop that wisdom eye in order to really see each other. Once we have that wisdom eye, then we will all appear to be buddhas to each other. Even dogs and cats will be buddhas to us!

Dogs will have lost their individual "dogness." Cats will no longer be just these small animals. All creatures will appear as buddhas when our vision is pure because all dualistic appearances will cease. But until then, we will continue to have an individual identity, which will then discriminate between ourselves and all of the objects of the universe.

Whether appearances become pure vision or impure vision depends entirely on whether we have achieved inner purity. The more inner purity we cultivate, the more we will see that purity reflected all around us. But if we have more and more impurity inside us, the whole world will appear defiled and seem to cause us tremendous suffering.

Intellectualizing reality, attachment to meditation experience,
cultivating and meditating on the actual true state
are causes of deviation.
Because attachment and aversion arose toward
conducive conditions, one is bound.

As we have been discussing, most of the scriptures written by scholars are very intellectual and do not stem from meditation experience. This is the nature of academia—the collecting of information and the amassing of knowledge.

If collecting information helps us to know ourselves and to awaken, then that is positive. But as we know, most of the time, collecting information and intellectualizing about philosophical ideas actually distracts us from the true process of awakening.

While we are engaged in study, most of the time we are actually ignoring our own inner development. We are caught up in learning about everything except ourselves. We may be spending all our mental energy on trying to find the true nature of reality through debate, through study, and through dissertations. Meanwhile we are missing the most effective method for accessing this truth: the examination of our own minds through meditation.

If we don't meditate, then every conclusion will remain merely intellectual. We may gain great knowledge through our studies, but there's no method to transform that knowledge into wisdom without engaging in meditation.

A Zen meditator once said that knowledge is like an onion with many layers. And he said wisdom is found when all those layers are peeled away. If you are a tantric practitioner, you can base everything on the *Heart Sutra*. All tantric sadhana practice is based on the four kinds of emptiness described in the *Heart Sutra*. Those four kinds of emptiness are like different layers of the onion that are peeled away to go completely beyond.

It is only meditation practice that will help us transform knowledge into wisdom. Philosophical books give us so much information, but if we don't bring this knowledge into our meditation, it will remain purely intellectual and will not lead to any direct awakening. Furthermore, if our meditation is based purely on an attachment to feeling good, to feeling relaxed, then we will not be making progress toward that wisdom either.

Oftentimes people say, "Oh, I had a great meditation session," because after the session they feel so calm and happy. But if you become too attached to that good feeling, it will actually obstruct your experience of ultimate truth. If you are meditating in order to feel good, it will not be reliable. Feelings are never reliable, and your attachment will become an obstacle.

There are many past yogis who did not go completely beyond in order to become buddhas because they were too attached to the bliss or joy of meditation. With that attachment, they remained in a meditative absorption for many, many years without achieving liberation. They were so attached to the blissful experience of meditation that they missed the insight that was required to see the truth. And when they eventually arose from that meditation, they still experienced suffering.

This is why even the state of nirvana, which is cultivated in the Hinayana, is not ultimate buddhahood. Nirvana is a state of permanent peace. But followers of the Hinayana are attached to that peace in the sense that they believe it is the ultimate, and so they remain there.

For Mahayana and Vajrayana practitioners, however, nirvana is not the ultimate. Only when you go beyond both nirvana and samsara will you see wisdom. Meditation should give us insight into that wisdom.

Meditation should not be a method for becoming attached to feelings. This is an important distinction for us to make, since we often use meditation here in the West as a method for relaxing from our stressful lives. This meditative relaxation has real health benefits and may improve our lives, but if we become attached to the positive feelings we experience, we will not actually see wisdom.

Of the three Buddhist trainings of wisdom, discipline, and meditation, it is interesting to note that only meditation has really gained interest here in the West. Why is the ethical training of discipline not popular here? And why is wisdom not discussed as frequently?

In the West, meditation has become more of a therapeutic way to release stress and to manage pain. If you are meditating for that sole purpose, then that is fine. But if you are meditating to achieve awakening like mystics do, then the therapeutic approach and the enjoyment of that relaxation can actually be a deviation from the path. Attachment to peaceful feelings can become an obstacle.

As we know, feelings are very powerful, and feelings are also blind. The more feelings we have, the more they will feed our root destructive emotions, which will generate more feelings. Feelings are rooted in desire. When our desire is fulfilled, then we feel pleasure and happiness. When our desire is not fulfilled, then we have pain and suffering. This pain and suffering gives rise to anger.

If we are using meditation to feel good and it is working, then we may be happy. But if we are struggling and no longer enjoy sitting there, then we may immediately blame our meditation practice. It may even become a cause of anger.

All feelings and root destructive emotions are interconnected. Without the three main afflictive emotions of desire, anger, and ignorance, you will not experience the whole range of more subtle feelings. Although we are inspired to pursue everything in our lives, based on our attachment to happy feelings, we need to know how they operate, and we need to recognize their limitations.

Desire, anger, and ignorance are the main sources of all our feelings. From attachment and desire we derive our feelings of pleasure. From anger painful feelings arise. And from ignorance we experience neutral feelings.

All of the more subtle feelings and mixed emotions that arise in our daily lives serve only to increase our root destructive emotions. When our root destructive emotions increase, generating more and more karma, we are bound in samsara. We remain trapped in that chain reaction between emotions, feelings, and karmic actions.

All negative disharmonious conditions are sublime siddhis
since negative conditions intensify the yogini's experience.

This is a very profound point Virupa is making. If we reflect back through our lives, we may realize that many of the best things we have learned were learned from our mistakes. If we have used those mistakes to grow, then our mistakes have actually helped us to mature and to gain some wisdom.

People who are more mature and who have more wisdom are often people who have made the most mistakes in their lives. But they have learned important lessons from them. The key is whether you will use your errors to transform yourself and to grow, or whether you will let your mistakes have a lasting negative effect on your life.

For yogis, all of these negative experiences are actually blessings. Suffering is the greatest teacher. Those who are very weak and unable to see the lesson in the midst of their pain can be destroyed by their suffering. But for those who have the strength to learn from it, suffering can be a tremendous blessing.

This is why yogis like Virupa say that without suffering, there's no compassion. Those who have suffered more have had more opportunity to cultivate compassion. We can observe this in our ordinary life. Those who have experienced great mental, emotional, or physical pain will truly understand what it is like to walk in the shoes of someone who is suffering.

Suffering is actually a source of energy for yogis. It helps them to cultivate higher states of realization. Even if we look at the Buddha's life, if he had never seen the sick person, the old person, and the dying person, he never would have begun meditating. He never would have abandoned his kingdom and gone to sit for six years under the Bodhi tree.

When we are faced with pain and obstacles, that is the best test of how much our spiritual and religious practice can help. From the Buddhist perspective, whenever we have pain and suffering, we should see it as a positive development. All the great teachers say that instead of growing discouraged and miserable, we should accept suffering knowing that negative karma has finally matured.

Our feelings are based on karma. Our suffering is the result of negative karma. So when we are suffering, it is an indication that we are exhausting our negative karma. We can view this as a very positive experience because of the negativities that are being released. Suffering can be very purifying in this way.

Negative experiences can be used to cultivate positive ones. Yogis use negative experiences as an opportunity to cultivate the positive within themselves. If negativities in your life are actually creating more negative actions and reactions, then you are not a yogi. But if you can use this suffering to transform yourself, if you can use it to benefit others, then that is a sign that you are gaining wisdom.

In fact, without obstacles, yogis cannot progress. If you want to make progress in your life, you actually need to be challenged. All of these challenges stem from the root negative emotions. Attachment is a challenge. Anger is a challenge. Ignorance is a challenge. And learning how to overcome the negative actions arising from these afflictive emotions is a great challenge.

At the same time, these afflictive emotions have potent energy, which can be harnessed and transformed into the positive. Ignorance can be transformed into wisdom. Anger and hatred can be transformed into loving-kindness. Attachment can be transformed into compassion.

All of these factors are interrelated. Without ignorance, there is no way we can learn to see wisdom. We must go through the afflictive emotion in order to achieve its opposite. We must use our current situation—all of our suffering and difficulties in life—to discover the maximum potentialities within ourselves.

16

Just As a Good Horse Is Encouraged

Since one understands the true state of negative conditions,
without avoiding them, train in them,
maintain that, and practice until coming to the conclusion
of experience and realization,
just as a good horse is encouraged by a quirt.

A QUIRT IS A RIDING whip used to goad the horse on. So according
to Virupa, all the disharmonious conditions can actually be used
to advance one's practice. All of this pain and suffering actually con-
tains sublime siddhis. For Virupa, anger is a siddhi because anger can
become a spiritual practice. Desire and ignorance can also become practices. Through all of these afflictive emotions, Virupa can see wisdom.

This method of transformation is at the core of tantric practice. In
Buddhist tantric iconography, you will see three different types of images.
You will see the very ornate deities decorated with many jewels and orna-
ments. Such deities represent the transformation of ignorance. You will

also see male and female buddhas and deities in union, representing the transformation of desire. And the third type of deities are those possessing a very wrathful form, who represent the transformation of anger.

How much wisdom do we have in our current lives? At our level we have desire and attachment, anger issues, and general confusion a lot of the time. This is why our minds are always wandering toward whatever represents these afflictive emotions to us.

If we are angry, then all we will be able to think about are our enemies. Our anger may be so strong that we may even see these enemies in our dreams. We may yell and throw things in our dreams if these emotions are strong. We may also experience sleeping emotions surfacing more in our dream life, even if we aren't aware of them during the day.

We can also see that if we have a lot of attachment and desire related with the sense organs and sense objects, those sensory experiences will populate our dreams. We may be full of insecurity about losing those attached objects, and we may have elaborate dreams of grief and loss. Whatever the object of our attachment may be, our mind will wander after it constantly.

If we have a lot of ignorance, our mind will always be confused and disoriented. Ignorance can be like a state of drunkenness. When you are drunk, all sorts of subconscious things may surface, and you may say and do all sorts of things out of confusion. But the next day, once your hangover is gone, you may not even remember your previous actions.

So this is the power of destructive emotions. They are actually destroying our minds. The Buddha observed this through deep meditation and realized how emotions dominate our experience. This is why he designed such effective methods for overcoming the source of these afflictions.

Mahasiddha Virupa is saying that these disharmonious conditions can become our spiritual achievements only when we have the proper methods. We must have the mental capacity and the meditation practice in order to achieve this.

Otherwise, when we get angry, we will create more enemies. And the more enemies we have, the more anger they will inspire in us. Anger itself becomes the enemy, but often we don't recognize this. Instead, this chain of action and reaction generates more and more pain and suffering and mental instability in us.

In a moment of anger and rage, how can we learn to see wisdom? Instead of reacting with more hatred, instead of being consumed by anger that harms ourselves and others, how can we transform this energy?

Meditation is the very best method for anger management. Through meditation you begin to get a handle on your reactions. When you gain some control over your emotions, then you will have real possibilities for spiritual growth.

It is said in the teachings that tantric practice is like turning poison to medicine. As I have mentioned earlier, medicines are generally poisonous. It is only the proportions that determine whether they are useful or deadly. Furthermore, we need to properly diagnose the illness in the first place in order for something to become an effective medicine.

Will our anger, desire, and ignorance become a medicine, or will they remain a poison and destroy us? This is the question at the very heart of our spiritual practice. Those who have practiced meditation for a long time may be able to transform any poison into medicine.

If the Buddha had remained within the luxury of the kingdom without ever seeing illness and death, he would never have discovered the truth. Only his awareness of suffering could inspire his spiritual growth. We can see this theme in many religions. Christianity believes that Jesus suffered for us, and out of his suffering came redemption. So here too is a way in which suffering was transformed.

Suffering has a lot to do with whether we choose to cultivate spirituality in our lives. Many people will go to the temple when there is some sickness in the family or some business problem. They will go to the lama for divination and instruction on rituals to practice. So these laypeople may perform rituals and pray to the Buddha, but when they feel better, they will forget all about the temple until the next hardship occurs.

That material approach to spiritual practice doesn't do much to cultivate spiritual qualities. It has nothing to do with transforming our destructive emotions. It is more like going to a doctor when we have the flu. After we receive treatment, we forget all about the need for medicine until the next time we get sick!

Here Virupa is saying that all the negative, disharmonious conditions are actually sublime siddhis. This will make sense only when we have wholeheartedly committed our lives to meditation. When meditation is at the center of our lives, then everything else in our lives becomes part of that practice.

In every moment of our lives there is some lesson to learn. Every situation can provide us with an opportunity to cultivate spiritual practice. If we watch TV or read the newspaper, we see that there is hardly any good news. There is death and violence and suffering everywhere. But how will we choose to approach that pain? How will we handle that suffering?

Will we let that suffering make us a better person, or will we let it make us bitter and angry? This is the difference between ordinary people and those on a spiritual path. In our regular lives, all our suffering increases our destructive emotions in this vicious cycle. We simply need to look around at our families, our neighbors, and our culture to see how destructive emotions create more and more pain and suffering.

But for the meditator, all this pain and suffering can become energy that fuels transformation and gives rise to positive qualities. In highest tantra, according to the iconography we discussed, there are deities representing the transformation of all of our afflictive emotions. If we are not ready to practice at that level, then the next best approach is to cultivate patience. If we are not ready to transform these afflictive energies, we can at least use suffering to practice patience.

Once there was a mystic who was dying. On his death bed, his son asked him if he had left any will behind or had any parting advice. Since he was a wandering mystic beggar, he did not have any material wealth to leave his son. But from his life experience he gave this advice. He said, "Whenever you are faced with negative circumstances or conditions, don't react right away. Wait for twenty-four hours and then see."

This is a wonderful teaching on patience. We know that when we are angry, we do not see things clearly. Anger has completely overtaken our minds. Anger has obscured our vision to the point where we will project that anger onto everything we interact with. Any immediate actions will come out of that emotion rather than out of a clear and spacious mind.

The whole of Mahayana practice is really the process of learning how to transform from the negative to the positive. According to Buddhist teachings, patience is the best antidote to anger. When we are angry, not only will we project that anger onto other humans and other living beings, even our environment will become an object of our anger. We may even find ourselves angry at the weather or at the heat or cold!

All negative conditions help to teach us patience if we are ready to learn. If someone is making a fire and it burns you, you may get very angry at that person. But if you have some common sense, then you will see that it is not the person but rather the fire itself that burned you. And no matter how much anger you feel toward the fire, you will still lose in that situation.

Any negative situation can be transformed into something positive. That is the Mahayana path. So if we study and practice the six paramitas, they instruct us on how to transform all of these negative situations into something more positive.

But if you have so much anger or desire that you cannot employ these methods, what should you do? This is where the Buddha taught the third approach. If you cannot transform these emotions through tantric practice, and if you do not have enough patience, then the third option is renunciation. If you cannot transform, then you can at least stay away from your enemy. If your enemy is making you so angry that you cannot practice patience, and you cannot see the Buddha in that enemy, then you should remove yourself from the situation.

These are the three different levels of practice the Buddha has taught. The whole Hinayana path is one of renunciation. If your enemy is making you angrier, then just try to forget him and stay away. But if seeing your enemy allows you to practice patience, then welcome him. Your enemy can be a very good teacher. And if you can see buddha nature in the enemy, that is the best thing. That is the tantric way.

How you will face a situation is entirely personal. Although the Buddha has given us all these different levels of practice, only the level that is suitable for you will be most effective.

It will not be good for your development if you attempt to practice the highest level of tantra when you have not yet cultivated patience and are not ready for it. We are all different. We all have different propensities and different levels of emotions. You must cultivate the method that works best for you.

Mahasiddha Virupa is a tantric practitioner, so the expressions in these mystical songs come from this highest level. To Virupa, the more poison there is, the more wisdom one gains. Virupa can see the Buddha in his enemies. This is the level of realization that he has attained, but it may not necessarily be suitable for us.

Since one understands the true state of negative conditions,
without avoiding them, train in them

This is very important advice. Often we go to the temple or church part time to be members of a community and to feel happier. But if something happens in that community or temple, and we no longer feel good there, then we may stop going. And if we don't feel good, if we are physically or mentally uncomfortable, we will never go into retreat.

If our spiritual practice is only connected to our wish to feel good and to feel happy, then if those feelings change, as all feelings do, we will stop going. We will stop practicing, and there will not be much transformation. There will not be much progress because our involvement is still connected with our feelings.

Although all we want is happiness, we must remember that happiness and unhappiness are interdependent. Although we are seeking pleasure, pleasure and pain are interdependent. We cannot find one without the other.

Our feelings are so strong, and when we feel something, we are sure that it is real. This is why feeling has so much control in our lives. But we need to recognize that feeling is illogical, irrational, and it's blind.

We don't want to know that pleasure is interdependent with pain. We don't want to be told that happiness is interdependent with unhappiness and suffering. But if we learn more about feeling, there is also a bright side to this interdependency. If we look closely, we will see that the suffering and pain that we experience also carry within them the potential for pleasure and happiness.

Why is this the case? We ought to ask this question of the Buddha. Why did he sit for six years under a tree in Bodhgaya in scorching heat and miserable conditions? Why did the Buddha stay under the Bodhi tree with barely any food under those extreme circumstances?

What the Buddha realized was that within that pain there was the potential for bliss and joy. Within that suffering there was the potential for freedom. Because he learned how to accept that pain at the mental level, his mind was at peace, and all of the physical discomforts faded.

If we look at images of the Buddha after those six years, he is so thin that he is almost a skeleton. His stomach is shrunken, his ribs are showing, and he is emaciated. Some may see this as abuse, as self-imposed torture or penance. But the Buddha came out of that experience stronger. Through physical pain and suffering he developed insight and wisdom. When we accept pain at the physical level, then we can gain real mental strength.

Those who experience physical deprivation and who live in poverty are often very strong mentally. When we live in wealth and luxury, when we are physically indulged, we actually become much weaker mentally. There are very high rates of depression in developed countries. People often feel less peace when they have too many options, when they are too physically comfortable, and when their senses are overfed.

If we know the nature of these feelings and integrate this understanding that happiness and unhappiness are interdependent, then this insight can actually bring a greater sense of peace.

The Buddha taught the four noble truths so that we could become familiar with every aspect of suffering. When we are feeling happy, we may not want to know about suffering. We may want to blindly believe this happiness will last. But the truth is that if we can really understand the nature of suffering, we have the potential for a much deeper form of happiness and freedom.

If we are in the midst of suffering, we may also have no interest in talking about suffering. Or if we watch the news, we may feel we already know about misery, and we may have no wish to talk about it. Instead we may be doing everything in our power to distract ourselves from our pain and the misfortunes in the world.

The question we can ask instead is how can we learn to use pain? When we learn how to transform these difficult feelings by understanding their nature, we will gain so much more freedom in our lives. If we understand how to transform difficult situations into positive growth, we will become like alchemists. The more suffering we have, the more potential we will have for joy.

This is why Virupa says that since we cannot avoid negative conditions, we must train in them. We cannot run away from suffering. The seeds of suffering exist in every cell in our bodies. Every moment these cells are changing; they are aging and dying. Even biologists accept that fact.

Some masters say that the moment we are conceived, we begin to die. We see that we cannot avoid change; it is built right into our bodies. Every moment we are aging. Every moment we are getting closer and closer to our own deaths.

The best thing we can do instead of despairing or growing apathetic is to learn the deep lesson in every moment. Here we should recall another story about an old Indian mystic. When he was dying, his students asked him for advice. They asked him if he had any regrets or wisdom to share. The mystic said, "In my next reincarnation, I want to make all my mistakes as soon as possible, so that I can also learn from them quickly. I don't want to wait until I'm too old to learn those lessons."

Our lives are full of mistakes, from the very moment of conception. We go blindly through life, lacking full awareness of what we are doing and why. Making mistakes is not what brings wisdom—it is the awareness we bring to those mistakes that will allow them to become lessons for us. If we examine the causes and antidotes to those mistakes, then we will develop insight, and this is how we will learn from our errors.

Until we gain this insight, whatever we are doing will stem from the core afflictive emotions of anger, desire, and ignorance. Everything we do in life arises from some combination of those root emotions. Without wisdom, our emotions make us do all sorts of destructive things, which then create more karma.

The best way to learn is first to accept the truth of suffering. As the great Kadampa masters have said, "Don't let suffering create more pain and anger in you. Instead, accept suffering with joy." Here joy means that every time you have a headache, every time you have the flu or any physical or mental suffering, you should rejoice, knowing that your negative karma is being exhausted.

All suffering—whether it is physical, emotional, mental, or spiritual—is due to negative karma. Through suffering, your karma is ripened. Through suffering you exhaust your karma; you are purified. This is a fact! This is not something that the Buddha made up. Karma is a natural law of cause and effect.

But this purification can only succeed if you don't react to suffering with even more destructive emotions. If you can suffer without allowing it to create more anger in you, then you can actually halt the process of generating more karma. For the first time you can actually gain some freedom.

The Kadampa masters said, "If you open up your heart when you are suffering, thinking about the suffering of all sentient beings, your own pain will become a practice to cultivate compassion." If you approach your own suffering with this generosity and open-heartedness, it will become a profound teaching in compassion.

In this way, suffering can become a great teacher. Suffering can lead to transformation, and it can exhaust our negative karma. There are many things we can learn from suffering. But if we don't use suffering in a positive way, then it will become a source for even greater bitterness and anger.

Whether something will become agreeable or not and whether we will learn from our disagreeable experiences is based largely on our outlook. In order to change our outlook, we have to experience this inner transformation. This is why Virupa states that we must practice in those negative conditions until we come to some realization.

Just as the sting of a quirt will push a horse to move forward, all of the suffering in our lives can help us to cultivate more meditation and spiritual practice. If we take that into account, then every moment of our lives can become part of our practice. Transformation cannot be a part-time practice, like going to church only on Sunday, or visiting a temple only when we are ill. To experience real transformation, every situation should become a spiritual practice.

Practice is not really related to our feelings. Practice is not an effort to feel good. The goal of practice is to become a buddha, to see that light inside us, to achieve awakening. With this aspiration, pain and pleasure, happiness and unhappiness, can become part of our practice. If our practice is limited only to our feelings, then it will not be a source of transformation. This is why Virupa says,

> If yogis with good experience lack the companion of conduct,
> as that is not possessed, it is like people without feet.

So we must ask, what is conduct? As we have discussed, the Buddha gave three trainings: the training of wisdom, the training of discipline or proper conduct, and the training of meditation. Conduct is the training that integrates our wisdom and meditation into every moment.

We can sit in meditation for ten minutes, an hour, or ten years, but after that, how will we respond to the world? When we go out into the market, when we are presented with difficult situations, how will we behave? This is where conduct is integral to our practice; it is the means by which we bring our meditation and wisdom into our daily lives.

Conduct is where we integrate the realizations we gain through study and meditation into every activity. We can bring these realizations into every experience, whether we are eating, walking, driving, swimming, or even playing golf!

Even the game of golf can become an effective practice of concentration and meditation. Only when you are in the middle, not too tight, not too loose, will your golf swing be effective. This is how we need to live our lives, not too tight, not too loose. We have to find the middle way.

Conduct should protect you in your worldly activities. When you really need direction, when you are angry, when you are obsessive, and even if you become intoxicated, if your conduct is strong, you can correct yourself. Through right conduct you can bring the wisdom of that inner witness to the situation and refrain from further destructive behaviors.

Without right conduct, your meditation will not progress. This is why Virupa says that if someone lacks discipline, it is like being without feet. Without feet, how can you get anywhere? Without a vehicle, how can you travel great distances? Without conduct, you cannot advance on the spiritual path. Conduct can transform your eating into eating yoga, your shower into bathing yoga, your sleep into dream yoga, and your waking into waking yoga. Conduct has the power to integrate meditation and wisdom into our lives, and therefore it is vital to our spiritual journeys.

17

Giving Up Nothing, Accomplishing Nothing

WE ARE ACCUSTOMED TO gaining knowledge based on gathering names, facts, and ideas, all of which are entirely dependent on language. But as we have discussed, names and language are merely a reference. We will not understand the true meaning of what they refer to until our experience prepares us.

Many of us spend all our time learning about the world through language. But to yogis and those who are great meditators, our appetite for information may seem completely absurd—a waste of time!

As I mentioned earlier, take for example the word for "sugar." There are thousands and thousands of words for this same substance. It would take months to gather all these words from different languages. And if you tried to memorize them all, it would take even longer. Then if you wanted to learn enough to communicate with the whole world, it would take forever. Furthermore, if we try to learn about sugar by investigating its components in a lab, we may be able to describe all its chemical properties, but will that actually help us understand the experience of sugar?

Everything we do as far as knowledge is concerned is based on language. But language is not truthful. Language is not ultimate. Language is something that humans have created out of necessity and utility, but it is unreliable.

This is why yogis don't rely on language for their understanding. They are very practical people. They want to experience things directly. Only when a yogi has personally tasted sugar will that yogi truly know what sugar is. How can you describe that experience of sweetness; how can you possibly express it in language? We can say, "sugar is sweet," but then how do we define sweetness?

On the other hand, even without language, a person who has experienced that taste will better understand its qualities. The personal experience of that sweetness will give you more wisdom than all of the books written about sugar and all of the thousands of names that have been created to refer to it. Personal experience is much closer to the wisdom.

Words and terms are the source of so much miscommunication, even when we are discussing the Dharma. Our confusion is because we have not personally experienced something. So although Mahasiddha Virupa had the original indescribable experience of mahamudra, which cannot be transmitted through language, he is offering us these dohas as encouragement. While he cannot give us personal experience, he can offer some reference to that realization of clarity and emptiness.

It is difficult to know, however, whether we are getting closer or farther away from that original experience when we use language to discuss it. Language is always trapped in time, place, culture, and our individual frame of reference. And the usage of language is always changing. Meaning is always shifting, even for the same words, depending on history or social change.

All this is to say that our meditation experience is more reliable and more truthful than any words. Words may help us to practice, but if we base our understanding merely on language and study, then we will never know what is real. To know sugar, you have to taste sugar. If you keep on learning different names for it, and for all of its properties, it will deter you from the actual experience.

The Buddha never taught the Dharma for the sake of knowledge. He said that the main purpose of studying the Dharma is to inspire your meditation. Out of study, reflection, and meditation, meditation has the greatest potential for spiritual growth. We should be studying for the sake of our meditation. However, if we stop meditating in order to focus on our studies, then we may gain a great deal of information, but we will have lost sight of the whole purpose of the Dharma.

> Train in the actual, ultimate, real state, free from attachment,
> giving up nothing, accomplishing nothing, attached to nothing,
> purifying nothing, rejecting nothing,
> the best of the very best conduct is whatever feels good to one's
> body.

How can we train ourselves to experience that ultimate state that is free from attachment? These mystical songs will just be a bunch of words unless we have had some experience in our meditation. They may even seem meaningless to us. When Virupa says "giving up nothing, accomplishing nothing," this may not make much sense or be relevant to us yet.

Because we have not yet experienced that ultimate state, we still have to give things up in our lives. We still need to give up old habits, additions, and negative behaviors. And often in our practice we remain focused on accomplishment until we have seen that inner space between our thoughts while in our deepest meditation. At that point we will have achieved freedom even from the need to accomplish anything.

As we have discussed, the mind is a constant river of thoughts. This is why meditation is so hard for us in the beginning. Focusing on one object can seem impossible because we have never seen that space within us. The moment we try to meditate, more thoughts will come.

Our minds are never present in the beginning; they are always wandering around to so many different objects.

Those like Virupa and the Buddha who have attained realization have seen the space between thoughts. When they remain in that inner space, there is nothing to give up. They have gone beyond. At our level, there is still a lot to give up. We have to give up all of those drops of thoughts. At our level, Virupa's words may even seem like a contradiction. For Virupa, there is nothing left to accomplish because he is in that state beyond thought. In that state there is nothing to achieve.

At our level, because our minds are so busy with thoughts, we still have so much we want to accomplish and achieve. With all of our mental activities and emotions, we want to achieve peace and happiness. Even our spiritual aspirations to achieve bliss are still based on motivation and accomplishment.

We are still filled with expectations when we meditate. And as we have discussed, here in the West it seems the main purpose of meditation is usually stress reduction and relaxation. But if we experience that profound inner space of the union of clarity and emptiness, then there is nothing to be attached to, nothing to achieve, nothing to accomplish.

In that state of inner space, there is nothing left to be attached to. All attachment has gone because mind has gone and all emotions have dissolved. When ignorance, desire, and anger have gone, who is left to do the attaching?

Attachment is present in our lives now because of our egos, because our selves and all our emotions want to be the subject of the universe. And because the "I" exists, we immediately want to possess other objects. But when the ego itself has gone and we are in that inner space, no one remains to do the attaching, and there is no object to be attached to. In the inner space between thoughts, both subject and object have dissolved, and we are in a timeless state beyond dualism.

This meditation we are doing now, like focusing on the breath or focusing on some object, is just the beginning of our practice. Perfecting shamatha meditation is only laying a foundation; it is not the ultimate purpose. When we have the final realization of emptiness in insight meditation, we no longer will rely on any object or visualization. All objects of shamatha meditation and all visualizations in Vajrayana sadhana practices will be dissolved in that ultimate state. This is the purpose of the completion practices in the sadhana—to dissolve both subject and object.

Given where we are now in our practice, we still need to do a lot of purification practices. We have to purify ignorance, and we have to purify attachment and anger. We also have to purify all our habitual patterns, which are based on the destructive emotions. This includes all of our addictions. But once we are in that inner space, then there is nothing to purify, there is nothing to accept and nothing to reject. At this stage we have gone beyond both. However, in our ordinary lives, we still have good things to accept and bad things to reject. But when someone has gone beyond both, this discrimination is no longer relevant. That is perfection.

So even the good activities—all the accumulations of merit—are still not perfection. Often we go to a church or temple and accumulate merit so that we can reject and confess our negative deeds. In regular life, we may kill, lie, or steal, and then we may go to a temple to make up for these negative actions by trying to purify ourselves.

In these cases, we are trying to purify our negativities by doing something good. But that dualism of good and bad is still not a perfection because it is still relative.

A meditator who is in a state of inner space has transcended this dualism. In that perfected state, there is no merit to be accumulated and there are no sins to confess. The great yogis have gone beyond karma.

When the buddhas and mahasiddhas are in that state of inner space, what is conduct? What is good for them? When Virupa says "whatever feels good to one's body," this does not mean indulging the senses. It means that these yogis have actually gone beyond feeling. There is no longer such a thing as something good or bad to feel because the feeler, the ego and self, have dissolved.

Now if you come out of that inner space and examine it, you may recognize it as the best feeling you have ever had because you didn't feel anything! Even in our ordinary lives we tend to feel happiest when we are doing an activity that makes us completely forget ourselves.

However, the problem with forgetting ourselves in ordinary life is that the minute we are finished with an activity, the self comes right back! We may go to a wonderful movie and have a great time for the hour or two in which we entirely forget ourselves. But when the movie is finished, and our ego comes back, we may suddenly feel miserable again and begin talking about ourselves and our feelings.

Any activity, including meditation, can distract us from ourselves temporarily. But if the self and ego are not fully dissolved, all of our emotions will resume after that break. In the inner space of deep meditation, however, the mind has become one with the wisdom of emptiness, and there is no question of forgetting oneself. One has now seen the true nature of oneself, which is space. It is selflessness.

This may all sound very illogical, but as we have already explored in teachings on buddha nature, it is said that we can look to outer space for some understanding of our inner state. Inner space and outer space are the same in that they are both unconditioned.

Now the question arises, if outer space is unconditioned, then how did the universe begin? How did all these stars and moons and planetary systems develop? The Buddha said there are limitless universes, and now scientists are agreeing that there are billions and billions of universes. How can we explain this?

The Buddha taught that all of these universes began from our karma, both our individual karma and our collective karma. Who created karma? Karma is created by our minds.

In some sense, we can understand the planet and even the outer universe by comparing it to how a bird creates its nest or how we build a new home. Doesn't our home always begin with a vision in our minds? Doesn't it begin with a dream of what we want to make?

Our house begins with a dream, and then we build it. In the same way, the whole universe is built from the individual and collective karma of sentient beings. Karma is created by emotions in the mind. This is why all these universes are always changing hands, like houses changing owners. Today this is my home. Tomorrow it might be foreclosed on, and then it will belong to someone else.

Even in one hundred years, everything that we have created now will be very different. Things change; everything comes and goes. New countries are created; old countries cease. But in all of this worldly change, has space ever changed? Space will always be there, because it is unconditioned. Everything else will be changing moment to moment.

The question remains: is all this space happening out there, or is it happening within us? That is a big question. Spiritualists, theologians, and quantum physicists are still debating these theories. But science is coming closer and closer to agreeing with what the Buddha taught thousands of years ago. As we discussed, physicists are now talking about the emptiness at the center of everything, which they call the "quantum vacuum."

The realization of emptiness is dependent upon your meditation. But until we have firsthand experience, then to increase our faith in that inner space, we can contemplate outer space. Outer space can serve as a mirror to reflect our inner space. Until we have this realization, then all that we experience will be based on our ego.

Our self and ego are the beginning of our lives, upon which we build everything else. If we regress back to when we were a mere fetus, or to the moment when we were first conceived, where is the material body? What exists of us in that first moment of conception? If we contemplate that first moment, we will have great insight into knowing whether the mind, or the material form, came first.

Buddhists would say that between the mind and the body, the mind always comes first. It is the mind that creates matter. But here, when we talk about space, it actually extends beyond the mind. So if mind has created our body, and envisioned and built our home, then if we go beyond mind, what is there?

Philosophers like Nagarjuna have said that where there is emptiness, there is everything. Everything is possible in emptiness. Here emptiness refers to inner space. When you see inner space, you are a buddha.

But when you don't see that inner emptiness, then interdependency emerges.

So according to a Buddhist understanding, evolution starts from not seeing this inner space. When you don't see this inner space, then your ego and emotions and everything will arise. As we have observed, even when we catch a glimpse of that inner space, we feel the best we have ever felt in our lives because we briefly step free of our egos. Any potential for healing inside of us also arises in that inner space.

When I hold the healing Chöd ceremonies in the West, often psychologists and therapists attend. While I perform the Chöd, everyone is just lying down, there is nothing to learn, and no information to take in. I am merely reciting Tibetan, which most people don't even understand.

I asked these people why the healing Chöd practice is so attractive to therapists and psychologists. They are not even Buddhists, so what draws them to attend? What I learned is that they are very tired of talking, very tired of hearing endless stories from patients. They are ready for peace and quiet.

Chöd has a meaning of "cutting through." The Chöd ceremony cuts through all of your thoughts and emotions, and then on a deeper level, it cuts through the ego.

So whether or not that is actually happening for these psychologists and therapists who attend the ritual, the chanting and rest may still bring some kind of peace. Briefly they may stop thinking. They may stop this circular chain of analyzing that is so necessary to their professions.

The Buddha said that life is a cycle. So even if we look back to our infancy and try to analyze that, how can we know what happened when we were in the womb? If we believe in past lives, we have to go even further back to analyze their causes and conditions.

This type of analysis can be productive, but it is also never-ending. In this way, it has the potential to become very exhausting. We have to find a method to cut through all of these layers of analysis, right down to wisdom. All that cutting down can be done through meditation. And when you discover that inner wisdom, it can cut through everything.

Inner space is wisdom. And wisdom has that healing potential. Inner space has the power to cut right through our egos, and through all our thoughts and habitual patterns. This is why it is so powerful and inspires the greatest healing that we have ever experienced in our lives. Now we are healing from the root. We are not merely treating a symptom. We are healing at the very core.

In the inner space of meditation, we feel most natural. We feel the best when we are freed from our egos. This is why meditation has such a profound potential to heal us. One moment of that experience of inner spaciousness and wisdom has more power to heal than many other methods. In that experience of wisdom, we are touching the core of our beings, and we are recognizing that deep inner freedom.

When Virupa says "the best of the very best conduct is whatever feels good to one's body," we should not misunderstand this as a feeling. What he is actually saying is that when you are in the most natural state of being, in that inner space, then you are most comfortable, most healed, most free, because you are beyond the body.

Though relatively,
the buddhas have the great confidence of a dead body,
they diligently do whatever possible
without abandoning the great mass of sentient beings.

This may seem like another paradox to us. If you are dead, then you have ceased to care. You have ceased to feel anything, right? Your whole life you have been accumulating possessions, feelings, identities, in order to live. But when you die, none of this matters. Everything stops being important.

The Buddha achieved a similar nonreactive state while he was still alive. Dead bodies of course don't care about anything because they are dead! But buddhas experience this state of freedom from engagement, this ability to be a witness to everything based on wisdom. Both a Buddha and a dead person share a similar freedom from attachment and aversion. But only a buddha remains a witness to everything, whereas a dead body cannot comprehend that state of awareness.

At our level, we are reacting every moment. When we see something we like, we immediately become attached and want to possess it. If we are confronted with something we don't like, we are immediately averse to it and may even get angry.

Life is a state of constantly conflicting emotions. We all know that there is a very thin line between love and hate. This is because the basis for both love and hate is rooted in the ego. When the desires of the ego are fulfilled, we grow happy. When these desires are not met, we feel pain and anger.

There is no ego for the Buddha. The Buddha's love is unconditional. Therefore it cannot turn to hatred. Even when the evil *maras* were attacking him, the Buddha did not become angry because his ego was gone. Buddhas don't react.

Now the question that challenges many a Buddhist scholar is if buddhas don't react, do they still see suffering? And when beings are suffering, do buddhas feel their pain? If we say the Buddha doesn't suffer, and doesn't know all of our suffering, then we are challenging one of the basic principles of Buddhism. If the Buddha is omniscient, and knows each and every thing, then the Buddha should know the suffering of all sentient beings.

The Sakya masters say that the Buddha doesn't suffer because he has gone beyond feelings. The Buddha doesn't suffer because he doesn't have any karma. But the Sakyas believe that the Buddha can still see suffering and can still know the pain of others.

This is the reason why the Buddha's wisdom has two aspects in reference to other beings. The Buddha is always in a state of wisdom within himself, which is why he never reacts. But whenever the Buddha sees the sufferings of others, out of his innate wisdom arises limitless compassion.

At our level, compassion does not arise from wisdom. Our compassion is based entirely on our emotions. We feel compassion if something happens to our loved ones or to someone close to us. But often we don't have compassion if something happens to our enemies. Our compassion is rooted in our emotions, and it is conditional.

> they diligently do whatever possible
> without abandoning the great mass of sentient beings.

So although the Buddha does not suffer, when he sees the suffering of others, his compassion arises toward all beings. The Buddha has unconditioned compassion toward limitless sentient beings.

The Buddha's compassion is like the sun. The sun is shining all the time, but sometimes here on earth we still experience darkness. The sun has not gone out at night, we simply can't see it for a while from where we are on the planet. It may be dark in America, but in India it is a bright sunny morning. It is the same sun always shining. Only our ability to see it changes.

Likewise, according to our inner conditions, some will experience darkness while others may almost always feel the light. It is neither the sun's fault nor the Buddha's fault that we cannot feel the light. It is due to our own circumstances and to how we are conditioned. If the Buddha has compassion for all sentient beings, and wants us to be free of all our suffering, then why don't we all experience that compassion all the time?

If the sun comes out, but you have something obscuring your vision, if something is covering your face, or you are in a windowless room, you will not experience that warmth or that light.

In a similar way, if the Buddha appears, but your karma is such that you are not ready to practice, then you will not receive the blessings of the Buddha's compassion.

> they diligently do whatever possible
> without abandoning the great mass of sentient beings.

What this is saying is that, as far as the Buddha is concerned, there is no discrimination between beings. It's not as if Buddha is only going to help Buddhists. The Buddha's compassion is limitless. The Buddha is ready to help everyone whether they are Hindu, Muslim, or atheist. Whether you will receive these blessings, however, depends upon your situation, and upon your inner conditions.

The Buddha achieved wisdom. Therefore he no longer suffers. But when he sees the suffering of other beings, that condition inspires the Buddha's limitless compassion for all sentient beings. This compassion stems from wisdom, not from the emotions that would create a feeling more like empathy. The Buddha does not feel our pain but nonetheless offers unconditional compassion, based on wisdom.

From our perspective, there may appear to be real contradictions between the relative and the ultimate, and between wisdom and compassion. The relative always works within the limits of interdependency. Ultimate truth, however, is beyond relativity.

Though fearless, without fearful thoughts toward samsara,
refrain from even the slightest wrong action.

Fear is one of the primary experiences in our lives. If we look closely, we see we are driven by all kinds of fears starting at birth: fear of failure, fear of pain, and fear of loss. But our deepest anxiety is due to the fact that at every moment we are confronted by death. Death is our biggest fear. When something threatens our lives, that is the most terrifying experience we can have. Deep down, we know we will die, and this is the cause of all our insecurity and fear.

Every moment we are dying. This is why every moment we have fear and anxiety deep down in our subconscious. Those fears are subdued when we are distracted from ourselves. This is why we keep so busy with other things! If we can forget ourselves, then our fear is also forgotten. But the moment we are confronted with ourselves once again, then that fear will come back.

Whenever that fear arises, instead of running away from it, we can reflect on it through meditation. We can examine why we are fearful. So much fear is based on our attachments. The whole system of capitalism is based on fear and greed, and capitalism magnifies both of them.

Here in the United States, we can see we are a very stressful and anxious country. Shouldn't such a developed nation be content and happy? Why are we so miserable? Why is there so much unemployment?

If we look at history, unemployment is a more recent phenomenon brought on by the Industrial Revolution. Before industrialization, children were more apt to do what their fathers did for work. Many times there wasn't even currency. People exchanged services and bartered. People lived with much less luxury than we have today, but mentally they were more content.

So capitalism is breeding fear and greed, which creates more instability. It also creates more anger. Here in the United States we are a very aggressive nation. Our fear creates pain, and our pain creates even more fear. Often fear exists because of our attachments. When our desires are not fulfilled, when our attachments are threatened, we experience pain, which leads to anger. This in turn fuels our aggression.

We are under the false impression that when we become more aggressive, it is a sign of strength and bravery and courage. But when we look more closely at the causes, we see that aggression is really just a much louder or more violent way of showing fear.

Anger can bring fear. Attachment can bring fear. And ignorance can bring so much fear due to the confusion of not understanding a situation. So we see that as long as we have these three basic emotions, we will have fear.

If we don't meditate, then that underlying fear will follow us from birth until death and even beyond. Children are born crying, and most people will die with a look of fear and confusion, not understanding what is happening. As long as we have these core destructive emotions, fear will be one of the main experiences of our lives whether or not we ever recognize it.

The Buddha has gone beyond these three emotions because they are rooted in the ego. Because the Buddha has seen selflessness, he is fearless. The Buddha has the inner wisdom to see the nature of the ego.

There is a legend that the Buddha had a miraculous birth and did not cry. When he passed away, he lay in the sleeping posture, very peacefully dying without pain. How many of us will experience that peace at the time of our death? The majority of people die with tremendous pain and fear. Or they die on such high doses of morphine that they are very ignorant of the entire process of death.

When Virupa says "refrain from even the slightest wrong action," he is saying that in that state of inner space, enlightened beings also do not commit any negative actions. This is because buddhas have gone beyond karma and beyond the ego that creates that karma.

Buddhas may still be eating, drinking, or sleeping, but none of these activities are done with desire, anger, or emotion. Even ordinary activities arise from the Buddha's wisdom, so those actions do not create karma.

Now if buddhas are fearless, why aren't they performing all sorts of feats to display their bravery? Buddhas don't need to display anything because they have seen wisdom. And in that wisdom, they are free from even the slightest wrong action. In our lives, even if we aren't committing any obvious negative deeds, even in the neutral state of sleep we are still creating karma. This is because even in sleep we generate all kinds of emotions and thoughts. But buddhas are beyond all karma and beyond all fear.

18

Give Up Attachment and Aversion

Though phenomena are realized to be empty like space,
free from an origin,
give up attachment and aversion,
having destroyed all strong grasping.

At our level, *phenomena* includes all of the objects and all of the efforts related with those objects. The universe consists of phenomena, and the action or effort occurs when all of the sense organs engage with that phenomena. We have eyes to grasp at visual objects. We have a nose to smell. We have ears to experience sound. All these sense organs generate both the action of perceiving and the actual objects themselves.

One of the great masters said, "First, one is attached to the self. Second, one is attached to phenomena." Because of our intense attachment to ourselves, we then form attachments to all phenomenal objects. This is what gives rise to all of our clinging to our possessions and to all of our identification with these objects. Our feelings of "I" and "mine" extend to all of the attachments we form and generate as well as all of our emotional involvement with phenomena.

At this point, we don't have any realization of the true nature of phenomena. We have very strong attachments to objects, especially to those central objects related with the central organs.

Our attachment is also what inspires us to give, to create, and to be formed in the first place. We are conceived based on attachments. According to Buddhist psychology, this attachment includes the attachment between our parents and also the attachment of our consciousness to a body. These attachments force us to be born again and again.

So we can see, attachment forces us to create things. In the Buddhist cosmology, the whole universe is created by attachment, especially our universe, our human experience, which we call the *desire realm*.

Why is it called the desire realm? In Buddhist cosmology we have the desire realm, the form realm, and the formless realm. Our phenomenal world is called the desire realm because in some sense even the way we are conceived and the way our birth is forced are all based on projections of desire. Throughout our lives, desire creates all of our dreams, all our expectations and excitement. Through desire being fulfilled we experience pleasure and happiness. We indulge ourselves with desire and attachment because we believe this will bring lasting happiness.

In the desire realm, happiness has become the ultimate dream for us. To some degree happiness has become the whole goal of our lives. But the problem is that the more we want happiness, the more misery that desire can invoke in us.

We all have experienced this to some extent. The harder we pursue happiness, the more that happiness begins to disappear. Here in the desire realm, although all we crave is happiness, the consequence is that we are often quite miserable and dissatisfied.

This is why the Buddha chose the four noble truths in his first turning of the wheel of Dharma. As we know, the first noble truth is the truth of suffering. That first noble truth examines all our feelings. Why do we want to experience so much happiness and pleasure? And why does this pursuit lead to so much unhappiness? Why does this desire only create more suffering and restlessness?

Now the purpose of contemplating the truth of suffering is that by truly knowing its causes there is a chance that we can free ourselves from it completely. The problem is that normally we don't really understand the nature of suffering or of happiness. Instead we are just pursuing a dream. And in the process, deep down we are never completely happy. We always have this underlying restlessness.

To some extent these feelings are blind. Pursuing happiness is actually only a myth. But this myth has come to define our entire lives. And deep down we really don't know what we are doing or why. Even bearing children is done without true understanding. We are overjoyed at the birth of a child, but what do we really know about that child's future life? How much power do we actually have to ensure our children's happiness?

Attachment is related to what we believe will bring us pleasure and happiness. We celebrate a new baby with so much delight, but how much of that happiness is lasting? If we could see the arc of that child's life from birth to death, and even beyond, how much true happiness will that child experience?

We are attached to phenomena. We are attached to all of the objects including family members, friends, and inanimate objects. We are clinging to the objects that bring us happiness. But the problem is that everything is conditioned. Everything is changing, aging, and decaying.

Why are we so averse to death? Why do we celebrate births but grieve deaths? Attachment and aversion are so mixed together, but if we understood what has been driving us from the beginning, it would be a very different story.

Since we don't have a full comprehension of the nature of reality, our desire creates our dreams, needs, and possessions. Due to this, pain and aversion are inevitable at the time of death. Everything that is created must decay. Everything that is born must die. But without a full understanding of this, we will experience so much sorrow and disbelief when confronted with death. We have lived in denial, almost letting ourselves believe that what we create and the attachments that we form will be eternal.

When Virupa says "free from an origin," it is because yogis know that everything is free from birth and death. But we have not seen that yet. That is why we still have so much attachment to birth and so much aversion to pain and death. All of the attachment and aversion is there because we don't really know what we are doing!

According to Buddhist psychology, you cannot have attachment or aversion without ignorance. And that ignorance is not knowing the nature of reality. If we have not seen the inner space, then we constantly project objects that we become attached to. We constantly change the objects in our lives, and even the people in our lives, but the underlying emotions remain the same. The emotions are even increased and magnified the more fixed our habitual patterns become.

Until we are completely free from grasping, our attachment and aversion will constantly be interacting with and reacting to everything in the phenomenal world. The only way to see the nature of phenomena is to see the nature of ourselves. As long as we don't see the true nature of ourselves through meditation, we will never be free from destructive emotions.

As we have already discussed, pain and pleasure and happiness and unhappiness are a result of destructive emotions. And destructive emotions are there because of the ego. Attachment to the ego and self can make desire and aversion interchangeable, giving rise to all of the other feelings. The only way to achieve real peace is by seeing the true nature of oneself through meditation.

None of this discussion of suffering is meant to imply that human life is worthless. Whether human life will become precious or whether it will be rendered useless depends largely on how well we come to understand its value.

There was one Indian yogi who would go down to a river every night. He was always throwing pebbles into the water. Early one morning, as the first light was touching the water, he tossed a pebble, and it shone in the sunlight like a diamond. Suddenly he felt so lost, realizing that all of these nights he had been wasting pebbles by throwing them in the dark when he could have seen that they were diamonds!

This is similar to our lives. Every moment in our lives can be misused. Every moment can be wasted, degraded, and cheapened by our choices. Or we can learn to see the tremendous preciousness of our lives and use every moment for our practice.

This is why we call the highest Vajrayana practices of tantra the *diamond path*. It is called *diamond* because our lives, and especially our physical bodies, have the potential to become like diamonds. But if we don't know the right methods, then we won't see the value in our human life. And if we don't understand the incredible potential within this lifetime, it will instead become the basis for all of our pain and suffering.

Once we recognize that this life is as precious as a diamond, then it can become a source of peace and enlightenment, bliss and emptiness. This is why our precious human life is called the "diamond body" because it has those profound potentialities for transformation.

Whether we will become a diamond or not depends on whether we can see the space inside us through meditation. Once we see the inner space and realize that we were not born and will never die, then we will become like diamonds!

Diamonds are the most lasting material in that they cannot easily be destroyed by other objects. As a result, diamonds represent something eternal. Something can become eternal only when it is free from birth and death.

We need to clarify the nature of birth and death. According to Buddhism, we do not choose our birth. We are forced to be reborn based on our desire. So although we celebrate birth, we all know birth is painful. It is painful for the mother and also for the child. This is why mothers and babies are screaming out at the time of birth. There is pain when something is forced because it is not happening willingly, and it is not occurring out of freedom.

When you have achieved that diamond state, although you are free from birth and death, it does not mean that you will cease to appear. Buddhas can choose to freely appear. Buddhas can choose birth based on wisdom and compassion They are not forced by karma and defilements to take form.

Virupa is saying that if we see the inner space through meditation, then we are free from birth and death. In empty space there is no interdependency. That space is free from relativity. If we could ask Einstein, he might agree with Buddhists that we cannot project relativity onto space itself.

Now on the other hand, what is happening within that space is all happening in relativity. This is the same inside of us. When we realize the inner space through meditation, that space is free from interdependency. It is free from relativity. This is the reason why it is also free from birth and death.

Until we see the inner space, we will have desire, anger, and all of the myriad feelings rooted in the ego and stemming from our basic ignorance about our true nature. In that ignorance, everything is still locked in interdependency and relativity.

This is the reason why the Buddha said that life is a cycle. In that cycle, we cannot see the first cause of birth, and we cannot find a last cause at the time of death. Because of this law of interdependency in the relative world, every cause needs another cause.

When we see the inner space within ourselves, we will also see the nature of outer space. But if we don't discover this inner space, then all we'll experience inside us and around us will be emotions, feelings, and ideas. And based on these feelings and concepts, we will generate all of our actions and reactions. We will constantly create and destroy things, endlessly. This is why the Buddha said that life is beginningless; in that interdependency you cannot find a first cause.

Life is beginningless, and samsara is also beginningless. But if we practice, and if we come to know that inner space, then there is a possible end to that cycle. In that realization of inner space, we may achieve freedom from all pain and suffering.

Though one realizes the meaning
of the great transparent dharmata, free from extremes,
while one has not attained stability,
keep one's experience and realization secret from others.

Virupa is cautioning us that even if we have some spiritual realization of wisdom and emptiness through our meditation, until that experience is stabilized, we should not go out declaring our realization.

Many teachers warn that people who claim a lot of spiritual progress have probably not reached a very high level of realization. Boasting publicly of one's experience is often a sign that the ego is still thriving and that the dissolution of the self and emotions has not really occurred.

According to the Buddhist path, it is vital to accumulate merit early in our spiritual practice. The accumulation of merit is a method to break down the chain reaction of the habitual patterns. Breaking these tendencies is especially important with regard to the negative habitual patterns, which we have developed mentally, physically, and verbally. To reverse the negative habitual patterns, we have to create more positive karma.

Positive karma is the accumulation of merit. If we have been killing sentient beings, then we make a resolution not to kill. Once we have made the resolution, then the act of not killing becomes a way of accumulating merit. These resolutions help us consciously break the chain reaction of negative habits. This is true for all of the resolutions we make, whether it's lying, stealing, intoxication etc. All of the accumulation of merit is an effort to weaken and ultimately overcome the cycle of negative habitual patterns.

The more faith we have, the easier it will become to accumulate merit. Faith can strengthen us to keep our moral conduct. If we have more faith in the Buddha, then taking the precept not to kill is deepened and reinforced by our devotion. Based on faith, we accumulate more and more merit, which will overpower these negativities and all destructive emotions.

At some point we will begin to see emptiness when we meditate. This is the beginning of seeing the true nature of ourselves. This is why it is called "the path of seeing." But that first glimpse of our emptiness and egolessness is not sufficient. We have to meditate continuously until that realization of emptiness becomes a deeply integrated part of our person.

Virupa is cautioning that without that integration, when we claim to have achieved some spiritual experience, our pride and egos only get bigger. These proclamations are an effort to make people respect or appreciate us, and they can foster even more arrogance.

This is why it is very important that we do not announce our realizations to the world until they have been profoundly stabilized. This privacy and humility is very different from the Western attitude toward achievement. Here in the West, we always feel that if we don't put all of our qualifications on our resumes, then we won't get the job! We won't get the respect!

We also find that teachers sometimes make outrageous claims about their spiritual powers in order to gain attention, fame, notoriety, and power. We have to be aware that it is not always the famous teachers who are the best teachers. Some of the most realized masters may be living in caves for most of their lives, deeply engaged in spiritual practice. Running a large center and having many followers is no real indication of a teacher's realization. Sometimes it is actually a sign that there is still a lot of ego, a lot of charisma, and a need for attention.

It is important to be mindful of the dangers of spiritual capitalism here in the West. Here we are expected to promote ourselves. Here we are supposed to advertise and make a name for ourselves in order to measure our success. Success here is defined in such a material way and is often not based on inner realization.

So we see a real contradiction between priorities in the West and traditional measures of spiritual progress. For yogis, success has very little to do with fame or with all of the trappings of spiritual capitalism. It has more to do with how much transformation they have achieved within themselves.

This is why true spiritual people make a distinction between worldly dharma and holy Dharma. We may do many seemingly holy Dharmic activities, but if they are for fame and other material gain, then they are not truly holy. We must know the correct methods.

Whether something will become holy Dharma or worldly dharma depends on how much transformation it will inspire. Yogis and true masters place all of their emphasis on holy Dharma. They actually see the eight worldly dharmas as a poison on the spiritual path. Fame is one of these poisons. Making a name for ourselves through our spiritual endeavors can actually pollute our spiritual path.

Holy beings are beyond any attachments to name and recognition. They are beyond all pride and avarice. Without that inner freedom, fame and attention can easily corrupt you. Fame can undo any positive transformation, unless you have gone beyond it.

Milarepa was one of the greatest yogis. He meditated in a cave for years, eating only nettles, renouncing everything. He said it was easy to let go of home and family and material things. But he said it was more difficult to let go of identity and not to react if someone said something bad about him. This was the most difficult attachment to overcome.

Names and reputation are very important to us. If we think about it, it is actually absurd that we are so attached to a name. We didn't bring this name with us from a previous life. This was not inherently our name. Somebody gave it to us at birth. So why do we feel so happy when someone says something complimentary about us? Why are we so destroyed when someone says something negative about us?

We are attached to our names because we think that they represent our selves. The more self-attachment there is, the more reactive and worldly we become. According to Buddhism, this whole samsaric world is merely an extension of our ego. We extend our territory all around us, claiming the world in relation to our sense of ownership. We say "my house," "my state," "my country," "my children," and so forth.

The bigger our ego grows, the more we want to extend its territory. This is why one of the great Indian masters said, "The rulers, all of the most powerful kings, possess the biggest egos." They want to subjugate everything and make everyone else become part of their ego. They become egomaniacs.

It is important to clarify here that a healthy ego is not a bad thing. We need confidence in ourselves in order to have a good career and do good work in the world. Even meditation and spiritual practice require a healthy ego and a belief in our abilities.

But whether that ego will become maniacal and destructive or help us to know ourselves depends on our level of spiritual transformation. This is the distinction we need to make. The Buddha used the ego to practice and to transcend. Genghis Khan and other ruthless dictators used the ego to kill millions of people and to bring tremendous pain and suffering. We need a healthy ego to begin with, but how we use it will make all the difference.

Buddhists have used the ego to see the true nature of ego itself. Once they saw the true nature of their own ego and self, they could see the true nature of others. This is how they achieved freedom. Ruthless dictators and corrupt politicians may have extended their egotistical territory around the world, but they die trapped, miserable, and paralyzed by their own creations.

They are miserable because they thought they would become so powerful, but in the end, they realize that they don't have control over their own lives. Regardless of all that they have conquered and attained, they have no power to escape the pain of their own death.

Once you are able to recognize the phases of the ego, and when the ego dissolves, that is the beginning of your recognition of the inner space. Once you have this experience, you make it part of your realization. But that dissolution of the ego is not some end result. You have to keep on meditating on that realization again and again until you reach the state of enlightenment in which you even see the egolessness of the ego. That egoless state is the nature of the mind.

Even after the Buddha was enlightened, he still hesitated to share his realization. He waited forty-nine days. People came to him and said, "Now you are the Buddha! Now you are enlightened! Please share your teachings with us!" The Buddha said, "Although I have realized this great wisdom, there are not many who can understand what I have realized."

So the Buddha waited for forty-nine days until he met some chosen disciples who were ready and worthy of hearing his teachings. When you are beginning to experience some inner transformation, then the Dharma will become more and more valuable. Teachers and buddhas may be teaching the same thing, but according to the different levels of readiness, and according to how much meditation students have done, each student will benefit from the same teachings in different ways.

This is why there is a saying in Tibet that you should listen to and study the same teachings again and again. According to your transformation, every time you listen, you will gain something new. The teacher is teaching the same thing, but according to your inner conditions, your experience will be very different.

Even in universities we can see that although hundreds of students may attend the same class, some will excel, and some will fail. The teacher has been teaching the same class to everyone, but each student has responded from an individual level of understanding and attention.

Though one realizes that ultimately both self and other do
    not exist,
relatively, think on the great benefit of migrating beings.

This is an important point to reiterate. If you are enlightened, your ego and self have dissolved, which means the concept of the other has also disappeared. If we have a right hand, then we must have a left hand. But if the right hand is gone, how will we project the left?

When you have dissolved the self and ego, you go beyond time and space, and you cease to project others. This is why even inner and outer space become the same. When you are enlightened, you see the unity of inner and outer space. You realize that your inner nature is the same as the inner nature of everything around you.

Enlightenment is a unified state in which there is no distance between self and other. But as we have discussed, buddhas still have compassion for all sentient beings. That compassion is coming from profound wisdom.

When Virupa says, "relatively, think on the great benefit of migrating beings," he is referring to this compassion of the buddhas. A buddha's most compassionate act is teaching. You might expect that if the Buddha were here, and if someone were starving, that the Buddha would give that person food. The Buddha himself was once a beggar, so surely he would understand this suffering!

But what the Buddha realized is that the teachings can inspire spiritual practice in a person, and that practice has the power to free a person, not only from suffering, but from the very causes of suffering. That is why the Buddha's teachings are his highest expressions of compassion. When buddhas give a teaching, they don't teach out of emotion. Their compassion comes from wisdom, which is limitless. The buddhas have compassion without an object.

The first level of compassion is empathy. As we have discussed, when we see someone experiencing pain and suffering, we feel this person's pain. That is compassion based on feeling and empathy. But that feeling of another's pain is not what's actually going to have the power to help that person. By feeling their pain and suffering, what are we doing to relieve their suffering?

The next stage of compassion is more active. If the person is sick, we try to provide some medicine. We try to take some action to treat the symptoms. Maybe that medicine can relieve that person's pain temporarily, but ultimately the person is still going to become old and sick and die. The medicine won't free that person from death.

What has the power to free that person from death and birth? The highest level of compassion will free us from birth and death because it is working at the causal level. According to this understanding, the Buddha's teaching is the highest expression of compassion because it is based on wisdom. Only wisdom has the power to free us from all of the causes and conditions of our suffering.

Every form of suffering has a cause. So whatever can uproot the cause is the most powerful offering. This is why the Buddha's most compassionate act is teaching. Even now, thousands of years after the Buddha's life, his compassion is still working for us. We are still acquiring wisdom through the Dharma. The Buddha's teachings are still inspiring our meditation practice.

If the Buddha's compassion had manifested only in a material way, like giving food to the hungry, it would not have had a lasting effect. We would not necessarily have learned how to free ourselves from the causes of suffering.

But the Buddha's teachings have helped us look at the sources of suffering. In this way, the gift of the Dharma is with us even now, showing us ways to transform our own suffering. Through methods of purification, we can slowly diminish our obscurations.

When we are purified, the universe will also be purified, and we will see the pure realms. In an enlightened state, we can interact with the buddhas. But until then, we rely on the Buddha's teachings through the generations. Even now the Buddha's words encourage our practice and alleviate so much suffering by showing us the root causes of that pain.

Of all of the Buddha's teachings, the most important is the law of karma. Until we are realized beings like the Buddha, or like Mahasiddha Virupa, we must respect the laws of cause and effect.

Enlightened beings can live outside of karmic law. Their actions may even seem strange or unusual at times. This is sometimes referred to as *crazy wisdom*. If we look at Virupa's life story, there are some feats and unusual activities that he undertook in order to teach that may seem unethical from our relative perspective.

But at our level, we must honor the natural law of karma. This is not just a theory. Karma is the truth of cause and result. If we do anything in anger, we must know that that anger will bring pain and suffering to ourselves and to others. And if we do something out of faith, then that will bring more merit and positivity.

Relatively, in the conditioned world of interdependency, we cannot break the natural law of karma. We must accumulate more positive merit to purify our negative karma. But once we become the embodiment of the accumulation of merit, that is, a fully realized being, then we can go beyond both positive and negative to see emptiness.

Until then we must rely on the Buddha's teachings, which at their very essence are teachings on karma. All of our spiritual practice revolves around this law of karma. The whole concept of accumulating merit is based on this understanding of interdependency and on cause and result.

We must have the highest regard for this natural law. Karma is not projected. It is not created by the Buddha. It is a fact based on our own thinking and what we do physically, mentally, and verbally. This is why the great Tibetan masters have said, "How you feel now is the result of what you have done in the past. And what you do now will determine your future."

Karma works in the three times of past, present, and future. Past causes have present results. Those present results will either exhaust the karma or create another cause for future results. What the present results may create is completely up to us.

If we have good karma from the past, we may be experiencing good results in the present. Maybe we want to use those good results to generate even more good results in the future. But if we have bad karma and presently are suffering bad results, then the best thing we can do is stop the negative cycle in the present moment. Instead of letting those negativities become the cause for future suffering, we have the choice to purify ourselves and transform.

19

Think on the Great Benefit of Migrating Beings

LET US RETURN TO these profound lines from the doha:

Though one realizes that ultimately both self and other
do not exist,
relatively, think on the great benefit of migrating beings.

Through the study of Buddhist philosophy and through meditative reflection we can come to the realization that the nature of the entire phenomenal world is emptiness. Ultimate truth is emptiness, and in it both self and other are dissolved.

Once we come to this conclusion about emptiness and conduct our lives accordingly, there is a real risk. If we conduct our lives with this belief in emptiness but without the stabilization of wisdom, there is a danger that we will disregard how karma works. There is a grave risk that we will even disregard the law of karma itself and how relativity functions.

So although the nature of ultimate truth is an empty state in which self, other, and all phenomena are equalized, until we are fully enlightened, we have to live according to the law of karma. Even if we become very good scholars with an intellectual understanding of emptiness, we must ground that emptiness in experience.

We have to engage in all formal spiritual practices if we want to realize wisdom. Wisdom is vital in order to complement the dangers of emptiness. Wisdom is the key to creating any true transformation in ourselves, and understanding karma encourages all of our positive spiritual endeavors.

It is important to monitor whether or not knowledge is helping to transform our minds. If knowledge is actually making us prouder and more arrogant, then the more we learn, the more narcissistic we will become. And the more we learn, the more we will esteem and defend our own conclusions. The Buddha cautioned that this clinging to our own opinions is one of the worst wrong views we can hold.

The Buddha described five different wrong views. This particular wrong view of esteeming your own conclusions is especially intended for scholars and academics. If we are poor, we may not have the luxury of a lot of time to study and formulate ideas. All these "isms" flourish only when our stomachs are full and we have a roof over our heads. If our basic needs are being met and we're not focused on survival, we have the time to fight over ideas.

The Buddha taught that in samsara there are two main reasons people fight. The most common is that all people and even animals fight over feelings. If we are lacking intelligence, then all of our fights may be based on feelings, both mental and physical.

All of the economic systems, whether it be capitalism, communism, or socialism, are based on the idea that we are only living for this one life. These systems do not function with any regard to past lives or future rebirths. These structures arise based on the flow and control of material things, and so much of this, at its root, is based on feeling. Citizens want to feel prosperous, safe, or happy. Leaders want to feel power and control the world's natural resources.

So we fight over resources in our attempt to feel good. There is a class struggle as people vie for opportunities and security. There are constant arguments between individuals over their miscommunicated feelings. Everything is based on feelings.

Feelings, as we know, are blind. Feelings don't have much logic or reason behind them. Buddhists would say that what we find agreeable to our physical bodies is based on our karma. What are the elements that our bodies find compatible? And what are the corresponding mental factors we find pleasing?

The Buddha said that the second cause of arguments, which arise in samsara, are arguments over ideas. This level of intellectual argument is a bit more elevated than the level of feeling. We can find scholars and yogis debating their views in far more philosophical kinds of disputes.

We can see that most of the fights between religions are based on ideas. The Buddha said that we cling to our ideas because we have become extremists due to our attachment to ideations. We need only think on the terrible suffering inflicted on heretics or the terrorism and atrocities throughout history to see the extremism these religious views create. Even Buddhists are at risk of becoming too attached to emptiness if there is not sufficient transformation within us!

So why do we have to try to be pure? Why can't we just do whatever we feel like doing and pursue whatever sensual pleasures we think will make us happy without regard for moral conduct or karma? Why can't we live according to the philosophy of the Charvakas?

The Charvakas believe only in this one life and in the pursuit of feeling good. They do not believe in karma. They disregard natural law. They believe you should do whatever makes you happy in the present.

So when we become extremists based on feelings, then we become very narcissistic and do whatever makes us personally happy. And when scholars become attached to their view, they also risk becoming extremists. In Buddhist philosophy we find that most intellectual extremes revolve around the idea of emptiness.

All four of the different levels of Buddhist philosophy are focused on recognizing emptiness. In the beginning, we try to prove the emptiness of matter. And then we try to prove the empty nature of the mind. Then we try to go beyond that. But ultimately, if we even become attached to the view that is beyond the extremes, then we are still caught in an extreme view because of that attachment! And if we disregard karma, then we will not transform.

We must remember that the whole purpose of studying Buddhist philosophy is to help our practice, which will then transform us. When we do the sadhana practice, it leads us through stages of spiritual development. First, we have the purification and accumulation of merit through all of the preliminary practices. Then we have the accumulation of wisdom in the sadhana. Next, out of emptiness we become the deity. And ultimately, we dissolve the deity back into emptiness.

So in our lives, if we merely study emptiness and we don't use that knowledge to transform ourselves, then we don't have any real spiritual view. Knowledge of emptiness alone won't help us to progress. We must cultivate our practice and develop a deep understanding of wisdom and compassion.

If the study of Buddhist philosophy remains purely academic and is not brought into actual practice, then there will be no spiritual cultivation. And if we don't believe in karma, then we won't believe in rebirth. And without a sense of rebirth and of cause and effect over time, we will have no incentive to accumulate merit, and we will not purify or transform ourselves.

If we conduct our philosophical studies with the understanding that this knowledge is all being gained to support our practice, then we will benefit. Reflecting on the knowledge that we acquire can inspire us and encourage our growth. But the main goal should always be the meditation practice itself.

Practice has to start from where we are in our lives right now. At our level, we are still living in relativity based on karma. So we must reflect on the relative world. We must examine how this cosmos and this universe are created and experienced individually by us. We must reflect on the causes of all of our emotions and actions.

If we look inside ourselves, we begin to see the sources for all of our feelings and ideas. And if we investigate our experience of the relative world in this way, we come to the conclusion that there must be some natural law. We see that karma is driving this interdependency.

By acknowledging and accepting relativity, we thereby accept karma. We can personally experience karma based on our feelings and experiences. The more positive things we do, the more positive results we will experience.

This does not mean that our lives will somehow immediately become easy as long as we do good deeds. And it doesn't mean that terrible things won't still happen. But if our approach to these events grows more and more transformative, then negativities will diminish. As Virupa has said, suffering can be a tremendous teacher. And the more positivity we cultivate in response to the difficulties in our lives, the more merit we accumulate and the more our karma is purified.

The accumulation of merit cultivates more spiritual qualities such as loving-kindness and compassion. And the more we perfect these spiritual qualities, the more fruition they will bring. This is why Buddhist spiritual practice is arranged in a particular order, with the accumulation of merit being the vital foundation for all other practices. We must purify our destructive emotions and habitual patterns before we can progress.

We must understand that karma is very important. And conducting our lives according to the natural law of karma is crucial. It is only through honoring this natural law that we will have the opportunity to recognize the spirituality inside us.

As the Buddha realized, by nature our minds are peaceful, loving, and compassionate. Our true nature is one of wisdom, but it is buried by all of these destructive emotions and karmic propensities. This is why we must do all of these spiritual practices in order to know our buddha nature.

Here in the midst of our lives, we may not see that true nature of love because we are filled with all of these other feelings of anger and resentment. We are always experiencing some combination of conflicting emotions. Although the nature of our mind is full of compassion, it is often clouded over by our more passionate attachments. Instead of knowing the wisdom of our nature, we are often filled with the confusion and ignorance of not understanding our lives or actions.

These conflicting feelings are all circumstantial. By nature our minds are pure. By nature we have all of these spiritual qualities inside us. By relying on the natural law of karma and perfecting our lives according to that understanding, we will increasingly discover these pure qualities inside of us. That is the transformation.

In that transformation, when we see wisdom, then like the Buddha taught, that wisdom will give rise to compassion. But that compassion is free of all attachment. It is limitless and unconditioned. It will be of endless benefit to migrating beings. So although we may gain some knowledge of emptiness, until we are fully awakened, we have to rely on relativity and the law of karma. And through our spiritual practice, we have to accumulate more and more merit. Without this accumulation of merit, and without a strong spiritual foundation, we will fall into an extreme view of emptiness and nihilism.

The opposite of nihilism is the extreme view of eternalism. In Buddhism there are four extremes you can fall into, and if you are trapped by any one of these extreme views, it will become an obstacle to your liberation.

The accumulation of merit can guard against these potential extremes. Now, these words "accumulation of merit" may sound very religious. Or we may mistake this accumulation as an act of penance, motivated by guilt and fear. Or we may misunderstand it as a sort of bargain we are making based on some philosophical theory or superstition. But really, if we look at the essence of what the accumulation of merit is, it is simply about changing our actions. And it is about ripening our conditions for further spiritual transformation.

If we have been acting out of anger, we can begin to counter that by acting more from a place of love. If we are living with a lot of attachment and addiction, then we can begin to act with more compassion.

The accumulation of merit is a way to change our individual patterns and personalities.

Often in our lives our conflicting feelings and actions have actually been accumulating more anger, stronger desire, and more ignorance in us. Accumulating merit is the antidote to these three destructive emotions. Each small positive choice we make, when faced with these negative emotions, becomes an antidote. And as this positivity grows, it begins to fundamentally change our lives one small step at a time.

As these profound changes unfold, negativities and destructive emotions will cease. For the first time, we may actually experience free will. We may have freedom not only from these destructive emotions but also from the actions created by those emotions. So that's why the accumulation of merit, based on relativity, is so important.

> Though one has the confidence
> that does not depend on the guidance of others,
> place the very kind guru on the crown of one's head.

As we have discussed, these dohas are coming from Virupa's experience of mahamudra. Mahamudra is the realization of the union of clarity and emptiness, cultivated through sadhana practice. When we practice the generation and completion stages of the sadhana, and when we see the true nature of our minds, then we see mahamudra.

The tantric path of Tibetan Buddhism is all based on the guru's presence. In the Theravada or Hinayana path there is no concept of the guru. The Hinayana refers to the teacher as a spiritual guide. And in Mahayana Buddhism the guru is also known as a spiritual friend.

The concept of the guru is only found in the Vajrayana. And the reason the guru is so critical is because it is the guru who can introduce us to our true nature. It is during the tantric empowerments that the guru shows us the nature of our minds.

Some initiations have three or four individual empowerments relating to enlightened body, speech, mind, and the fourth, respectively. And through these spiritual means, through these ancient rituals, preserved and passed down from a lineage of masters, we gain a glimpse of the clear and empty nature of our minds.

During the initiation, you are introduced to the buddha nature of your body, speech, and mind. You are also given the method for how to carry what was introduced to you into meditation and the path. And by relying on the path, you can reach buddhahood. You can achieve that complete transformation.

So the guru is very important, being the one who shows us this true nature of our minds. And the Vajrayana practice of guru yoga is also a very powerful method in one's spiritual path. Guru yoga is part of the uncommon foundation practices. For people who have unshakeable faith and devotion to the guru, it is said that guru yoga alone can inspire complete awakening.

For those who don't have unshakeable faith and devotion, guru yoga can simply be a foundational practice for accumulating merit. It is said that the only way to awaken the buddha nature or wisdom within us is through the accumulation of merit and through the blessings of the guru. Due to your faith and devotion, the guru's blessing is transferred to you. Then your ordinary mind and the Buddha's wisdom become one. These are the ways to achieve enlightenment. One cannot reach enlightenment based only on knowledge.

Since the guru is vital to our Vajrayana practice, we must make sure that we don't misunderstand the role of the guru or become attached to the guru as in an ordinary relationship. Also, due to our experiences here in the West and the stories we've heard of false gurus behaving in destructive ways, we may even bring some fear to our concept of the guru. We may feel that following a guru is almost like joining a cult.

In Vajrayana Buddhism, however, the guru represents the entire lineage from the Buddha until now. The guru is emblematic of an unbroken line of teachings passed from master to disciple for thousands of years. The guru represents that lineage of wisdom and compassion.

When we are in the presence of the guru, it becomes easier to believe in the reality of wisdom and compassion. Through taking refuge and through doing guru yoga, we are still relying on the relative guru. But with more practice and more blessings, we will ultimately see the true nature of our own minds. That true nature is the ultimate guru. So all of these practices are ultimately intended to allow us to recognize the guru within us.

This is an important point to make. Since the whole purpose of devotion to the guru is ultimately to see the guru within us, we cannot practice with a false attachment to something outside of us. We must do guru yoga with the understanding that we are buddhas. We all have buddha nature. All of our practices are intended to create stronger connections with our buddha nature.

This is the reason why we visualize the guru in the form of Vajradhara Buddha when we do guru yoga rather than in some ordinary human form. By nature, we are all buddhas. The more we make a connection to the enlightened vision of the Buddha by visualizing the guru as a buddha, the more drawn we will be to the buddha nature inside us.

This ultimate buddha nature of our minds has very little to do with the dualistic objects we project during our visualization practice. It has more to do with the inner process of purification. The more that our air, other elements and channels, and our mind of awakening are purified, the more space there will be for our buddha nature to emerge. Then we will see freedom.

If we can grow to see the purity inside ourselves, then we will see the purity around us also. If we have that inner freedom, then we will also feel free in the outside world. These are the skills and methods that we need to cultivate in order to see more purity in the world around us.

This is the reason why, even if we are great scholars filled with confidence in our knowledge, if we don't have faith, we cannot achieve buddhahood. We must rely on faith to truly awaken to our nature.

Some may think that Buddhism's emphasis on faith is illogical. But really all logic leads back to faith. We are so accustomed to proving why something makes us happy based on our brains that it may be very hard to accept the power of faith. But when faith enters through the heart, it has the force to change people much more quickly.

Although the Buddha encouraged practice arising from both the brain and the heart, it is the heart-oriented practice based on faith that can transform us much more quickly. Vajrayana is a spiritual path that aims at the heart with devotion. Although we make hundreds of choices using reason, ultimately, we tend to make the biggest decisions of our lives based on our hearts. Our hearts seem to have the biggest impact on who we love and how our lives unfold.

When Virupa says to "place the very kind guru on the crown of one's head," this is so that the guru can transform us as soon as possible. Our very strong devotion and faith can become the conditions to receive blessings and to merge with wisdom instantaneously. Even if one experiences a single moment of strong faith during an empowerment, that faith has the power to cut through all of these mental obscurations.

Normally our minds are filled with thoughts, and in that constant mental activity we rarely see any glimpse of the inner space. Occasionally, when we are completely lost in an object, our self and ego diminish, and we may have a fleeting moment of peace.

This is similar to receiving the blessings of the guru. When we bring our very strong focus and devotion to the object of our faith, the guru, then we can also be shown that inner space very quickly. We may access it much more easily than through meditation alone. When we become one with the object of faith, we receive all of its blessings.

And with those blessings, we can then see the inner space. The inner space is the nature of your ordinary mind, seen with the guru's wisdom—the Buddha's wisdom. This is what occurs when we do the empowerment of enlightened wisdom. And this is also the blessing we receive through strong faith and devotion. When we place the guru on the crown of our heads, our ordinary mind and the guru's wisdom become inseparable.

The one with attachment and grasping will debate everyone.

As we have discussed, when we have a strong attachment to our point of view and when we cling to our conclusions, then we will constantly defend our ideas. Whenever people are arguing all the time, it means they are very attached to their particular point of view. They may actually constantly need someone to argue with! If their opponent is kind, they may still fight them. People with attachment to their views might even argue with the Buddha if they could!

Productive arguments to discover the truth can be good. But arguments for the sake of defending our points of view may actually further obscure the truth. Many times, we have philosophical arguments instead of the practice of meditation, and then there is no end to the argument. We cannot see the ultimate truth through debate.

So much of our legal process and other disputes in society don't actually have much to do with the truth. These disputes are based much more on evidence and proof. We rely on proof to solve a case, but there is rarely any real truth reached in these processes.

Ultimate truth cannot be proven with words or evidence. How can you prove emptiness when it is beyond words, thoughts, and everything? You cannot. Proof only exists at the relative level. That is why most interpersonal, judicial, and philosophical arguments will never end. In the relative world, arguments are a way of expressing attachment to your point of view and imposing your point of view on others.

All of these disputes play out in the realm of attachment and aversion. Without meditative practice there will be so many debates and arguments based on our attachment and aversion. Sometimes, to prove our point if our ego is very strong, we may even deviate from the teachings of the spiritual tradition and from the lineage. This is why Virupa says,

Contrary conduct not in conformity with tradition is a
   deviation.

Because of our limited perspective, we may see some human quality, something fallible in the teachings, and we may decide that the whole tradition is of no value.

The only way to prove the validity of the Buddhist teachings is to ascertain that they are coming from the enlightened Buddha. This is why lineage is so crucial. We must rely on an unbroken lineage of masters in order to know that the purity of the teachings remains. When the lineage is pure, then we can practice with confidence, knowing that we can reach enlightenment because we are following the Buddha's experience.

But if we don't have a pure lineage to rely on, then whatever knowledge we base our practices on may not be valid. If the teachings are not coming from an enlightened source, then how can we be confident the teachings will help us to achieve liberation? A teacher who is not enlightened may create many wonderful words and teach with great conviction and charisma, but there is a very real danger that those teachings are not giving us a valid method.

That is why Virupa is saying that if we don't practice according to the lineage and tradition, then there is a deviation. All Tibetan masters try to prove the validity of their practice or lineage because they know these methods must be coming from a realized source in order to be effective.

Many masters are opposed to teachings without a genuine lineage going back to the Buddha. Sakya Pandita was completely against any new teachings being created, that is, teachings that could not be traced back to a highly enlightened master. When you know the purity of the lineage, you can have much greater confidence in the practice. You can be assured that these words and methods have not been created by someone with the wrong motivation or intentions. You can be confident that they are an effective means to liberation.

Now, throughout Buddhist history in Tibet and India, there have been various ways in which the teachings have appeared. There are the hidden teachings known as the *termas*, which some masters have claimed to receive in their dreams or to have found in Dharma texts hidden in a log or in a cave somewhere.

Some of these discovered treasure teachings are actually valid.

Padmasambhava and other enlightened masters did indeed hide some teachings in advance, warning that great destruction would come in the future. But there have also been cases where people faked these discoveries in order to promote themselves. This is why masters like Sakya Pandita stressed the importance of lineage in preserving the purity of the Buddha's words.

Now some have taken issue with this emphasis on lineage because it all gets traced back to the Buddha in India. Some people feel that if we view all of these teachings as arising from India, then there is no credit given to Tibet. Some people who lean more toward nationalism want to feel pride in Tibet's spiritual identity, and they don't want to trace all of this wisdom culture to India.

But for the spiritualists who only wish to achieve buddhahood, nation is meaningless. To the spiritual person, whether something is coming from an enlightened source is far more important than what country it is from. But sometimes there are tensions between the nationalists and the spiritualists over this issue.

As practitioners, though, we have to choose a practice that has an unbroken lineage coming from the Buddha. Until we are fully transformed, we must be able to put complete faith in the teachings of the lineage.

Imagine, for example, that you really want to go to New York. Some people have worked very hard to create maps and guidebooks about New York. Because these resources come from an authority, we don't need to make our own maps; we can just follow the directions and focus on driving.

Likewise, all of these spiritual maps—all of these methods we are taught—come from beings who have worked very hard to become enlightened. They have then created maps and guides for us. If we rely on them and put our complete faith in them, then we will have a good journey.

On the other hand, some people want to know everything before they can place their trust in something. Some people might need to know how to build a car before they would even agree to drive it to New York! Some might want to rebuild all the roads themselves and rewrite all the maps.

But how can we progress if we don't put some faith in a process that others have shown us to be valid? How can we move forward in our journey if we don't trust the roads and maps that have been passed down to us? This is why lineage is so vital to our spiritual development.

20

Difference Is Liberated in Its Own State

Since there is no object of perception and no perceiver,
difference is liberated in its own state.

For an enlightened being like Mahasiddha Virupa, this freedom from perception and perceiver makes perfect sense. Virupa is liberated. He has gone beyond both subject and object. But this may not be the case for us. At our level there are still perceptions and perceivers, and that is how we function.

There have even been studies lately proving that conventionally attractive people seem to have an advantage over others when it comes to success. This is proof that our eyes are eager for pleasing objects. Whatever is more beautiful sells more quickly and is more popular. Beautiful music becomes successful. Even beautiful food may seem to be more delicious to us because our eyes are informing our experience.

But we must remember that nothing is perfect in samsara. What is beautiful one moment can easily change depending on our inner conditions, projections, and the actions of others. Everything has two sides.

According to Buddhist beliefs, beauty is the result of merit and good karma. The Buddha said that we become more beautiful if we practice patience. So beautiful people must have practiced a lot of patience in a past life!

The more patience we practice, the more beautiful we become. And the more beautiful we are, the more popular we may be. We may use that popularity to make others happy, and as a result, it may be a bit easier for us to get things done.

Now on the other hand, we know all too well that even a very beautiful person can become angry and can suddenly seem very ugly to us. So if beauty is the result of patience, then ugliness is the result of anger. The angrier we are, the more unattractive we will appear, and the less popular we will be.

What is interesting to observe is how one person can be perceived in two different ways according to their emotions. As the saying goes, "beauty is in the eye of the beholder." As a result, it is very difficult to agree on any kind of universal definition of attractiveness or ugliness because they are different for every person and dependent on so many conditions.

How do we determine what is beautiful music or what is delicious food? In general, it seems we enjoy experiences and objects that are agreeable to our senses. When they are agreeable, these objects tend to make us feel happy. So as long as we are made happy by an object, we will consider it good. But the minute it becomes disagreeable, we will be angry and experience pain and frustration. At that point, we will want nothing to do with that object.

So what is projected between the perceiver and perception depends largely on our inner conditions and on our emotions. All of this dualism of subject and object has much more to do with our inner conditions than with the outer objects themselves.

But we always tend to think that the reality of the experience exists in those outer objects. If something is disagreeable to us, we automatically assume that the inherent qualities of the object are ugly. Rarely do we realize that it is our perception based on our emotions and inner conditions that is causing the object to be either attractive or unappealing.

In our lives, both the perceiver who is the subject and the perceived object are very powerful. They are powerful because we are driven by desire. With desire we pursue so many objects. When we consume them, they make us happy, and we feel pleasure, which is why we pursue them endlessly. That is why we are caught in a vicious cycle that extends across the three times: past, present, and future. As long as we are in this dualism of perceiver and perception, there will always be something for us to chase after.

This relationship with desirable objects doesn't just exist in the moment we are pursuing or consuming them. While we are engaged with these objects, we may feel very satisfied, pleased, and beautiful. But when the objects we've enjoyed are gone, we still carry them in our heads and in our hearts. They may actually take on way more power in our minds after they've been consumed than they did while we were actively chasing them. This is because we are still desiring them, and we are stuck with the memories inside of us, which cannot recreate that experience.

So we are tortured because now not only is the object inside us a memory, it is also gone, and we are still as restless as we were before. Maybe we are even more restless because we want to have that experience again so badly, and we cannot make that happen. This is the nature of so much of our life in samsara.

In our Buddhist practice, we have developed very skillful means to counter this cycle. Even when we set up our shrine offerings, they include objects for all of the different senses. So by offering these sense objects, we are symbolizing the transformation of our basic emotions. The desire with which we consume everything can be brought into our spiritual practice and transformed.

We all know that we cannot live without eating and drinking. At some point, can we manage to consume and enjoy something and then let it go easily without it increasing our desire? Or will consumption only make us more attached to the desirable experiences, which we will continue to chase endlessly?

As for the great mahasiddhas like Virupa, such enlightened beings have seen the true nature of subject and the object, and since there is no longer a perception or a perceiver, they are liberated.

In the *Heart Sutra* it says "form is emptiness." But that realization is not sufficient. The sutra goes on to say "emptiness is form." But even that is not enough, so the sutra says "form is no other than emptiness. Emptiness is no other than form."

When we see the unity of subject and object, the unity of appearance and emptiness, we have gone beyond both. Until we can go beyond both, our lives will be characterized by this drama between subject and object. And the more that desirable emotions are evoked by an object, the more beautiful it will become. This is why beauty is so highly esteemed in samsaric life.

But for yogis, beauty and ugliness are no different. They are the same in the sense that their nature is appearance and emptiness. Yogis have gone beyond both because the subject, who is the projector, is gone. Therefore the projected object is also gone, and the emotions that arise when subject and object are seen as separate have dissolved.

When attachment is gone, the desire with which you perceive is also gone. This is why for yogis there is no such thing as beauty or ugliness. What they see instead is the perfection in the ugliness and the perfection in the beauty. Perfection lies in both.

Beauty and ugliness are only projections based on our inner emotions. Even if someone very beautiful is sitting next to us, if we are having a bad day or feeling angry, we will not see that person's beauty. Or if the beautiful person becomes angry, we will also not see their beauty.

So even in one object, according to the state of our emotions, we will see either beauty or ugliness. This is why illusion works. It's why movies are so engaging and can so readily manipulate our perceptions throughout the plot. Illusion always works, and the biggest illusion of all is samsara.

For the meditator who has gone beyond and who has seen the fourth level of the *Heart Sutra* in which "emptiness is no other than form, form is no other than emptiness," this is the state of mahamudra.

From this state, the yogi sees everything with equanimity. There is no such thing as something to be accepted or rejected. There is no longer something agreeable or something disagreeable. They are equal.

This is why in the *Four Limitless Prayers* the highest wish for beings is equanimity. Equanimity is higher than love, which makes you happy. Equanimity is higher than compassion and joy. It is the highest level because equanimity is the experience of seeing the union of wisdom and compassion.

In order to progress spiritually, we have to start where we are, with our current experiences and feelings. But we should never presume that what we experience and what we feel is the ultimate truth. These emotions and intuitions may be so strong. They may be a part of every aspect of our lives and may appear so real, but they are not reliable. There is a whole other dimension to experience that unfolds at the level of equanimity.

When you experience everything with equanimity, there is no difference between perception and perceiver. Everything is the same, which is why Virupa says "difference is liberated in its own state."

Both beauty and ugliness are empty. Beauty is no other than emptiness, and emptiness is no other than beauty. Likewise, ugliness is no other than emptiness, and emptiness is no other than ugliness. There is no difference between them.

At this level, then, even between wisdom and craziness there is no difference. This is why some of the great mystics and mahasiddhas perform all manner of crazy activities out of their wisdom. They appear crazy to us because they've gone beyond the normal conduct and etiquette of the relative world. Only another highly evolved person can tell the difference between a mahasiddha and a madman!

Since the experiencer is destroyed,
one is freed from all effort and practice.

Many yogis think that the moment of enlightenment is the ultimate death. Now, we are not at that enlightened level yet. We are alive and hold certain concepts about death. But for an enlightened yogi, death is not actually death. Death is still living. That is the difference between an ordinary person's way of looking at life and death and an enlightened yogi's understanding. For highly realized beings, death is not the end of their life; death is not a cessation. The greatest death is when they achieve nirvana. Then they are completely gone. But we are not mahasiddhas, and we are not enlightened. So what we experience is the ordinary cycle of birth and death.

A great saint once said, "Until death, there is no end to our activities." We see this in our own lives. We always seem to need to keep busy doing something. And when we have nothing to do, when we feel bored, we actually invent activities in order to distract ourselves! We would rather make up some activity than just sit still. And every busy activity will create another corresponding chore because busyness is part of a chain of cause and result.

So we create the conditions for something to occur. Then the result of that occurrence will make us do something else, which will create more conditions for the next activity. There is no end to this cycle! Because we exist, we need a home. We need to eat. We desire family. We create a community. All of these things keep evolving and expanding. But all of this effort we expend becomes a great source of stress and suffering.

This is why the Buddha said that life is suffering. Most of the activities we do in samsara are driven by our afflictive emotions. Because of this, even apparently pleasurable activities become the cause of so much stress. For us it isn't until the day we die that our activities are finished. We wait until death to realize we have no use for the roof over our heads and no use for the physical body. The day the experiencer is gone is the day when our efforts stop. All our accumulations of worldly objects cease.

According to the Buddhist understanding, however, even after we die and leave our home, family, and physical body, we still carry things into death in our mental continuum. The strongest impressions that life has imprinted on our mind streams will go with us into the bardo and even into the next rebirth.

If we spend our lives treasuring our attachment to our families and possessions instead of to the Buddha, then that attachment will follow us into our next life. We will carry traces of that desire in our mental continuum, and those memories will force us to pursue all of those objects of our attachment over and over again. We will be driven to attain a new family, another home, and all of the things we held so dear to us in our previous lives.

When will this cycle end? Each time one life ends, we will be forced by desire to take rebirth, and we will immediately begin trying to attain the things we desired all over again. Only when we achieve great awakening and see mahamudra will we be freed from this cycle.

This is why the yogis and mahasiddhas say that the greatest death is when you achieve nirvana. They say this because only then will samsara cease. Until enlightenment, even death won't truly free us, since we will be compelled to quickly start the cycle again.

Everything stems from what we carry in our minds. For those yogis who have achieved enlightenment, even death is not really an end to anything. It is just another feature of samsaric life. Death just marks the end of one chapter and the beginning of the next.

The experience after death is very mysterious to us because we can't remember it. But according to the *Tibetan Book of the Dead*, the best way to learn about death is through observing our sleep. They say that sleep is the gateway to understanding death.

Sleep is the window through which we can witness the experience of death, and our waking hours are a window into our experience of rebirth. Death is only a short period of sleep before we wake up again, in a new birth, in a new body. But most of us lose consciousness at the time of death, and we have no memory of that sleeping stage or of the dreamlike experiences of the bardo. And when we arise in a new body, we have no clear idea of where our mind has come from.

Those who are enlightened don't experience life or death the way we do. For us, we still have no choice. We have to sleep or die. We have to wake up or take rebirth. The sun rises, the sun sets—this is the nature of our unawakened lives.

But for those who have realized the state of mahamudra, the "experiencer is destroyed" because the individual is destroyed. Nirvana means the destruction of the person. Enlightenment is that destruction of the personality and of all of its attachment to the phenomenal world. When that individuality is destroyed, one is free from all efforts and practice. There is no more dreaming to propel one toward the creation of more forms and activities. One has gone beyond.

So although Virupa is teaching out of his profound realization, and although we are not up to that level yet, we should not confine our minds to the limits of our own experience. There is so much more to become aware of.

Virupa's words can encourage us to meditate more, and they can give us a glimpse of what is possible. Then we need to do all of these sadhanas, visualizations, and other spiritual practices. Until we achieve those ultimate realizations through our meditation, our lives will continue to be a vicious cycle.

> Since the result to attain is destroyed,
> one is liberated from all hope and fear.

Our lives right now are very goal-oriented, very result-oriented. Due to this, we are filled with hope and fear about the future. We are filled with expectations about what we wish to achieve. But in many respects these hopes are actually rooted in emotions of attachment and greed.

So why is there so much greed and fear in our lives? And why do we accept it as the norm? Even if we look at someone incredibly successful and wealthy, we see how this success also breeds insecurity.

The more we have, the more we also feel is at stake. The more wealth we amass, the more expectations we have for it to fulfill us, and the more insecurity we have that we might lose it. The higher we go, the more afraid we become of falling down.

So why is all of this greed, fear, and expectation plaguing us? These feelings exist because we want to achieve something. We have dreams of who we could become and what we might accomplish. But often these goals, instead of inspiring more joy in our present lives, seem to torture and distract us instead.

Some research has revealed that the most miserable part of our lives is generally between college and midlife, when we are still obsessed with achievement. We spend the prime of our lives struggling to make a name for ourselves and struggling to succeed. And what researchers have discovered is that it is usually the retirement years that are the most satisfying for people, after they've let go of all their ambitions.

By the time people reach retirement, they have pursued so many things and perhaps have exhausted their egos to some extent. Maybe they have realized that these accomplishments are no longer as important as they once thought. Or maybe they have made so many mistakes in life that they have finally gained some wisdom!

Whatever the reason, people seem to grow more peaceful later in life, after they have let go of their worldly dreams. When we are young, we still have so many expectations and plans. When we are in midlife, after some of our dreams have been fulfilled, we become very afraid we could lose what we've achieved. Sometimes the least satisfying part of our lives is when we are living our dreams because we are so afraid. This is our pattern: fear, greed, and hope are very present in our lives.

On the other hand, the mahasiddhas and yogis who have achieved the highest realization are free from hope and fear because they've realized there is nothing to achieve on the outside. Once they have seen the true nature of their minds—mahamudra—there is nothing left to accomplish.

Because there is nothing to strive for, nothing to attain, there is no hope or fear for these yogis. They don't even fear death. It is said again and again in the teachings that the best meditators welcome death joyfully because death is one of the best times to achieve enlightenment.

But if you don't practice meditation, then death is something unknown and very mysterious. The prospect of death is confusing and even quite scary for most people.

Although there are circumstantial causes for fear, if we look deep down, most of our fear is related to what is somehow life-threatening. Anything related to death is a tremendous cause of fear in us. When we talk about emergencies, we are almost always talking about something life-threatening. It is the basic impulse of sentient beings to want to live.

So the basis of all hope and fear, for ordinary beings, is life and death. All our dreams and expectations are related to life. All our fears are related to death. But the great yogis have realized there is no such thing as life or death because they have gone beyond both.

What is left to hope for or fear when you have gone beyond life and death? What is left to fear once you have gone beyond all attachments? Once you have gone beyond ignorance and all of the other emotions, you are truly liberated. You are truly free.

It is important to understand that enlightenment is not something up there in the future, which we must go out and achieve. Enlightenment is here, in the midst of life; it is here within us.

Academia has trained us to believe that education is all about studying things outside of us. But while we are busily learning about the world around us, we are often completely ignoring ourselves, and that is why we are not experiencing any personal transformation within our current education system.

Now yogis have realized that before they can learn about others, they must first learn about themselves. Meditation is the best way to learn about ourselves. Through focusing our attention, we try to see what is happening in our minds and emotions.

The end result is that we discover who we truly are. This is a realization that we cannot go out and achieve somewhere else. There is no such thing as finding buddhahood somewhere else. That buddha nature is inside of us. Once we realize this, we no longer have any need to go looking for truth in the outside world.

But if we don't know that the truth is within us, then we go looking for knowledge. We devote ourselves to our education, which only feeds our appetite. The more information we gather, the further we often wander from any examination of ourselves. The more knowledge we gain, the further from the truth we seem to go.

But someone who has discovered the inner buddha nature has nothing left to achieve in the world. That itself is liberation.

Having totally uprooted I and mine,
one is victorious in the war with Mara.

Once we have discovered the buddha nature inside ourselves, the true nature of the mind, we will also know others. Until you know yourself, there is no way you will know others. But when you know yourself, and you have that wisdom, there is a much better chance to truly know others. And when you know yourself and others, then "I" and "mine" are completely dissolved.

This dissolution of the self is much like peeling away an onion. If you peel away the onion layer by layer, then at the center you cannot find the onion anymore. The onion was merely a product of all of these layers.

Likewise, if we peel away the layers of all five aggregates, the body, feelings, ideas, karma, and consciousness, there is no "I" left at the center. Without any basis in the aggregates, there is no way to project an "I" or "mine." The sense of "I" exists only when you have not yet peeled away the layers.

And the onion of the self is not merely a result of the five aggregates. We also pile on so many more layers of identity throughout our lives. We have layers for race, for nation, for religion, for gender, for knowledge, for all of these "isms" in our culture. The onion of identity and ego can grow bigger and bigger.

One of the great masters said that with your destructive emotions, first you get attached to the "I" and the self. Next you get attached to objects of the mind. Then you become attached to identities such as my home, my country, my race, my religion. So the concept of "mine" is actually just an expansion of that ego.

But when "I" and "mine" begin to extend their territories, they are bound to face conflicts. We can see this on a more global level between countries like Tibet and China or India and Pakistan. Throughout human history we have always been in conflict over territory. And if we look closely, all of these disputes over boundaries are actually based on attachments to "I" and "mine."

So who are our enemies? When "I" and "mine" are threatened, we project this idea of enemy. Whoever is threatening our attachment becomes our enemy, and this is why we are always at war.

But those yogis who have gone beyond "I" and "mine" don't have an "other" at all. There is no one to become an enemy. This is why they have even gone beyond the maras.

Mara has many meanings. Mara can mean your destructive emotions. Buddhists believe that as long as you have anger, you will always have an enemy. And as long as you have destructive emotions, you will create the karma to suffer, and you will also die. In this way, death is also mara. So we can see there are several maras.

But if you go deeper into meditation, you see that the sources of destructive emotions, karma, life, and death are rooted in the ego. Attachment to the ego gives rise to anger and pain when the ego is threatened. And the ego remains because of our basic ignorance of not knowing our true self.

As long as you have a self, you will think that you are right, and that you are winning. But even if you are Genghis Khan and you win the greatest battle in human history, you still will be defeated according to the standards of the mahasiddhas.

Conquest is based on the expansion of "mine." Genghis Khan wanted a universal empire, but that will never happen. To become a universal emperor, you would need to have boundless merit. You cannot accumulate that much merit in one lifetime. This is why all of the empires have come and gone, and no one has been able to rule the world. Power always comes and goes. Empires rise and fall.

So while the bodhisattvas and mahasiddhas lose everything, including the self, spiritually they are the victors. This is why the Buddha is also called "victorious," because the greatest victory is over one's own ego. None of the world's most powerful rulers have achieved this. But the mahasiddhas who have seen mahamudra, the union of clarity and emptiness, have triumphed over the ego, and all notions of self and other have dissolved.

21

Since Realism Is Destroyed in Its Own State

Since realism is destroyed in its own state,
one is liberated from samsara and nirvana.

As WE HAVE ESTABLISHED, mahamudra is the state that has
gone beyond both samsara and nirvana. In saying this, however,
we need to know a little bit more about samsara.

Samsara means "wheel of life." The imagery of the wheel of life
depicts how we are circling again and again through birth, life, death,
and the intermediate stage of the bardo. Samsara is this cycle that we
are trapped in.

The wheel of life has twelve different branches or limbs. Each
branch is explained by a different name, but they can all be included
under karma, emotions, mind, and body. Due to the interdependency
between these components, our body and mind play out all of these
karmic activities based on destructive emotions, which propel us

moment to moment and life to life. In this way, we circle through the three times of past, present, and future in this endless chain of samsara.

The nature of samsara is suffering. Recognizing this suffering is very important. When we acknowledge the pain and suffering of samsara, we are compelled to move beyond it to achieve nirvana.

The Buddhist understanding of nirvana is very much based on the four noble truths. Nirvana is freedom from suffering, and the four noble truths recognize this suffering and describe a way out of it.

To reach nirvana we have to reverse these twelve interdependent links and free ourselves from the interdependency of these four: mind, body, karma, and emotions. When we have achieved freedom, it is called nirvana, which literally means "cessation."

So what is ceasing is this interdependency that has been perpetuating our continued suffering throughout countless lifetimes. One of the most basic ways to acknowledge the truth of suffering, even if our lives seem generally happy, is to accept the truth that we are all dying. Every moment we are dying. That fact alone is a cause of great suffering.

But if we go one step deeper, we begin to realize that even all of the good feelings we have such as pleasure and happiness are still part of suffering. As long as we have any feelings, even if they are pleasurable or neutral, those feelings can be considered part of our suffering.

Once we have that realization about all of the feelings in our lives, we can begin to reverse the cycle of samsara. Buddhists always say that to achieve nirvana, you have to produce renunciation. Renunciation, however, doesn't mean that you have to put on some robes and join the monastery.

Renunciation here has more to do with knowing the nature of feelings. We have this tendency to always go looking for happiness. But the more we look, and the harder we try, instead of becoming happier, we achieve a frustrating mixture of pleasure and pain. So renunciation has to do with understanding that happiness and unhappiness are inseparable.

If we found lasting pleasure in samsara, which was a constant source of happiness, then that would be fine. That would essentially be nirvana. But most of the pleasurable feelings we experience are actually the causes for whatever pain comes next. The same is true of happiness. No sooner have we achieved the happiness we thought we wanted then that happiness itself becomes a cause for the next feeling of unhappiness.

If we reflect honestly on our personal experiences up until this point in life, we can verify that most of the pain and suffering we've experienced has been intricately related to all of the pleasure and happiness we've known. None of our positive experiences can last forever. They are always changing, and inevitably they become the source of much longing, pain, and misery.

As practitioners, we have to closely examine whether our feelings are also driving us in our spiritual practice. Are we meditating to feel happy? Are we joining a religion and going to a church or temple in order to feel pleasure and happiness? As long as we are actively pursuing a feeling, we will always be disappointed.

If we don't really know what we are looking for, or if we look in the wrong place, we may actually become more miserable. As long as happiness and pleasure are feelings, they will remain caught in interdependency. As long as we are busy pursuing happiness, we will not discover the pure joy and freedom of truly knowing the nature of our own minds.

So this basic ignorance of not knowing the causes of suffering is why samsara is so filled with misery. But if we reach the point of recognizing the truth of suffering, it can inspire the cultivation of a deep spirituality within us. This is the reason why Buddhism is so focused on impermanence and death. These contemplations are an effort to know the true nature of our lives in order to progress on the spiritual path.

The moment we see the true nature of our lives, our journey toward nirvana begins. The moment we accept that life is impermanent and that pain and death are inevitable, we will be inspired to move beyond that suffering. This moment of recognition is where the reversion of samsara can begin. And then, through the trainings of discipline, meditation, and wisdom, we can reverse the afflictive emotions.

In some sense, samsara and nirvana are interdependent. They are related in that once we know that the nature of life is suffering, that suffering can be used as an energy to cultivate something more positive. That transformation, that positive energy, is what Buddhists call renunciation. So renunciation does not mean abandoning your life or becoming a monastic. Renunciation has more to do with understanding the nature of your life and then beginning this process of transformation based on developing positive qualities.

It is our human nature to have very strong attachments. Due to this tendency, we are always attached to some object or experience. We interact with the whole universe based on our sense organs, which are always attached to feelings of sensual pleasure and desire.

So when Virupa says that "realism is destroyed," he is talking about moving beyond all attachment. "Realism" is a rough translation; the Tibetan word means something more like "grasping." Normally when we are attached to an object it is because we have convinced ourselves that that object is real. Because if an object is not real, then how attached could we really become? How much can we really grasp onto something that does not exist?

We cannot experience any freedom because of our attachment. We want to achieve happiness and pleasure because we have strong attachment. And that attachment is connected with a strong grasping. You cannot have attachment without grasping. And all of the grasping, as we have discussed in the previous chapter, is rooted in the ego and in the sense of "I" and "mine." Grasping is actually one of the main obstacles obscuring our vision.

When there is strong grasping and attachment, not only do we want to make objects real, but even at the conceptual level we want to make all "isms" real too. Even Buddhism can become an ism when mixed with our ego, and then it can become a major obstacle to our liberation. As one of the great Sakya masters said, "When grasping arises in your mind, you do not have the right view."

You may say you are a great philosopher, and you may try to explain all kinds of philosophies, but if those explanations are mixed with your own grasping, then you do not have the right view and you will never have the freedom. You will remain in samsara.

Mahamudra is when you have gone beyond isms. Mahamudra is when you have gone beyond all forms of grasping. Because mahamudra is a union of awareness and emptiness, at the subjective level, then that state frees your mind from any grasping, or any attachment to any isms.

When Virupa says "since realism is destroyed in its own state," it is important to explore what is meant by "its own state." The true nature of the mind is free from grasping and free from attachment. But because we have not discovered the true nature of our minds yet, we are still living with this mixture of ignorance, attachment, and anger.

A philosopher once said, "Man is born free, but everywhere he is in chains." But according to Buddhism, man is not born free. Man is forced by karma and destructive emotions to take rebirth again and again. Only the buddhas can be born out of their own free will to help sentient beings.

Now when children are young, they are very naive and innocent. That innocence may give them a certain level of freedom. But then their family and society immediately begin to train them. They are told, "You cannot do this, you cannot do that." We create so many restrictions for children.

So society, and then education, begin to train this naïve person into a very conditioned little mind. And as we have discussed, our system of education is so based on knowledge. We are given all of these incentives in school, encouraged to learn the most information possible. While this may give us certain opportunities in life, it does nothing to help us to achieve even a basic state of freedom.

So while Buddhists don't believe that we are born free, Buddhism does state that the basic nature of the mind is free from ignorance, anger, and attachment. Rediscovering that truth is the greatest freedom of all. And when you are finally free from all destructive emotions, then the wisdom and compassion of mahamudra will arise. And in mahamudra your mind will finally be freed from the cycle of birth and death.

You will be freed from samsara because the very root cause of samsara—ignorance—has been destroyed by your wisdom. Not only are you free from samsara, but you are also free from nirvana. Nirvana is merely the cessation of birth and death, the absence of suffering. But mahamudra, due to wisdom and compassion, is a state beyond even nirvana.

Mahamudra is the wisdom of seeing the true nature of yourself, as well as seeing the true nature of others. Mahamudra is a state beyond all feelings because it has gone beyond the ego. Mahamudra is an ego-less state. And since all feelings are rooted in the ego, then without the ego, they naturally dissolve.

If we were to really simplify things, we could say that samsara is suffering, nirvana is freedom from suffering, and mahamudra is going beyond both. Mahamudra is much higher than nirvana. Although once you achieve nirvana you no longer suffer, you also do not reincarnate to benefit others. It is the limitless compassion and wisdom of mahamudra that activates you to take rebirth for the sake of all sentient beings.

The next lines of the doha are very profound. They are referring to the whole Hinayana path, how to reverse it, and also describing the state of mahamudra:

Since rigpa is pure in the basis, it is called perfect buddhahood.

Rigpa is another word for a state of mahamudra. The term *rigpa*, however, emphasizes the clarity aspect of the mind. Mahamudra is more comprehensive because it describes the union of clarity and emptiness, that is, wisdom and compassion.

To achieve nirvana, we have to go through samsara. We have to know that samsara is suffering. Only with that realization, and based on renunciation, will we practice the four noble truths and achieve nirvana.

On the other hand, the state of rigpa or mahamudra in tantra is based on the premise that from the very beginning our basic nature itself is perfect buddhahood. This is why during tantric empowerments you are introduced to your physical body as the buddha's body, your speech as the buddha's mantra, and your mind as the buddha's wisdom. You are introduced to that pure nature. And when you carry these introductions onto the spiritual path, then that becomes your practice. In this sense, the very result itself—buddhahood—is the path. But in Hinayana Buddhism, you are traveling from samsara to nirvana, and so the path and result are two separate states.

So according to the higher tantric teachings, we are already buddhas. As we carry on our practice, after receiving the necessary empowerments, we have to continue to see ourselves as buddhas. This perfect buddhahood is there from the beginning. Because if we were not pure from the beginning, how could we ever purify ourselves? If something is dirty by nature, then we can never fully clean it.

But the truth is that we are all pure by nature. We are pure from beginningless time. All this karma, all this suffering, and all these emotions are circumstantial. That is why these impurities can be purified through practice. And then when we discover the original buddha nature within us, there is no need to go out looking for buddhahood. There is no faraway place called a pure land where we go to reach buddhahood. Once we see the buddha inside us, then we can see that the pure land is right here around us and everyone is already buddha!

The more tantric practice we do, the more this pure vision becomes visible to us. All of our sensory experiences are based on the energies we carry in the channels inside us. If we have impurities in our channels, then we see with impure vision. If we have pure things inside us, if all of the channels are pure and our mind is wisdom, then we see everything as pure.

When great yogis have this pure vision, it is not something that is happening from the outside. It is based on their own purity. When water is very dirty, you cannot see anything clearly. But when the water is very pure, you can see everything. Likewise, if there is no blockage and the energies inside you are pure, if the air is pure, if the channels and the red and white elements in those channels are pure, then everything will appear equally pure around you.

All of these pure visions that the yogis talk about are based on discovering that original purity inside ourselves. Due to this discovery, we are then able to see the purity in others and in the whole universe. If we have never seen that purity, then the world is simply a projection of our karma and emotions. So what we will see, and how we will experience it, is all dependent on us.

We must keep remembering that we have buddha nature inside us. That belief in our innate purity is the foundation that gives us greater confidence in our spiritual practice. If we know this purity already exists in us, we will be more inspired to work to uncover it.

Some social scientists will say that our human nature is actually to be aggressive. But if our basic nature were violent and angry, then there would be no way that anyone could achieve buddhahood. The Buddha said that even an animal's basic nature is not aggressive. All sentient beings are pure by nature. Buddhists do not believe that we originate from sin and are sinners at our core. If we perform negative actions, they are circumstantial; they are related with our karma and defilements. But our essential nature is pure.

That purity in our minds is continuously there. That is why tantra has the meaning of "continuum." What is continuing is our inner purity. The wisdom and purity of our mental continuum is there all the time. If we don't see it now, it is because circumstantially we have so many emotions.

If we are filled with anger and desire, we will never see our inherent purity. What we will experience instead is based entirely on those afflictive emotions and mental activities and all of the concepts and wandering thoughts they provoke. But those beings who not only see our purity but also remain in that purity are the true masters, the great yogis.

Since phenomena and mind are exhausted
in the state of exhaustion,
therefore it is explained as nirvana

As discussed above, if we achieve nirvana, it is seen as the greatest death we have experienced. This is because in ordinary death, only our physical body is exhausted, but our mind continues. Our mind is not dead, and with all those remaining mental activities, it begins looking for new parents and is forced into rebirth in a new body. So ordinarily our mind continues after death.

But when you achieve nirvana, not only have you exhausted the gross physical body, but you have also killed your mind! This must be why those who have achieved nirvana are called *arhats*. Arhat means "killer of the enemy." Arhat has a meaning of death because when you have achieved nirvana, for the first time you are free from your ordinary mind. Not only is the mind exhausted, but the rest of the five aggregates including your feelings, thoughts, gross physical body with its blood and elements, and karma are all exhausted. Nirvana is the exhaustion of all phenomena as well as the mind and all the aggregates.

Now some may be wondering if nirvana is a kind of nihilism. If all the five aggregates have ceased, then what is left? The Buddha taught that although the five aggregates have expired, what remains is wisdom. Because of wisdom, we don't have any of the destructive emotions that force us to be reborn again and again. That is why nirvana is a state that is free from birth and death.

One characteristic of nirvana is that it is permanent. Permanent in the sense that it is free from all conditions and causes—all of the emotions that force us to be reborn again and again.

The next lines of the doha describe the state of mahamudra, which is:

uncontrived, unchanging, totally liberated
from everything to be given up or to attain.

Mahamudra is perfect buddhahood, which is complete liberation. This liberation is not artificial. It is unchanging, and it is unconditioned. In the natural state of mahamudra, there is nothing to be abandoned and nothing to be accepted. It is a state that is completely free from all conditioned things.

We may get a glimpse of that space in our meditation. Back to our earlier example of water: if we let muddy water sit still long enough, the dirt will all begin to settle , and the water will become pure again.

In a similar way, when we let our minds relax in meditation, then all those active emotions will settle down, until at some point we can even go beyond the sleeping emotions.

When we are in that inner space between thoughts, we are beyond time, space, and conditions. It is a changeless state of genuine pure happiness and complete freedom. Once yogis experience that bliss, then there is nothing else in samsara remotely comparable.

Once yogis have experienced that state of mahamudra, they can experience it everywhere. This is why Virupa explains that in that state there is no effort necessary because there is nothing to accept and nothing to reject. There is no more karma. It is a state that is free from all stress and effort.

While we still have emotions and karma, we will always have likes and dislikes. There will always be things that we find agreeable or disagreeable. We will always alternate between attachment and aversion. But when we have gone beyond all of that, when we are in the state of mahamudra, we will have complete freedom and peace.

22

Who Realizes Selflessness?

That great profound term mahamudra,
whatever its basis of designation is,
also has the label "empty."
As moments are empty by nature,
who realizes selflessness?

THESE LINES ARE REFERRING to our preconceptions of buddhahood. Through our meditation practice, we are all trying to
achieve buddhahood and realize the true nature of ourselves. But when
we become a buddha, it is quite possible that buddhahood is a completely different experience from what we were expecting!

According to Vajrayana Buddhism, mahamudra is the result. It is
the realization of buddhahood. During an empowerment, the guru
introduces you to your true buddha nature. The guru shows you that
your physical body is actually light and emptiness, your speech is actually sound and emptiness, and the nature of your mind is wisdom and
emptiness.

Ordinarily we don't have any experience of the emptiness of these three aspects of ourselves. At our level, sound is something real when it reaches our ears. When we experience it, it exists. Ordinarily we don't recognize the empty nature of sound, which is like an echo, having no reality.

The same is true with our bodies. Our karmic conditions and projections are such that we perceive the physical body as made up of flesh and bone. Ordinarily we don't see the empty nature in those bones and in that flesh and blood. Nor do we experience the empty nature of our minds. Instead, we experience a constant stream of wandering thoughts. Even when we are meditating, we will notice the mind is filled with inner chatter.

If we have some experience of emptiness at these three levels, however, then these mystical songs may resonate with us. But if we don't have any experience of the empty aspects of ourselves, then mahamudra is beyond our understanding and may not make any sense. Instead, we will remain firmly rooted in a reality of flesh, bone, sound, and thoughts.

But when great meditators like Virupa have some experience of the emptiness of the mind, in that inner space, where is thought? In that inner space, where is the mind? For that matter, where is buddhahood?

If we recognize the empty nature of body, speech, and mind, then all of the phenomena of the universe—everything that we perceive through our body, speech, and mind—will also be empty. Though we may see color and shape, within that, there is still emptiness. The same applies to all our sensory perceptions of sound, smell, taste, touch, and thought. All of these objects are by nature empty.

Deep in meditation, resting in that inner space beyond all thoughts, where is this notion of buddhahood? Where is the person who realizes emptiness?

Those who have not realized this state may assume that there is still a "person" achieving "buddhahood." We can project all kinds of things from our limited perspective, but the reality is that when you are in that inner space, you cannot find mind, thoughts, or feelings. You have gone beyond all five aggregates and can no longer find a person in that space. If you cannot find a person anymore, then who is it that realizes buddhahood?

This is the absurdity of the paradox of relativity and ultimate truth. These two truths are together all the time, but when you have realized the ultimate, you are speechless, and you have gone beyond all thought. In ultimate truth, there is nothing that you can express or communicate to anyone.

For this reason, we must remember that all of the philosophical books that describe emptiness and buddhahood are only a reference. They cannot give us the real experience of emptiness. As we have discussed with the simile of sugar, until we taste sugar with our own tongue, no matter how much we read or study, it will remain intellectual knowledge. Until we taste it, we will never truly know what it is. And once you have tasted the sweetness of it, then all the other information you have gathered about sugar won't be necessary anymore.

Once you have tasted that sweetness, how will you possibly express it to someone else? All of the experiences of the different sense organs are this way. There is no way to communicate entirely our sensory perceptions to anyone else. So we see that even within the relative world, we are still unable to fully express our experiences to one another.

When we experience the ultimate truth of mahamudra, then our sense of ourselves is gone, time is dissolved, and there is nothing left to express. It is no longer even possible to say "this is mahamudra" or "this is buddhahood." This is why Virupa asks, "As moments are empty by nature, who realizes selflessness?"

At our level, through our experience of the present moment, we prove that things exist. Just one single moment is, relatively speaking, a way to prove we exist. This is dependent upon our timeline. How can you prove that one present moment exists without a past and a future?

Back to the river analogy we've explored in earlier chapters: a river is nothing more than a continuation of billions of drops of water. When these drops come together and are moving, we call them a river. But when you analyze that massive river down to a single drop, you cannot say that a single drop is a river.

Furthermore, if you analyze that single drop down to the subatomic level, you will find that the drop is composed of many different elements. If you separate those elements of earth, air, water, and fire, then at a certain point you cannot even find the drop itself anymore. So where is the drop now? Where is the river?

We think that there is a drop, and we think that there is a moment in time because we have a subjective mind, which is projecting the timeline and the interdependency of all objects. The subjective mind gives rise to the otherness of the phenomenal world. The sense of self is the root of this dualistic interaction with the universe. As long as we exist, our universe exists. But once we are gone, the universe that we have projected is also gone.

So we can see that the existence of the moment and the existence of the drop are dependent entirely on a subjective person. And looking deeper into the mind, Buddhists have detected three different levels of mind.

First there is the gross mind, which is interdependently interacting with the object. Then there is the subtle mind, which functions irrespective of the sense organs, for example, while we are dreaming or remembering something. Third is the very subtle mind, which is even beyond the mind itself. That third level is mahamudra, the very subtle mind that is only found deep in that inner space of meditation.

When you are operating with your gross mind and with your subtle mind, you can experience the phenomenal world. But when you are experiencing the very subtle mind of mahamudra, you no longer experience yourself as a person or perceive any other phenomena in the universe. There is no longer a projector and nothing to project.

Right now, because we are functioning in this universe based on our gross and subtle minds, we are always projecting and evaluating everything, based on our karmic vision. And our karma is mixed with all our emotions, and so the karma and emotions are determining everything.

Even when we talk about divine things like buddhahood, heaven, or mahamudra, these notions are still coming from the gross and subtle minds. As I have reiterated so many times with regard to the doha, the mystical realizations of the very subtle mind are inexpressible. That is why philosophers can write these exhaustive explorations of mahamudra and always conclude by saying that the ultimate is inexpressible! Just as we cannot properly express the sweetness of sugar, so too there is no way to express something that is beyond our experience.

There is no realizer, just a name, a term, a label.
Also that is not perfect, a projection of disciples.

Until we have experienced this space, then all these terms like buddhahood or ultimate are just imperfect labels. As far as our experiences here in the relative world are concerned, we have these two types of vision that we have explored earlier. We have experiences of both perfect and imperfect relative truth, perfect relative truth being that the majority of us have agreed that snow is white, and imperfect relative truth being that for some people, due to say an illness like jaundice, snow may appear yellow or some other color entirely.

But both of these perfect and imperfect visions of snow are still only relative truths. Relative to our human eye organ, we are seeing these appearances as a result of our karmic vision. Snow is not necessarily even the same to all other sentient beings who possess eyes. Creatures perceive color in so many different ways, even on this one small planet. It is our shared human karma that makes the majority agree upon a perfect relative truth, like snow appearing to be white. So relative truth has perfect and imperfect vision.

Likewise, it is worth reiterating that there are two kinds of ultimate truth as well, namely, the perfect and imperfect. Everything that has ever been written about perfect truth, everything that we can study, everything that we can learn from the *Heart Sutra* or from reading every philosophy book ever written is still only imperfect ultimate truth. It is imperfect even though it is referencing perfect truth. It is only through our experience of the inner space of mahamudra that we will ever really know perfect ultimate truth.

Until we have the realization of mahamudra, both perfect relative truth and imperfect ultimate truth are still not perfect! Perfection refers to when you experience realization. So when the *Heart Sutra* talks about the perfection of giving, it clearly states that the perfection is the realization that there is "no giver, no receiver, and no gift."

So what the sutra is really saying is that in order to perfect giving, the person who is the giver has to realize his or her own selflessness. Only after the dissolution of the self will the giving become perfected. Otherwise, if the giver hasn't realized selflessness, then the act of giving will always be tied to some emotions.

So the word "perfect" here in the doha is also referring to realization. If you do not have realization, then the truth is just "a projection of disciples." It is the emotional and karmic projection of the practitioners. But if the space is completely purified within you, then there is the chance for perfection to arise.

To see a perfect universe, we must first have the realization of perfection within ourselves. Otherwise everything is merely karmic vision. And at our level, most of what we experience does not arise from wisdom. It is a karmic projection based on emotions.

Also in disciples there is no self,
similar with illusions and emanations.
"Mahamudra" is a mental imputation of the childish.

The words "childish" and "noble" are two terms that seem always to appear in Buddhist sutras. Here, "childish" refers to whenever you are acting out your karma, based on your emotions. This lack of awareness is referred to as "childish."

And according to Buddhism, until you have reached the path of seeing emptiness, you have not become ennobled. So the noble truth is based on the realization of those who have seen emptiness. When the noble ones see all of us acting out of our karma and emotions, we appear very childish.

As mentioned, the root of all feelings are the three destructive emotions of ignorance, anger, and attachment. Whenever actions are based predominantly on these three emotions, we become very childish because we are not acting out of wisdom.

Until we see a glimpse of emptiness, whenever we talk about buddhahood, mahamudra, and all of these ultimate experiences, we are still only expressing our emotions based on our karma.

Some may take offense to this, but one of the Indian mystics once said, "God is the projection of our fear and faith." How truthful this is or not is up for personal inquiry. But we can observe that many of us go to church, temple, or holy places when we are experiencing more fear and suffering.

When we have more fear, then we feel much more comforted by faith objects and by the support of our spiritual community. According to Buddhist tantra, in the beginning when we have more fear and more emotions, then these negative emotions still need an object. This is why, in the first levels of tantra, in kriya tantra and in charya tantra, we invite Tara from the pure land to appear in front of us. Then we perform a Tara puja and do various practices.

In these beginning practices, it is more like the Buddha is our friend or a benevolent king or leader. Early in our spiritual lives, the Buddha is still somebody located outside of us. When we don't have much wisdom yet, and when we still have a lot of fear and suffering, it is far more comforting to have an imagined external buddha to rely on.

But when we go to the higher levels of tantric practice, we generate ourselves as the Buddha. And when we get to the level of anuttarayoga tantra sadhanas, then we even go beyond buddhahood to mahamudra.

These experiences all depend on how many emotions we still have. So when that Indian mystic said that God is a projection we make based on our fear and on our need for protection, maybe there is some truth there. Whenever we have fear, we want something to rely on.

Even before Buddhism came to Tibet, there was an older native religion called Bönpo or Bön. Bön is a very shamanistic religion, in which everything is an expression of God. The sky is God. The trees are God. All of nature is filled with divine spirits, and in this sense, practitioners of Bön find profound protection in their environment.

When we have gone beyond ourselves, beyond our egos, our karma, and all our emotions, our experience of everything will be different. Subject and object are gone, and we are completely free from dualism. When we look back from that state at all the actions we have performed in our lives, we may appear to have been very childish.

It is a common life pattern that as we progress through life and make more and more mistakes, we often also learn from them and gather more wisdom. From that mature perspective, when we look back at our lives, we may see the stupidity in so many of our choices and actions!

If we possess the right approach, then the more experiences we have, the more wisdom we can gain. There is an old saying in Tibet that when you are young, you have lots of energy, but when you are older you have more advanced methods based on all that you have learned in life.

So which is more important? The youthful always think that energy is more important. But the older you get, the more you often see that knowledge and wisdom based on your experience is far more important. So there is always this paradigm shift between the young and the old.

Many energies are based on the physical elements, but wisdom is based in the mind. In his collection of "elegant sayings"—a genre known as *lekshé* in Tibetan—Sakya Pandita wrote that even if one is going to die tomorrow, one should still keep on learning today. Because what we have learned will be carried in our mindstream into the next life.

We will always carry whatever we have experienced, learned, and impressed into our mental continua. Yet none of the physical energies based on our physical elements can be carried with us after death.

So where is your focus? If your focus is on spiritual practice and rebirth, then whatever you do on the mental level, including meditation, has long-lasting benefit. But whatever you do at the physical level has much shorter benefit.

This is why the evolution of knowledge and wisdom should be valued over physical development. Meditation serves to cultivate all of these lasting qualities in the mental continuum. This is why we actually close off most of our sense organs during meditation in order to focus solely on the mind, without being distracted by physical things.

In this way, mental realizations and wisdom have a lasting benefit. This is one reason why a great Sakya master taught the "parting from the four attachments." He emphasized that if we have attachment to this life, we are not a spiritual practitioner.

Now this may sound somehow contrary to what we've been discussing here, but if we study it line by line, there is no contradiction. What is life? Life is when your mind and body come together. So where is life before conception? And where is life after death? Life is the time between the moment of conception and the moment when we exhale and die.

So in some sense, if we are attached to this life, it refers more to attachment than to the materialistic and physical components of our beings. It refers more to that life force, the *pranavayu* air that keeps the mind and body together in our lives.

If all of our spiritual practice is focused only on this one life, only for the purpose of material and physical gains, then we are not true spiritual practitioners. We will not really cultivate those lasting mental qualities.

Is our life only a physical body and only a material phenomenon? We are born and we die—is that all there is to life? Many people focus their spiritual practice on this life only because they think this is all we have. Most of us don't remember our past lives, and we don't know whether there is a future after death. Because of these two unknowns, we think everything we do should benefit our current lifetime.

If we honestly look deep down, most of us are not really convinced that there is such a thing as an immaterial mind. Maybe for us the mind is the brain, our emotion is just the heart, and all of it depends upon a physical body. If that is our belief, and if we don't have any confidence in an immaterial mind that will survive the body, then our focus will only be on this one life.

When our spiritual practice is only for this life, only for the material, only for the brain and heart and not for the immaterial mind, then our basic spiritual foundation is not very sound. In fact it is very shaky.

On the other hand, according to Buddhist teachings, those who have strong faith and strong belief make the distinction between the physical body and the immaterial mind. If our spiritual practice is focused on that immaterial mind, then what Sakya Pandita said about continuing our practice, even if we know we'll die tomorrow, makes perfect sense. This study and practice is like credit we are earning for the next life.

Spiritual practice has to be focused on cultivating all spiritual qualities within us. Those are qualities like love, compassion, and wisdom. We have to discover whether these qualities can be found in our brains, our hearts, or somewhere else. Only when we are absolutely certain that these qualities reside in our mental stream will our practice become strong.

If we are still very emotional, then even our spiritual practice will just be another projection of those mental emotions. These projections may appear to be spiritual practice from the outside, but they do not give rise to a true spiritual experience.

All of these spiritual projections will be a "mental imputation of the childish" until the profound experience of inner space unfolds. In that inner space, beyond time, where the self is completely dissolved and all dualism has ceased, we will finally know mahamudra. It is there, in that awakened state, that we will experience the marriage of wisdom and compassion, the union of clarity and emptiness.

23

Nothing Exists in Peaceful and Pure Space

"Delusion" and "nondelusion" are mere names, mere labels.
Who is the person to feel or be aware of delusion?

HERE VIRUPA IS ASKING who exactly feels or is aware of delusion. This is a question that philosophers and spiritual people have been asking throughout the centuries. Does the self even exist?

So many complex philosophies and religions have developed around trying to answer these fundamental questions, but I don't know how much these systems of belief have actually helped us to know ourselves.

These philosophical inquiries definitely help to give us some reference points. Buddhist philosophers ask, "Why do we have this strong clinging to the 'I' and to the 'self?'" And as we discussed earlier, we see how all of this strong clinging and grasping to the self gives rise to all of our clinging to our material possessions, to our cars, our homes, our countries, and even to our planet.

But does this concept of "I" and "my" actually exist? Or is it merely something we've projected onto that object? Buddhists have attempted to answer this not only through philosophical inquiry, but also through deep reflection and meditation. And through meditation, when they have had some realization of wisdom, then they have a better sense for whether or not the self exists.

Without realizing wisdom, without realizing mahamudra, it is difficult to have any perspective because our concepts of "I" and "my" are so firmly rooted in our lives. Because of that strong ego connected with grasping and attachment, there is constant affirmation of some existing self and of all of its possessions.

According to a Buddhist understanding, we can examine what a person is through studying the five aggregates. First there is matter, which is the physical body and the physicality of the material world. In the lower Buddhist philosophies, the materialists reduce everything down to the smallest unit. And at the level of particles, the materialists can demonstrate that most identification of things is lost through that reduction.

Recently scientists have been talking about the discovery of the Higgs boson, which they call the "God particle." So even the divine is being reduced to a particle. It is almost implied that the particle is the creator of the universe.

Now the materialists in Buddhist philosophy have come to a similar conclusion. They have concluded that everything, when reduced to particulate matter, loses the identifications of the gross material. Even the materials of the human body can be reduced to a mere pound of dust after cremation. And in that smallest dust, can we recognize a person? If that smallest dust is not the person, then where has the person gone?

So everything in the material world can be reduced to that subatomic level that science has proven. At that level, can we establish whether a person is there, whether a car is there, or whether a phone is there? I don't think we can identify any gross material at the level of the particle.

Returning to the five aggregates, we find that a person is more than just matter. While we are living we have feelings, and this sets us apart from some of the other material objects in the phenomenal world. I don't think that if we were to hit a rock, for example, that the rock would complain! Rocks don't experience pain or any feelings in the way that living beings do.

So Buddhists go beyond matter to the second aggregate, which is feeling. We examine feelings and ask the same question. Is there any self to be found inherently existing in those feelings?

If we have a headache, do we say that the headache is who we are? Where is the person in that experience of pain?

Buddhists then look further to the third aggregate, which is ideation. We have so many concepts. We have so many isms. We are constantly thinking. We create all kinds of theories, all kinds of principles, and so many systems for understanding the world.

But if we look into all of these ideas, are we able to find the self? Although the Buddha may have inspired the belief system of Buddhism, can we actually find the Buddha within the ism? Can we prove an existing self in any ism?

The fourth aggregate is that of formation. If we look into all of our mental, physical, and verbal activities, is there a self in any of those? We may be acting and reacting mentally, verbally, and physically, but do we actually exist in those formations? Can we find the person, the doer, in any of these habitual patterns?

The fifth aggregate is that of consciousness. If we look into the mind itself, consciousness itself, can we prove an existing self there either?

To some extent science is intent on dissecting everything. If we follow their example, and if we intellectually dissect every part of the person, the material part, the feeling part, the idea part, the activity part, and the mind, can we find a self in any of these aggregates?

The paradox is that we can only find the true nature of the self when we are in a meditative state. At the moment, we still have so much delusion, and maybe our clinging to the self gets stronger and stronger the more we examine it. Without meditation, our ego can become bigger. Our territory gets bigger, and as a result, we want to climb higher and higher and accumulate more wealth, knowledge, and possessions.

But if we sit in meditation, everything begins to dissolve. The stronger our meditation and the more profound our experience, the more we begin to dissolve all of the aggregates. We dissolve matter, feeling, ideas, activities, and even the mind and consciousness itself.

When you have dissolved all five aggregates and you have gone beyond all five, then where is the self? Now you have become impersonal.

When we have a strong attachment to the self, we are filled with delusion. And this also creates the duality of "nondelusion." But from that impersonal state of inner space during meditation, in the state of mahamudra when you have gone beyond all five aggregates, how can you say "this is delusion" or "this is not delusion?"

This is the reason why, in the deepest realization of meditation, whatever is false and relative will fall apart. Everything will dissolve. But until we have the profound experience of mahamudra, there will still be relativity, and we will still have a sense that the self inherently exists.

If you are in that profound state of mahamudra, then you come to the realization that all these old methods for understanding existence are mere projections, names, and concepts. Everything is projected from your inner conditions of the five aggregates of physicality, feeling, ideation, karmic action, and consciousness.

In our own lives we usually determine whether something is good or bad based on how it affects us personally. And in greater philosophical debates logic is used to try to prove whether something is valid or invalid.

But if someone has gone beyond the confines of logic, how can this person determine what is valid or invalid? This dichotomy of delusions and nondelusions is also an extreme. Someone who is in a state of profound meditation has gone beyond both delusion and nondelusion. There is no longer any paradox—no conflicts or extremes for the enlightened person. In that enlightened state, you are actually one with the universe. So there's no dualistic projection because the projector has dissolved.

So this is the reason why Virupa asks, "Who is the person to feel or be aware of delusion?" Virupa is trying to help us realize the answer. When you have become selfless, there's no longer any feeling to feel; there's no personal awareness to be conscious of. You have gone beyond the person. You are in the ecstatic state of bliss of the union of clarity and emptiness, of wisdom and compassion. There is no human being left in that state.

Someone who has gone beyond ignorance has even gone beyond life itself. The wheel of life begins with the ignorance. So someone who has transcended ignorance is free from this whole forced cycle of death and rebirth.

As we have discussed, life is the *pranavayu*, the fundamental life-force air, which helps to keep our minds and our bodies together. For someone who has gone beyond life, all these distinctions like delusion, nondelusion, and the five aggregates don't even arise.

In the state of mahamudra, one has gone beyond individuality and is free from the self and ego. When one sees that the nature of the self is selfless, and the nature of the ego is egoless, the individual has completely disappeared. Some of these seemingly paradoxical lines from the doha are intended to help us go beyond all of our assumptions about reality.

> If not even an iota of the result—nirvana—exists,
> and is not perceived,
> "liberation and nonliberation" is an adventitious reification.

The previous lines were trying to bring mahamudra realization and insight to the level we are at now in samsaric life. But these lines have more to do with how to integrate mahamudra at the level of the result.

In our current lives, when we practice, when we do meditation, we want to achieve something. We have some goal in mind. It's such a paradoxical situation because from our current state, since we have not achieved nirvana, we think nirvana is something in the future that we are working toward.

We may be very surprised to discover, however, that nirvana is not what we believed it to be. Nirvana is actually the cessation of the five aggregates. When all of the aggregates have ceased, when they all have dissolved, then where can we locate nirvana? Who is experiencing that state?

When a person is reduced to ashes at the time of cremation, can we find the person in that dust? In the same way, when all five aggregates have ceased, we have achieved that state of nirvana. But when we achieve that state, is there some material thing in that cessation that we can call nirvana?

We cannot find nirvana. That is the trick. Often we need to have some lofty goal in order to inspire our practice. But as I have mentioned before, when you have gone beyond the bridge and you have reached the other shore, then the bridge is no longer necessary. Even the water is irrelevant, and also, for that matter, I think all the methods are no longer existent.

Mahamudra is beyond even the eternalism of the nirvana. So that's why Virupa says, "'liberation and nonliberation' is an adventitious reification." It is just a projection. To say that one is liberated would be the equivalent of shouting to tell people to keep quiet!

At the level of mahamudra, all this dualism of liberation and nonliberation is just projection. The ultimate mahamudra is beyond samsara and nirvana. From the mahamudra perspective, even nirvana is not a state free from extremes.

Nothing exists in peaceful and pure space,
so what is the path of liberation?

Space is pure as well as peaceful. If we are on an airplane or a spaceship, and we have gone beyond all of those stormy clouds, at that high altitude there is great peace.

Imagine if that space, free of all clouds and storms, could be revealed inside of you. Just by gazing at the sky and contemplating space, you can have a glimpse of peace, a glimpse of clarity, and a glimpse of that emptiness.

In that space, nothing exists. Inner space and outer space become one. There's no conflict between subject and object, and that's why it's so peaceful. Whenever we have experienced any peaceful state inside us, that is when we have been temporarily free of the tensions of dualism.

The original buddha nature inside all of us is that state of purity and goodness. Space is the nature of our minds. Through meditation we are trying to reveal that space again. But it is not something that we acquire. It is naturally there all along, free from karma and afflictive emotions. Through our practice, we can gradually dissolve all of our obscurations to reveal that original purity again.

If we were inherently sinners from the very beginning, there would be no time in which we could be completely free. Sin would be the nature of our minds. But this is not the case. By nature we are pure. All of the afflictive emotions merely come and go, just like clouds come and go. But space is always pure.

Within us, anger comes and goes, jealousy comes and goes, desire comes and goes. All of the positive and negative emotions come and go, but they are all circumstantial. They are not in the nature of the mind. This is the reason why it is possible for us to overcome them and go beyond them. That is mahamudra.

If our original buddha nature is already liberated, then what is liberation? There's no such thing as liberating anything! In fact, we see that even the nature of the clouds, even the nature of the afflictive emotions, is already emptiness.

Within anger there is wisdom. Within desire there is wisdom. Within ignorance there is wisdom. All of these are merely expressions of that emptiness. Space provides room for all of these things to unfold. If there were no space, then none of these planetary systems would even have room to exist. If there were no space, then we could not even build a home.

So we ought to ask, did home come first, or did space come first? Similarly, did all of these emotions inside us happen first, or did our original nature happen first? In both cases, space and that original purity came first. In fact there isn't even such a thing as "first," because space is unconditioned and beginningless.

There was no cause, and there were no conditions. Space is beyond any concept of a beginning. It is free from time and also free from obstructions. That's why space is pure and peaceful. Nothing exists there.

We cannot say that liberation is achieved or that it exists somewhere. That inner space of mahamudra is beyond liberation and nonliberation. We have used this example often, but if you don't have a right hand, then how can you project a left hand? If there is no liberation, then there is also no nonliberation in the state of mahamudra.

"Ultimate" and "relative" are also just emphatic labels.
But the two truths don't exist in the dharmadhatu.
The dharmadhatu does not exist.

For the sake of our practice, and to provide us with a graduated path, the Buddha taught about perfect and imperfect relative truth. He described how all of these relative perceptions are just karmic vision. What humans see, what humans are experiencing, is not a universal experience. It is based on our particular karma.

If we examine our lives, within relative truth there are many imperfect relative truths. A democratic country is a good example of this. Whether or not the majority is smarter, it will always win. The reality of the majority will dominate the relative truth.

So this is how we create things in the relative world. It is like the popular story of the blind men and the elephant. A few blind people were trying to identify what an elephant was. One person touched the elephant's tail and said, "An elephant is like a rope." Another person touched the elephant's leg and said, "Oh, an elephant is like a pillar." In this way, we construct our reality based entirely on our own perfect and imperfect relative truths. This is how we project and identify things.

There is no universal agreement about reality. Starting from our individual karma, and generated by our collective karma, we share human experiences. We have all of these characteristics that we use to define ourselves as humans, but this is not how other animals perceive us.

This is how society is. It's all karmic vision. Within these karmic visions, there are perfect relative truths, namely, what the majority has agreed upon, and imperfect relative truths, that is, what the minority experiences. But neither relative truth is the ultimate truth. Relatively they are perfect and imperfect, but they are still interdependent. They are not ultimate.

Ultimate truth is what we are studying in the scriptures. We are studying different levels of philosophy. At the objective level we examine ideas, we talk about matter, we talk about mind, we talk about Madhyamaka, and all of those things. But again, these are just discussions, just dialogues. We are referring to something profound, but until we have that experience inside us, then all this study is only a reference.

Even the wisdom we receive from a teacher or guru is still only a carbon copy of somebody else's experience. It cannot become our own personal experience automatically. We have to become buddhas in order to have the Buddha's experience. If we just mimic the Buddha, then we don't experience the buddha inside us.

Early in our sadhana practice we use visualizations to help us imagine ourselves in the form of a buddha. But even those visualizations are not reliable. That is why we have to do the completion practices at the end of the sadhana, to go beyond, and to dissolve that deity back into emptiness. Without the proper dissolution, the sadhana visualization could be dangerous. It could actually generate a false sense of pride in being that deity.

So, as we have established, all of the philosophical books and all of the methods are just imperfect ultimate truth. The perfect ultimate truth is when you become a buddha.

When you have the realization of mahamudra, then you see that the imperfect ultimate truth and the perfect and imperfect relative truths are all just "emphatic labels." They have been strongly supported with logic and with the very sharp intelligence of scholars. They are certified labels, but still, the state of mahamudra has gone beyond both relative and ultimate truth; there is no dualism.

> But the two truths don't exist in the dharmadhatu.
> The dharmadhatu does not exist.

When you are in that state of dharmadhatu, which is mahamudra, you cannot express anything. You cannot say that dharmadhatu exists, does not exist, both, or neither. In that state you are speechless. You are free from all states and free from all extremes.

All of the most profound experiences in our lives are difficult to express. The moment we express them, we are actually limiting those experiences.

Even just the experience of the senses is difficult to describe. Can you explain all of the beauty you have seen through your eyes? Can you ever really describe the sweet tastes you have tasted on your tongue?

The more you try to express these sensations, the further you will get from the actual experiences because there is no way you can fully express them. We could go around and around, chasing our meaning. We could say sweetness is like sugar. Sugar is like honey. Honey is like syrup. But until you taste the sweetness yourself, no matter how many descriptions you hear, the references will always be inaccurate.

The only way to have a universal experience of sweetness is for everyone to taste it and to go beyond all of the names, all of the descriptions, all of the language. At best, language is merely a method to communicate relativity. Language cannot communicate ultimate realization.

We cannot prove dharmadhatu, that is, mahamudra. It is a state that can only be experienced through deep meditation. And when we have experienced it, that experience is beyond all words, all concepts, and beyond even the mind and consciousness. Because of this, dharmadhatu, the realization of mahamudra, is beyond all extremes.

Virupa has used these doha to begin to break down some of our misconceptions. Through these profound mystical songs, he has given us a window into what is possible. And he has reminded us again and again that the profound realization can never be reached through language or through study. In fact it cannot be reached as long as there is a self or an ego striving to reach it!

Mahamudra, that union of clarity and emptiness, wisdom and compassion, can only be experienced in the deepest meditation, when everything has dissolved back into that clear space.

Complete Translation of Virupa's *Treasury of Dohas*

Homage to Shri Vajrasattva.
Homage to blessed Nairatmya.

E ma ho!
The mahamudra of samsara and nirvana
is completely pure by nature, like space.
Since the reality of the demonstrated object does not exist,
it cannot be expressed through the medium of conventional
    words.
The essence without proliferation
by nature is free from all dependent phenomena.
It cannot be investigated or examined,
it is free from demonstrative examples,
it is also not abiding in freedom from examples,
beyond the domain of the mind,
not eternal, not annihilated, not samsara or nirvana,
not apparent, not empty, not real, not unreal, not nonarising,
not the original dharmata, and also not beyond mind,
also not nonbeing because being and nonbeing

cannot be expressed with the mind,
not connected with any dualistic phenomena,
originally homogeneous.
Even the explanation of the activities of defining the essence,
equivalent with the fallacy of those false horns of a rabbit
    being sharp or dull,
all phenomena are not different from that characterization.
The relative phenomena of the world, however they appear,
are without essence, mere names, mere sounds, mere
    designations.
Not the slightest bit of difference between names and meanings
    exists.
Innate from the beginning, not to be sought elsewhere,
the nature of the mind, without a name, mahamudra
free from proliferation,
equivalent with the nature of space, without a name
from the beginning,
nonarisen by nature, free from the proliferation of signs,
all-pervading, unmoving, and unchanging like space,
empty throughout all time and always selfless,
not the characteristic of concept, like a mirage of a river,
not bound, not liberated, having never moved from
the original state.

All sentient beings are emanations of mahamudra.
The essence of those emanations is the forever nonarising
    dharmadhatu.
Also all characteristics of dualistic appearances, happiness,
    suffering and so on,
are the play of mahamudra, the original dharmata.

Because there is no truth and nothing on which to rely
    in play itself,
reality never transcends the seal of emptiness.

Some are completely tortured with empowerment rites,
some always count their rosary saying *hum phat*,
some consume shit, piss, blood, semen, and meat,
some meditate in the yoga of *nadi* and *vayu*, but all are
    deluded.

E ma ho!
Having been connected with a sublime guru,
one should realize as follows:
because there is some kind of delusion,
true realization does not exist.
Free from any extremes of partiality or bias,
since there is nothing to realize and no realization,
the homogeneous original state is neither
with nor without extremes.
If one realizes in this way,
there is definitely no one else to ask.
Since diversity appears as the dharmakaya,
a mind that accepts and rejects never arises.
There is nothing to meditate or not meditate,
and nothing is covered with characteristics.
One should never depend on apparent
and nonapparent objects.
A mind with action and agent does not exist,
free from all objects.
A mind with hope and fear does not exist,
turned away from all attachments,
if one realizes the original reality shown by the guru.
The diversity of recollection and awareness
automatically dissolves into the dharmadhatu.
Consciousness does not remain on an object,
since one is free from all attachment and grasping.
All phenomena are liberated in the uncontrived
    original state.

If one is not attached to anything,
free from the stain of pride and so on,
devoted, totally connected with the sublime ones,
and free from mental activity of any kind,
there is no doubt one will be immaculate.
Because one is purified of a knower and objects of knowledge,
the direct perception of dharmata will arise.
If one has not realized original mahamudra,
since one is always attached to everything
because of the power of dualistic grasping,
thoughts arise in the mind like a stream
of the variety of blurred vision.
Not abiding in the nonerroneous ultimate,
one cycles and wanders in samsara.
Because of attachment and grasping
to all the fame and offerings,
and the arising of great hearing,
reflection, and intellectual comprehension,
good experience, siddhis, blessings, and the signs of power,
the contrived path is ultimately a stain.
The wise do not entrust their minds to those.
If one is interested in those things
and falls into the two extremes,
because it is the root of cycling in the cycle of samsara,
look, what is the mountain of the mind that is the root of
    everything?
If one becomes free from the mind
because it is not seen when looking,
liberation is certain.

Since the mind does not indicate "the dharmadhatu is this,"
both meditation and an object of meditation do not exist
    in that.
Rest in the undistracted state without any concepts

of existence and nonexistence.

If one intellectualizes emptiness, nonarising, beyond mind,

freedom from extremes, and so on in any way,

not dwelling in actual reality, one will be very distracted.

Rest in a relaxed state, disregarding empty or not empty.

Letting go in the state of independence

without meditating or not meditating,

be just like a zombie without a mind that accepts or rejects.

If one dwells in my state through knowing reality as it is,

the traces of the characteristics of dualistic appearances

will quickly be destroyed.

If one is distracted by characteristics

without dwelling in the state of realization,

one will not be able to avert the traces

of the characteristics of dualistic appearances.

Though it seems a particle is in the eye of one with
    ophthalmia,

the ophthalmic appearance cannot be repaired

without curing the eye disease.

Intellectualizing reality, attachment to meditation experience,

cultivating and meditating on the actual true state

are causes of deviation.

Because attachment and aversion arose toward

conducive conditions, one is bound.

All negative disharmonious conditions are sublime siddhis

since negative conditions intensify the yogini's experience.

Since one understands the true state of negative conditions,

without avoiding them, train in them,

maintain that, and practice until coming to the conclusion

of experience and realization,

just as a good horse is encouraged by a quirt.

If yogis with good experience lack the companion of conduct,

as that is not possessed, it is like people without feet.

Train in the actual, ultimate, real state, free from attachment,

giving up nothing, accomplishing nothing, attached to nothing,
purifying nothing, rejecting nothing,
the best of the very best conduct is whatever feels good to one's
    body.
Though relatively,
the buddhas have the great confidence of a dead body,
they diligently do whatever possible
without abandoning the great mass of sentient beings.

Though fearless, without fearful thoughts toward samsara,
refrain from even the slightest wrong action.
Though phenomena are realized to be empty like space,
free from an origin, give up attachment and aversion,
having destroyed all strong grasping.

Though one realizes the meaning
of the great transparent dharmata free from extremes,
while one has not attained stability,
keep one's experience and realization secret from others.
Though one realizes that ultimately both self and other do not
    exist,
relatively, think on the great benefit of migrating beings.
Though one has the confidence
that does not depend on the guidance of others,
place the very kind guru on the crown of one's head.
The one with attachment and grasping will debate everyone.
Contrary conduct not in conformity with tradition is a
    deviation.
Since there is no object of perception and no perceiver,
difference is liberated in its own state.
Since the experiencer is destroyed,
one is freed from all effort and practice.
Since the result to attain is destroyed,

one is liberated from all hope and fear.
Having totally uprooted I and mine,
one is victorious in the war with Mara.
Since realism is destroyed in its own state,
one is liberated from samsara and nirvana.
Since rigpa is pure in the basis, it is called perfect
    buddhahood.
Since phenomena and mind are exhausted
in the state of exhaustion,
therefore it is explained as nirvana,
uncontrived, unchanging, totally liberated
from everything to be given up or to attain.

E ma ho!
That great profound term mahamudra,
whatever its basis of designation is,
also has the label "empty."
As moments are empty by nature,
who realizes selflessness?
There is no realizer, just a name, a term, a label.
Also that is not perfect, a projection of disciples.
Also in disciples there is no self,
similar with illusions and emanations.
"Mahamudra" is a mental imputation of the childish.

"Delusion" and "nondelusion" are mere names, mere labels.
Who is the person to feel or be aware of delusion?
If not even an iota of the result—nirvana—exists,
and is not perceived,
"liberation and nonliberation" is an adventitious reification.
Nothing exists in peaceful and pure space,
so what is the path of liberation?

"Ultimate" and "relative" are also just emphatic labels.
But the two truths don't exist in the dharmadhatu.
The dharmadhatu does not exist.

The *Treasury of Dohas* composed by the Lord of Yogins,
Virupa, is complete.

Complete Translation of Sachen Kunga Nyingpo's *Praise to Virupa*

Namo Virupaya

A la la
From the innate, free from proliferation,
this one, very brilliant, gloriously blazing beyond imagining,
he who is called Jetsun Virupa
has become our lord.
E ma ho!

Freed from all concepts by your brilliance,
having increased the four joys with the airs of the three doors,
chaotic activities have transformed into bliss and emptiness.
Then, having awakened,
I shall offer a brief praise in commemoration.

The lord who has joined together
the two complete benefits of wellness and excellence,

having shown the supreme path to fortunate disciples
with wisdom and love, placing them in nirvana.
I prostrate to the one at play in the supreme unmoving state.

Someone in this world from a royal family,
a monk who completed the five sciences,
the spiritual guide of the millions of members
of the order of his Sangha.
I prostrate with devotion to the one famed as Elder
    Dharmapala.

Never defeated by opponents, the lord of the teaching
of the shastras of the great founders
that have the meaning of the three trainings,
pillar of the doctrine, the second omniscient one,
I prostrate to the one beyond dispute in the world.

During the day, a great assembly was satisfied
with the nectar of the teachings of the stages of the path.
In the evening, liberated by practicing secret conduct.
I bow to the one who realized the sixth bhumi
by following Nairatmya.

In order to guide living beings through unconventional
    conduct,
leaving the monastic sangha, with vulgar conduct,
wandering through all the towns and roads.
I prostrate to the one famed to all as Virupa.

Reversing the Ganges and taming a wicked king
after halting the sun, drinking the kingdom's wine
without getting drunk, splitting a linga, taming witches.
I prostrate to the powerful lord.

As such, at the end of demonstrating his limitless abilities,
having tamed Kartika in Saurashta,
I prostrate to the one who is at play in the great bliss
    of union
pervading the whole expanse of space
with objectless great compassion.

Having shown the profound path with the four oral
    transmissions,
the method of quickly realizing phenomena
as the reality of the utter purity of bliss and emptiness,
I prostrate to the one who ripens and liberates the fortunate.

E ma, while my mind has not attained the stage
    of liberation,
in the utterly pure expanse,
in your presence, Jetsun,
please embrace me like this again and again.

As such, having increased the stream of nectar
of that which is produced
as a byproduct of your compassion,
I supplicate you to accomplish my goals.

Also, whoever follows your example
should never part from the two stages.
May there be no obstacles on the path.
Please benefit the doctrine.

The airs of the pure three doors
increase the four joys;
after the four movements dissolve into the central vein,
may one obtain the stage of powerful vajra holder.

Also the fame of this residence,
pervades the earth [Sa-] and sky;
white [-kya] like the moon or jasmine,
glorious virtue is to be enjoyed.

Lord Virupa himself, with the white earth behind him, covering the area in between Bal ravine and Mon ravine, was seated cross-legged with the mudra of teaching. On his right was Krishnapa, on his left was Gayadhara, behind him was Kokkalipa, and in front was Vinasa. They were seen as being actually present. Then he bestowed the blessing of the four empowerments explained as the *Concealed Path*. He gave the empowerment of Vajravidarana. And he gave the reading transmission for 72 divisions of tantra: the *Intimate Instruction of the Path with the Result*, the *Ten Great Accomplishments*, and the *Eight Subtle Ones*. The words of the praise arose from the strength of Sachen's experience.

Sampatamithi.

Index

mystical, 35
of yogis and ordinary beings, differences between, 36–37, 178
perfection of giving, 276
permanence, 20–22, 67, 118, 269
phenomena
attachment to, 219–20, 221–22
empty nature of, 54, 150, 272, 294, 298
exhaustion of, 268–69, 299
liberating, 147, 295
relative, 83, 91, 93, 94, 95, 100, 294
selflessness of, 60
philosophy, Buddhist
analysis and logic in, 33, 53–54
limitations of, 45–46, 170–72, 176
nontheism of, 89
purpose of, 93, 233, 236
schools of, 92–93
on self, existence of, 281–85
See also Madhyamaka; Vaibhashika school
present moment, 7, 44–45, 119, 156–57, 170, 232, 273–74
pride
divine, 68
freedom from, 148, 296
in scholarship, 172, 234
in spiritual experience, 225–26
projections, 13, 21, 84–85, 105, 145, 274
of desire, 220
emotions and, 40, 93, 155, 250
existence as, 284
in guru-student relationship, 125–26
inner conditions and, 121, 179, 180–81
karma and, 276
perfect relative truth and, 77–78
source of, 109–10, 121, 164
in spiritual practice, 280

as transformational method, 128
projector and projection, 168, 250, 274, 285
psychology
Buddhist, 171, 220, 222
modern, 117
pure lands/realms, 231, 267
purification practices, 184, 209, 231, 236, 241, 267
purity, 35–36, 184, 187, 268, 287, 288

Q
quantum vacuum, 129, 130, 211

R
realism, 9, 92, 261, 264, 265, 299
rebirth, 23, 236
attachment and, 36, 65
of buddhas and ordinary beings, differences between, 25, 42, 265
causes of, 110
consciousness at, 23–24, 43–44, 70, 278
economic systems and, 234
focus on, 278–80
mental continuum at, 43
See also bardo (intermediate stage)
recollection, 145, 295
refuge, 41, 127, 240
relative truth, 81, 82
extremes and, 67
imperfect, 76, 79, 275, 288
as labels, 288, 289–90, 300
logic and, 177
perfect, 76–79, 275, 276, 288
See also under ultimate truth
relativity, 10, 34, 209
going beyond, 91, 216
ignorance and, 224
karma and, 120, 233, 236–37, 238
of merit, 239
paradox of, 273

About the Author

LAMA MIGMAR TSETEN was born in Tibet and fled to India in 1959, where he lived as a refugee. He received both a traditional and a contemporary education, graduating from the Central Institute of Higher Tibetan Studies at Sanskrit University in Varanasi. He served as the head of the Sakya Center in Rajpur, India, and the Sakya Monastery in Puruwalla. He has served as Buddhist chaplain at Harvard University since 1997. Lama Migmar has supervised the editing and publication of more than fifty rare volumes of Sakya literature and is the author of many books, including *Awakening to the Noble Truth*, *Wisdom Gone Beyond*, and *The Tibetan Book of Awakening*. As the founder of the Sakya Institute for Buddhist Studies in Cambridge, Massachusetts, Lama Migmar teaches throughout North America and Europe. Learn more at https://www.lamamigmar.net.

What to Read Next
from Wisdom Publications

Mahamudra
A Practical Guide
His Eminence the Twelfth Zurmang Gharwang Rinpoche

In his first major book, His Eminence Zurmang Gharwang Rinpoche, the head of the Zurmang Kagyu lineage of Tibetan Buddhism, unpacks the marrow of a crucial teaching.

Mahamudra
How to Discover Our True Nature
Lama Thubten Yeshe

Lama Yeshe tells us that mahamudra is "the universal reality of emptiness, of nonduality" and its unique characteristic is its emphasis on meditation: "With mahamudra meditation there is no doctrine, no theology, no philosophy, no God, no Buddha. Mahamudra is only experience."

The Mind of Mahāmudrā
Advice from the Kagyu Masters
Translated and introduced by Peter Alan Roberts

"Quite simply, the best anthology of Tibetan Mahāmudrā texts yet to appear." —Roger R. Jackson, Carleton College, author of *Tantric Treasures*

Essentials of Mahamudra
Looking Directly at the Mind
Khenchen Thrangu Rinpoche

"Makes the practice of mahamudra, one of the most advanced forms of meditation, easily accessible to Westerners' everyday lives. A wonderful way of bringing us to the path."—*Mandala*

Mastering Meditation
Instructions on Calm Abiding and Mahāmudrā
His Eminence Chöden Rinpoché
Foreword by His Holiness the Dalai Lama

"Kyabjé Chöden Rinpoché was more kind to me than all the three times' buddhas. His teachings are not just words but come from a learned mind—and from experience." —Lama Zopa Rinpoche

Mind Seeing Mind
Mahāmudrā and the Geluk Tradition of Tibetan Buddhism
Roger Jackson

"From the origins of the Mahāmudrā teaching in India, through its refinement and development among the Kagyü masters of Tibet, to its transmission to Jé Tsongkhapa and his Gelukpa successors down to the present day, Jackson guides the reader on a journey resembling the exploration of a great river from its turbulent headwaters to the spreading streams of its delta. *Mind Seeing Mind* is a model study of the historical and doctrinal literature of Buddhism in Tibet." —Matthew T. Kapstein, École Pratique des Hautes Études, Paris, and the University of Chicago

Becoming the Compassion Buddha
Tantric Mahamudra for Everyday Life
Lama Thubten Yeshe
Edited by Robina Courtin

"An intimate book, so clear and compassionate, you know you are listening to the unforgettable voice of Lama Yeshe, one of the great teachers of our time."—Sogyal Rinpoche

Freeing the Heart and Mind
Part One: Introduction to the Buddhist Path
His Holiness the Sakya Trichen

His Holiness the Sakya Trizin, the head of the glorious Sakya lineage, one of the four primary schools of Tibetan Buddhism, presents here the essential Buddhist teachings of the four noble truths, universal compassion, and the proper motivation for practice.

Freeing the Heart and Mind
Part Two: Chögyal Phagpa on the Buddhist Path
His Holiness the Sakya Trichen

His Holiness the Sakya Trichen, the forty-first head of the Sakya school of Tibetan Buddhism, with his trademark clarity and deep wisdom here unpacks two texts by the legendary thirteenth-century Drogön Chögyal Phagpa.

About Wisdom Publications

Wisdom Publications is the leading publisher of classic and contemporary Buddhist books and practical works on mindfulness. To learn more about us or to explore our other books, please visit our website at wisdomexperience.org or contact us at the address below.

Wisdom Publications
199 Elm Street
Somerville, MA 02144 USA

We are a 501(c)(3) organization, and donations in support of our mission are tax deductible.

Wisdom Publications is affiliated with the Foundation for the Preservation of the Mahayana Tradition (FPMT).